WOMEN, DEVELOPMENT, AND COMMUNITIES FOR EMPOWERMENT IN APPALACHIA

SUNY Series in Gender and Society
Cornelia Butler Flora, editor

WOMEN, DEVELOPMENT, AND COMMUNITIES FOR EMPOWERMENT IN APPALACHIA

Virginia Rinaldo Seitz

STATE UNIVERSITY OF NEW YORK PRESS

Published by
State University of New York Press, Albany

© 1995 State University of New York

For information, address State University of New York Press,
State University Plaza, Albany, NY 12246

Production by Christine Lynch
Marketing by Theresa Abad Swierzowski

Library of Congress Cataloging-in-Publication Data

Seitz, Virginia Rinaldo.
    Women, development, and communities for empowerment in Appalachia
/ Virginia Rinaldo Seitz.
        p.   cm. — (SUNY series in gender and society)
    Includes bibliographical references and index.
    ISBN 0-7914-2377-8 (acid-free paper). — ISBN 0-7914-2378-6 (pbk.
: acid-free paper)
    1. Women—Appalachian Region—Social conditions.   2. Appalachian
Region—Social conditions.   I. Title.   II. Series.
HQ1438.A127S45   1995
305.42'0974—dc20   94-15704
                                                                          CIP

10 9 8 7 6 5 4 3 2 1

CONTENTS

ACKNOWLEDGMENTS

I am grateful to the women of Southwest Virginia who shared their friendship, families, and their lives with me. In the telling of their stories, they have helped me to understand and appreciate how women struggle for development and change in all societies. I also thank the women in grassroots associations who read and commented on this manuscript.

I want to especially acknowledge Cornelia Butler Flora who was my major advisor for the dissertation that is the basis of this book. Her enthusiastic support for my research project made it possible to accomplish. I have many friends and colleagues whom I would like to mention personally for their much-appreciated friendship and helpful critique: Nancy Alexander, Katherine Allen, Elizabeth Bounds, Patricia Brady, Ellen Brown, Gladys Buenavista, Carol Burger, Toni Calasanti, Tracy Chew, Jackie Counts, Sharon Fisher, Ann Kilkelly, Nancy Lawrence, Tim Luke, Woody Leach, Carol Moore, Nancy Robinson, Ruth Rohr-Zanker, Mary Rojas, Susan Shome, Cosby Totten, Pat Tracy, Maxine Waller, Whit Watts, Tena Willemsma, and Anna Zajicek.

I also appreciate the consent of three notable publications to reprint excerpts in this book. These excerpts and the publications are: 1) Hall, Jacquelyn Dowd. "Disorderly Women: Gender and Labor Militancy in the Appalachian South." *Journal of American History*, 73 (Sept. 1986), 354–382; 2) Safa, Helen Icken. "Women's Social Movements in Latin America." *Gender and Society*, 4(3): 354–369; 3) Buvinic, Mayra. "Projects for Women in the Third World: Explaining their Misbehavior." *World Development*, 14(5): 653–664.

Finally, I dedicate this book to my daughters, Joanna and Juliet Seitz, whose lives are enriched by the women who have come before them, including those who have shared their stories for this book.

The research for this book was funded in-part by the Women's Research Institute, Virginia Tech, Blacksburg, Virginia.

CHAPTER ONE

Introduction

We have learned from our experiences . . . that the political
will for serious action by those in power is contingent on
women organizing to demand and promote change. We therefore need to assert our claim in shaping the major social
and economic issues facing our times. (Sen and Grown
1987:22)

A STORY OF GENDER AND SOCIAL CHANGE

This is a story of women and collective activism in the coalfields
and nearby mining areas of Southwest Virginia. Based on qualitative research conducted in the Central Appalachian mountains between 1990 and 1992, it explores the life histories of working-class
women in order to understand their class and gender conditions
and their positions of marginalization. The story also explores how
women struggle for development and change in grassroots associations, and how this struggle may lead to their empowerment.

The subjects of the story and the study are women in Southwest Virginia who came together in grassroots community development, income generation, and labor support groups. Through life
history interviews and informal conversations, these women shared
with the author their experiences and analyses of their personal
and collective lives. Twelve women participated in the intensive
interviews, while many others contributed to the study through
conversations with the author in many different settings inside
and outside of their collective associations. Together, we have pieced
together a story of gender and social change from the standpoint of
Appalachian working-class women.

What follows is an iterative and reflexive exploration of change;
consequently, the presentation is not linear. Following the introduction (Chapter One) and discussion of the research methodology
(Chapter Two), there are three chapters that deepen our under-

1

standing of Appalachian women's lives in the context of family (Chapter Three), work (Chapter Four), and community (Chapter Five). Because part of the operative definition of empowerment is collective action (see page 7), Chapter Five shifts our attention to community, referring back to Chapter Two because women's collective identity is rooted in the family. Analyses of women's participation in grassroots groups continues in the next three chapters. Chapter Six reveals problems inherent in top-down strategies and groups that are constrained to focus on only one of women's roles. Chapter Seven presents the challenges to class and gender hierarchies that have come from women in a grassroots labor-support group. Chapter Eight looks at the flexibility of community development groups and how their sucesses may contradict conventional development assumptions. The final chapter (Nine) summarizes what we have learned about women, community, and alternative visions for development and empowerment.

THE RESEARCH PROJECT

Gender is a central category of social difference that affects and is affected by women's relationship to the means of production. In this study, gender and class are examined in the context of women's collective social practices. The research project sought to answer the following questions:

1) How are women marginalized and oppressed on the basis of their class, gender and other positions of difference?
2) How do women theorize an understanding of class and gender?
3) Under what conditions do women come together collectively for social change?
4) What associations provide contexts for women's empowerment? (and)
5) How are women empowered through their grassroots collective practices?

A derived question relates the study to theory produced by women in the geographic periphery of the capitalist global economy (Sen and Grown 1987; Mohanty 1991) and by women of color in the United States (Collins 1989, 1990; Davis 1990; Moraga 1986; Moraga and Anzaldua 1981; hooks 1981, 1989):

6) Does the feminism (as theory and practice) of women in this research setting share standpoints with third world feminisms?[1]

The scholarly discussion of the research findings draws on socialist feminist theory and women in development planning literature. The central theoretical concern is how women may be empowered when they participate in grassroots associations that aim to further their development. Analysis is integrated with theory and is grounded in thick descriptions of women's everyday lives and work in families and communities. By examining the economic, social, political, and ideological dimensions of the process of change these women have experienced in collective associations, we can better understand the relationship between capitalism and patriarchy and how this relationship affects our understanding of empowerment. Defining empowerment, a concern in the women in development (WID) literature, has implications for social policy and planning interventions, as does the affirmation of women's agency in movements for social change.

THE SETTING

The research was conducted in the coalfields and contiguous economically depressed areas of Southwest Virginia in the Central Appalachian mountains. Because of the region's historic underdevelopment and dependency on extractive industries and the outside ownership and control of its productive resources, it is helpful to recognize structural similarities to other contexts, including the third world, that are expressed in the relationships of dependency that affect women's lives.

In this peripheral region of the United States, working-class women are organizing in response to structural trends in the economy that threaten the security of their families and contribute to their economic, social, and political impoverishment. The coal industry, its once powerful union, and the secondary industries coal once attracted, are on the decline. Manufacturing industries no longer stop in the mountains as they move south beyond U.S. borders. Centralization and bureaucratization of political and administrative authority have effectively excluded working-class participation in public discourse. Whatever social welfare benefits were won with the struggles of the union and the 'war on poverty' are in peril.

According to Kraybill, Johnson, and Deaton's (1987) study of socioeconomic indicators in Virginia coal counties compared to the state as a whole, the region is characterized by two-thirds more poverty and nearly that much more dependency on transfer incomes. There is much more unemployment, underemployment, and undereducation (Kraybill, Johnson, and Deaton 1987). The conditions of life in the coal counties (Buchanan, Dickenson, Lee, Russell, Scott, Tazewell, and Wise), a portion of the seventeen-county region of Southwest Virginia, support the assertion of the marginalization of women in this study.

LISTENING TO APPALACHIAN WOMEN

For the past twenty years or more, feminist scholarship has been concerned with the qualitative differences between women's and men's experiences of social life and how women's experiences have been left out of received knowledge and discourse (Harding 1987; Jaggar 1988; Jaggar and Rothenberg 1984; Smith 1987). Socialist feminist theorists have fundamentally challenged Marxist political economy by insisting on the theoretical relevance of reproductive work (Hartmann 1981). They have introduced psychoanalytic concepts to explore patriarchy as the ideological form of women's oppression (Mitchell 1971), or patriarchy as a social structure that unites with capitalism to alienate women in gender-specific ways (Jaggar 1988). They have offered a division-of-labor analysis of the unifying systems of capitalism and patriarchy (Young 1980; Mies 1986) and introduced radical feminist insights on the sexual basis for women's oppression (MacKinnon 1982, 1987).

This study contributes to the body of literature in socialist feminism because it addresses the gendered division of labor, the unity of women's productive and reproductive work, and women's sexuality as the nexus of gender and class oppression. It is also concerned with consciousness as a site of feminist oppositional politics (Hartsock 1983) and the relationship of consciousness and the collective (Mies 1986).

In recent years, feminist theory has been challenged from within for essentializing women's experiences (Spelman 1988; hooks 1981; Mohanty 1991). Women of color in the United States and in the geographic third world have deepened feminist critique, challenged epistemological universals, and opened the possibilities for more inclusive yet indigenous social movements (Collins 1990; Davis 1990; Moraga 1986; Sen and Grown 1987). Although feminist discourse has opened to other voices, it has not yet listened to Appalachian women. This study enlarges the conversations in feminist theory to include the unique voices of women in an historically marginalized region and for whom gender is constructed within a distinctive regional culture and political economy.

Appalachian studies as an interdisciplinary field has countered the stereotypes of Appalachian people and the construction of an Appalachian culture of poverty (Billings 1974; Fisher 1991; Walls and Billings 1991). Structural accounts of the regional political economy (Clavel 1983; Gaventa 1980) have sometimes acknowledged gender differences (Lewis 1970; Lewis, Kobak, and Johnson 1978; Gaventa 1990) but have not yet explored the explanatory potential of feminist social and political theory. As feminist theory empirically grounded in the standpoint of Appalachian women, this study contributes to a new area in Appalachian studies (Maggard 1986).

Just as feminist theory has challenged Marxist political economy, it has also challenged theories of development and under-development and the grand narratives of human progress (Maguire 1984; Jaquette 1982; Sen and Grown 1987; Mohanty 1991). Yet, the mainstream of "women in development" planning literature resists the implications of feminist scholarship, particularly in the area of economic development planning (Buvinic 1986; Tinker 1990). Moser (1989) has looked to organizations of third world women for empirical evidence of more holistic and alternative strategies for economic development (Sen and Grown 1987), yet discussions of the organizations of marginalized women in the United States have not yet entered the discourse.

By locating women in development issues in the Appalachian region of the United States, this research contributes to recent commitments in the field to engage in a "South-North dialogue," and to recognize the marginalization of women in core countries and their connection to women in the South through the new international division of labor (Mies 1986).

Finally, the use of a feminist research methodology (Nielsen 1990; Reinharz 1992) in this study offers alternatives to positivist science in a field (planning) where the construction of knowledge is directly related to policy formulation and planning intervention. By challenging the quantification of knowledge and the separation of values from meaning, feminist research allows for emancipatory planning practice.

This study gives a voice to women in grassroots associations in their work to change their consciousness and their material conditions. In this sense, respondents are actively involved in the construction of theory, and the researcher is their first audience. Beyond the community of scholars, there is a community of participants in grassroots associations and their enablers in private and voluntary organizations, public institutions and social services agencies, and in solidarity and religious groups. Understanding how women individually and collectively address the structural constraints of gender and class can inform future strategies for women and community development.

Exploring the process of change among marginalized women's groups in the United States will inform domestic and international planners involved in formulating economic, social and political development policies. If those policies aim to ameliorate or eradicate the conditions that contribute to the marginalization of women, planners can learn how women work towards those goals in collective associations. In understanding how women define empowerment, the work of collective associations will be substantively reinforced.

WORKING DEFINITIONS OF CENTRAL CONCEPTS:

Marginalization

> marginalize. *v.* To cause to live on the edges of society by excluding from participation in any group effort. (The New Lexicon Webster's Dictionary of the English Language 1990:610)

This study is about people who have been prohibited from full participation in social, economic, and political life, and whose experiences, contributions, concerns, and dreams are rarely considered in planning for the future. Because they are women, because they are working-class, and because they are ethnically defined as Appalachian, these people have been relegated to the margins of the social and political discourse that surrounds policymakers and scholars seeking to solve the economic, social, and political crises of end of the twentieth century.

Marginalization is defined as both a position and condition of women (Young 1988). As women, the respondents in this study are marginalized by the social construction of subordinate female gender roles and their accompanying ideology. These women are further marginalized by the depressed socio-economic conditions of the region of Southwest Virginia (Kraybill, Johnson, and Deaton 1987; Gaventa, Smith, and Willingham 1990; Shifflett 1991). Whether they are unemployed household heads, low-wage service sector workers without benefits, wives of high-wage (for the region), high-risk, and income-insecure mine workers, or miners themselves, the women in this study are affected by the relative socio-economic deprivation of the region and by industrial responses to boom-and-bust cycles in the coal industry.

Marginalization is a struggle concept. It is understood by acknowledging that there are interactions and contradictions in the kinds and levels of class and gender marginalization. Therefore, the marginalization of women on the basis of class and gender is not additive (Spelman 1988): you cannot study working-class persons, then "add women, and stir" (Smith 1974; Andersen 1988:13–16). To do so would ignore the epistemological implications of placing women's experiences at the center of our analysis, where our goal is not to speak "about" or "for" women but to speak "out" for them (Klein 1983 cited in Reinharz 1992:16). When we speak out for women we can move beyond the construction of women as victims of oppression to the affirmation of women as social actors. Marginalization, then, can also provide women the position on the edges of society that allows for critique; it can be the place to imagine more just and creative solutions to the problems of development.

Empowerment

(E)mpowerment is a *process* aimed at consolidating, maintaining, or changing the nature and distribution of power in a particular cultural context. The process is rarely a linear one. It takes twists and turns, includes both resistance and consent, and ebbs and flows as groups with different relations to structures and sources of power come into conflict. (Morgen and Bookman 1988:4)

Empowerment is a term often used to represent a positive material change in the condition of an individual, particularly when discussing the improved economic efficiency of women in third world settings. Emphases on individualism and the separation of the material and ideological dimensions of change through an economistic lens are problematic in feminist theory. The understanding of empowerment in this study is open and reflexive: it is also a struggle concept, defined by those who make the struggle. Grounded theory-building (Glaser and Strauss 1967) allows a central concept to take shape through analysis and is particularly suited to feminist research because it maximizes women's agency in the research process. Therefore, informed by feminist social and political theory (Morgen and Bookman 1988; Hartsock 1983; Mies 1986), empowerment will be partially and tentatively defined as a process and as an outcome of collective identity and political praxis.

Empowerment is a capacity in thought and action to address the condition and position of marginalization. Women are empowered when they recognize and act on strategic (relational) interests as well as practical (material) interests (Molyneux 1986): not only do women in collective association work to materially improve the conditions of life, they challenge the power relationships inherent in their gendered and class position. Thus, a portion of the operative definition is collective action.

Empowerment will further be defined as an outcome of a challenge to androcentric ideology expressed in a bifurcated consciousness that separates the personal and political, public and private spheres, and gender from class consciousness.

GENDER AND DEVELOPMENT PLANNING

If empowerment is more than economic improvement, it will require social and political as well as economic development. In writing about the setting of this study, Kraybill, Johnson, and Deaton (1987) remind us that "human capital and industrial location in a region are jointly determined" (6), linking social and community development to economic development on more than feminist grounds. From the experience of women in development planning, we can expect that women's associations will address the problems of education, health, nutrition, and housing as well as income generation in defining their practical gender needs (March and Taqqu 1982; Buvinic 1986; Moser 1989). When gender analysis reveals the complex interactions of women's productive and reproductive work, the importance of holistic development strategies becomes even more clear.

Women in development (WID) has emerged as an area in development policy and planning within the last twenty years, in the period roughly equivalent to the emergence of feminist scholarship and the second wave of a women's movement in the United States. Partly in response to pressures from women who were development professionals in the United States, and partly in response to worldwide interest in women's productive capacities during the United Nations Decade for Women (1976–1985), bilateral, multilateral, private and voluntary, and nongovernmental development organizations almost uniformly require consideration of women as a separate class or group in development policy (Tinker 1990). Yet a "conceptual awareness of the issues of 'gender and development' has not necessarily resulted in its translation into planning practice" (Moser 1989:1799). The women in development (WID) focus of development policy has not addressed issues of *gender* as a central category of social difference: women may be isolated in their own projects or integrated into others, but the structural relationship of gender may be unexamined.

As a policy arena, the rationale for WID has been developed by the United States Agency for International Development (USAID) and extended in other bilateral and multilateral institutions and in government and nongovernmental agencies. Over time, it has become a reductionist rationale that finally sees women as an under utilized resource: the purpose of "integrating" women into development, finally, is to enhance the economic efficiency of planning interventions (as in USAID, World Bank policy papers).

The subject of WID literature has been characterized by Young (1988) as the "condition" of women, "the material state in which women find themselves, their poverty, their lack of education and training." This allows development practitioners to find "ways of improving women's condition by targeting ameliorative resources rather than by radically changing underlying structures" (Young 1988:1–2). By focusing on the "condition" of women, one can ignore the "position" of women in relation to men, and how this affects the position of women in other power relationships, such as class, race, ethnicity, and region. By "treating" women out of context, the category "women" is ultimately invalidated, "since in every case it has to be modified by other social signifiers, class . . . , age . . . , civil status, race . . . and so on" (Young 1988:4).

Even when gender, the social relationship and relative position of women and men, is considered in development planning, it is usually limited to assessing the failure of projects to utilize gender analysis to draw women into the development process. With exceptions like an early critique of the development industry by Rogers (1979), an often cited monograph by Maguire (1984), and Mohanty's highly theoretical (1991) essay "Under Western Eyes," rarely are development assumptions questioned. If development planning were truly gendered, the social relations of power in all of their manifestations would be subject to critique, including assumptions about who are the subjects of development.

With the emancipation of women as her goal, Moser (1989) offers a conceptual framework for what she calls "gender planning" that corrects the tendency to treat women irrespective of their relationship to men and without an analysis of power. As interest grows in addressing the feminization of poverty in the United States (Weiss 1990; Rothenberg 1992) under conditions of global economic restructuring, gender planning can be extended to reflect the needs of marginalized women in Appalachia.

Gender planning is based on the validity of women as a category because gender expresses the socially constructed and unequal relationship between men and women. But it also offers planners "room to maneuver for addressing needs" without necessarily challenging the "specific sociopolitical context" and the "engendered position (of women) in the sexual division of labor" (Moser 1989:1804). Moser (1989) proposes that gender planning must take into account women's reproductive, productive, and community management work, and the strategic as well as practical gender needs of women (after Molyneux 1986):

> Strategic gender needs are those needs which are formulated from the analysis of women's subordination to men, and deriving out of this the strategic gender interest identified for an alternative, more equal and satisfactory organization of society than that which exists at present, in terms of both the structure and nature of relationships between men and women.
>
> • • •
>
> In contrast, practical gender needs are those needs which are formulated from the concrete conditions women experience, in their engendered position within the sexual division of labor, and deriving out of this their practical gender interests for human survival (Moser 1989:1803).

Strategic gender interests "arise not from women's attempts to fulfill traditional, or even modern, obligations imposed by the sexual division of labour, but from women's growing recognition that the age old structures of male dominance and privilege are not sacrosanct, nor indeed given in the genetic inheritance, but are social impositions, and as such amenable to change" (Young 1988:8).

Working in this conceptual milieu, Moser develops an analysis of five policy approaches in women in development (WID), and evaluates each in the context of meeting practical and strategic gender needs.

1) the welfare approach
2) the equity approach
3) the anti-poverty approach
4) the efficiency approach
5) the empowerment approach

Moser's discussion of empowerment breaks out of the limitations of the social reform tradition of planning (Friedmann 1987) where the other WID approaches can be located. An empowerment approach is not grounded in market rationality that ultimately promotes individualism over collective interest. Rather, it is based on a recognition of planning as social mobilization, partly in response to the accumulation crisis and decline of the welfare state in core countries and to structural adjustment policies in the periphery. Planning as social mobilization also resists the tendency in women in development planning to conflate women's equity with economic participation.

For Moser, and for the third world women's association of activists, professionals and scholars that has become its most visible advocate, Development Alternatives with Women for a New Era (DAWN), the empowerment approach "emphasizes that fact that women experience oppression differently according to their race, class, colonial history, and current position in the international economic order. It therefore maintains that women have to challenge oppressive structures and situations simultaneously at different levels" (Moser 1989:1815).

The discussion of planning as empowerment is emerging out of third world feminist scholarship and grassroots organizing (Sen & Grown 1987; Beneria & Sen 1986; Barrios de Chungara 1978; Afonja 1990), and aims to enable self-reliance and indigenous control by addressing both women's strategic and practical gender needs.

(It) questions some of the fundamental assumptions concerning the interrelationship between power and development that underlie previous approaches. While it acknowledges the importance for women to increase their power, it seeks to identify power less in terms of domination over others (with its implicit assumption that a gain for women implies a loss for men), and more in terms of the capacity of women to increase their own self-reliance and internal strength. This is identified as the right to determine choices in life and to influence the direction of change, through the ability to gain control over crucial material and nonmaterial resources (Moser 1989:1815).

Even though the research context for this study is not the geographic third world, the feminism growing out of women's grassroots mobilization in marginalized areas of the United States may have more in common with third world than middle-class North American agendas. When planners advocate the strategic gender interests of women, they enter the terrain of planning Friedmann (1987) calls "emancipatory practice" which falls within the "grand counter-tradition" (p. 307) of planning as social mobilization:

Its aim is the structural transformation of industrial capitalism toward the self-production of life, the recovery of political community, and the achievement of collective self-reliance in the context of common global concerns. In this context, our task is to wrest from the political terrain still held by the state and corporate capital expanding zones of liberation in which the new and self-reliant ways of production and democratic governance can flourish. (Friedmann 1987:412).

Because the goal of social mobilization is transformative, it is antithetical to reformist planning, and it is an oppositional practice that must include historically conscious subjects. For Friedmann (1987), "its starting point is social criticism. And it relies on action from below. . . . It requires the overcoming of resistance (through) (e)mancipatory struggle (which) is always particularized and historical . . . A key principle . . . is that no group can be free until freedom has been achieved for every group (leading) to results that will always be partial and contradictory. . . . Because it is oppositional, radical practice . . . cannot be organized and sponsored by the state. The impulse for it must come from within the community itself" (p. 297–301).

It is also an engaged position for scholars and planners that challenges both professional and scholarly canons. In addressing the apparent contradiction between "planning" and a radical and oppositional practice, Friedmann argues for planners "never far removed from the action:"

> Action needs to be undergirded by structures of meaning or ideology, which is the point of both departure and return for radical practice. The meanings articulated by ideology . . . function . . . to legitimate emancipatory practice, to sustain this practice in adversity, and to disarm and de-legitimize the opposition. Planners who become integrally a part of mobilized groups—in Gramsci's language, organic intellectuals—may have the necessary skills to put together statements that will serve these several purposes (Friedmann 1987:305–6).

Reporting on the Ivanhoe Civic League, one of the associations in this study, Gaventa and Lewis (1988) bring Friedmann's radical planning practice to a local context:

> Economic developers who work at building the infrastructure—sewage systems, water, roads—necessary for industrial development emphasize in their economic education technical training to do business plans, feasibility studies, marketing analyses. As important as these may be if one wants to become incorporated into the existent system, there is another infrastructure more basic and more integral to the community if one is interested in looking to alternative systems for more fundamental change. This is the infrastructure which includes education for human development, cultural creativity, democratic decision making, and understanding our history and our religious and political symbols. Then people can rebuild their own communities, can make their own theater, write their own poems, carry out their own research, be their own theologians, build their own economies (p. 2).

CHAPTER TWO

Methodology

PUTTING AWAY THE MASTER'S TOOLS

The master's tools will never dismantle the master's house. They may allow us to temporarily beat him at his own game, but they will never allow us to bring about genuine change. (Lorde 1984:112)

******

Investigating the subjugated knowledge of subordinate groups . . . requires more ingenuity than that needed to examine the standpoints and thought of dominant groups. I found my training as a social scientist inadequate . . . This is because subordinate groups have long had to use alternative ways to create independent self-definitions and self-valuations and to rearticulate them through (their) own specialists. (Collins 1990:202)

Feminist research aims to bring the subjugated knowledge of women to the foreground; the creative challenge for feminist methodology is to develop the tools to do so, and to reveal and open up the politics of the production of knowledge (Collins 1990). Reinharz (1992) says that feminist research is concerned with "questions of *identity* (what are feminist research methods?) and of *difference* (what is the difference between feminist research methods and other research methods . . . ?)" (p. 1). Noting the variation in definitions of feminist research, she suggests a self-definition of feminist research methods guided by statements from self-identified feminists and feminist research publications.

The simple criterion of self-identification deliberately bypasses the danger of applying a one-sided definition to *all* feminist researchers. . . . This approach rejects the notion of

15

a transcendent authority that decides what constitutes 'feminist,' consistent with the antihierarchical nature of many feminist organizations and much feminist spirit (Reinharz 1992:7).

Bookman and Morgen (1988) also argue for the need to create models for "activist research." Noting the "false equation . . . between distance, disengagement, and objectivity on the one hand, and quality scholarship on the other", they describe their personal understanding of feminist research:

We were trained in the social sciences *and* in the mass movements of the 1960s and 1970s. We are insiders and outsiders. The line between participation to *understand* and participation to *further* the efforts of women struggling for survival and justice often disappeared (p. ix).

In this spirit, this study is feminist research because it is a social analysis of gender, development, and change that advances the knowledge and interests of working-class women in Southwest Virginia. It has interpretive and critical dimensions that locate it within the post-positivist paradigm for social research. Importance is placed on the meanings women give to their experiences and intentional explanations of actions, not action unfettered by interpretation. Equally important are the historical processes and structural contradictions that those interpretations uncover.[1]

The contribution of the interpretive or phenomenological approach to social research (Schutz 1967; Denzin 1978, 1989; Lofland and Lofland 1984) is a recognition of the indivisibility of meaning and action: "(Human) action is intrinsically meaningful; it is endowed with meaning by human intentionality, i.e., by consciousness. . . . We are continuously ordering, classifying, and interpreting our ongoing experiences according to various interpretive schemes" (Bernstein in Nielsen 1990:8).

Despite its usefulness as an alternative to positivist science, particularly in its research strategy of participant observation, the interpretive method has been found inadequate to delimit critical and feminist inquiry. Fay (1986) criticizes the interpretive model for failing to offer quasi-causal accounts, or "a means whereby one can study the relationships between the structural elements of a social order and the possible forms of behavior and beliefs which such elements engender" (83–84). Fay (1986) also argues that interpretive social science may be implicitly conservative because it "assumes an inherent continuity in a particular society, i.e. systematically ignores the possible structures of conflict within a society, structures that would generate change. . . . In a time of upheaval, the interpretive model would lead people to seek to *change the way they think about what they and others are doing*, rather than provide them with a theory by means of which they could *change what they or others are doing*, and in this way it supports the *status quo*" (90–91).

Although there is "an interpretive dimension" in feminist research, Nielsen (1990A) notes that the reluctance in interpretive science to abandon the "subjective-objective distinction" creates problems for feminists whose research is grounded in the standpoint epistemology of critical theory. These feminists argue for a more "passionate scholarship" (DuBois 1985) where the boundaries between researcher and subject are more tentative (Cook and Fonow 1990).

The critical theory of the Frankfurt School and the work of Habermas in particular bring to feminist research both a commitment to emancipatory goals and a rejection of the assumption that there is an objective truth that can be known through science (Jay 1973; Habermas 1976; Fay 1986, 1987). "Every group's knowledge is grounded in history and social structure," but the knowledge "that should prevail" is the knowledge of oppressed classes and groups (Nielsen 1990 A:10). For Fay (1986), "a critical social science is one which attempts to account for the sufferings and felt needs of the actors of a social group by seeing them as the result of certain structural conflicts in the social order" (96). The commitment of social theory to political practice becomes the most important characteristic of critical social science, and it implies the involvement or validation by the subjects or social actors themselves.

Critical theory proposes that not only must all explanations of social action refer to phenomenological experience, but that they must also reveal latent meaning, historical process, and structural contradictions. Since it is concerned with the superstructural domain of class struggle, there is at least the possibility in critical theory of a position outside of the dominant ideology of the ruling class. Yet, even though critical theorists are concerned with the latent contradictions of class (Habermas 1976), it is feminists who have turned our attention to the latent contradictions of gender.

THE FEMINIST STANDPOINT AND WOMEN'S LIFE STORIES

If all knowledge is socially constructed, we are left with the question of whose knowledge should prevail. Friedmann (1987) and Smith (1987) argue that the production of knowledge is *for* particular groups, and that the knowledge of oppressed groups is privileged. The possibility of standing outside of the dominant ideology has been elaborated by socialist feminists working in the critical tradition (Smith 1987; Harding 1987; Hartsock 1983; Jaggar 1988). Because women are oppressed, they are capable of "double vision" or "double consciousness—a knowledge of, and sensitivity to both the dominant world view of the society and their own minority . . . perspective" (Nielsen 1990:10). Not only does material life structure consciousness, the "double vision" of the oppressed provides the potential for a more complete, and therefore privileged knowledge of society. (See also Freire 1972.)[2] Consequently, oppressed groups must also be involved in knowledge construction: the research strategy must allow them speak, and the researcher to speak *out* on their behalf.

Intensive interviews, continuously open to revision by the respondents as well as the researcher, provide opportunities for women to tell their life stories and participate in the construction of knowledge. Because my aim is to generate grounded theory (Glaser and Strauss 1967), I have used this method for collecting data. Reinharz (1992:18–45) claims that the open-ended interview[3] "allows researchers to make full use of differences among people" (19) and is particularly suited to female researchers and respondents; it allows for feelings, non-verbal information and "is consistent with many women's interest in avoiding control over others and in developing a sense of connectedness with people" (20).

The usefulness of life stories is connected to the tradition of the life history method in social research. According to Denzin (1978), "a central assumption of the life history is that human conduct is to be studied and understood from the perspective of the persons involved. . . . Not to take the role of the other is, potentially, to substitute the researcher's interpretations for the interpretations of those studied, and thereby slip into the fallacy of objectivism" (216). In interpretive research, the starting point for critical inquiry, life stories "get at the inner life" (Park in Denzin 1978:215). As a study concerned with the process of change, the research strategy assumed that change can be communicated in both thought and action, and that consciousness-raising is a necessary constituent of transformational praxis (Freire 1972; Westcott 1990). In linking experience and consciousness, the life story interview can explicate (Smith 1987:126) women's "consciousness (as) not simply the act of interpreting but also of constructing the world" (Stanley and Wise 1983:130–131). In the reconstruction of her past, a woman is constructing a conscious understanding of change.

In characterizing the intensive interview as a personal narrative, it is possible to act on the feminist admonition to *privilege* women's *stories*. In "emphasiz(ing) the fictions of self-representation," (224–225) as Behar (1990) does in her "reading" of the life histories of Mexican market women, the life story is a "version of the self constructed by a subject" (227). The life story becomes the text for revealing and analyzing cultural themes (Behar 1990), or drawing out of women's representation of their experience the "extralocal relationships" and structural constraints on women's lives (Smith 1987:69).

A FEMINIST RESEARCH PROCESS

During an twenty-three month period from June 1990 to April 1992, I met, individually and in groups, numerous women from Southwest Virginia.[4] I attended their meetings and celebrations, observed them working, went out with them for coffee, and visited their homes. They graciously welcomed me into their associations, homes, families, and communities as an "outsider within" (Collins 1990:11–13): I was an outsider, not restricted by ties of kinship and place in an uncertain economic environment, and outside the commitments of their collective associations.

The women had much experience with outsiders, from the church and community development workers who came to Appalachia to battle poverty to the scholars and entrepreneurs who followed to document and capitalize on those efforts. The women had analyzed the position of outsider and knew it to be a contradictory one; they had reason to be wary. Yet, I was also a woman and a divorced single parent, with experiential knowledge that placed me "within" a world they knew. These women, including the twelve that became respondents in my research project, came to accept my interest in them as persons and as members of communities of change, and to identify with me as a woman.

Our interactions were part of a feminist research process that centered around the intensive interviews of twelve women. Selecting key informants, collective associations, and individual respondents was a process that was part of my fifteen years of living and working in Southwest Virginia. Using my own experiences, I identified and contacted more than twenty key informants, women who work in community development, education, religious communities, labor organizations, and social service agencies; some are cultural workers and activists, and all are "development catalysts" (Chambers 1983) who have lived for many years in the region.

I asked key informants to identify associations that satisfied the following criteria: 1) that a clear majority of the membership be women although not necessarily by definition, and that if men are involved, they not be in positions of leadership; 2) that the membership of the association be overwhelmingly working-class women for whom economic security is a central concern in their lives; 3) that the majority of the work done in these associations be voluntary, or, in the case of income-generation groups, that there be a collective purpose beyond income-generation; and 4) that the associations are informally organized, or have substantive purposes beyond those formally described. Even if the groups have a charter, bylaws, paid staff, funding, or an institutional setting, that their actual practices and methods of decisionmaking be counterintuitive to an understanding of bureaucratic practices.[5]

Discussions with key informants and my own knowledge of the region led me to select four types of associations that could provide collective contexts for women's empowerment in the coalfields:[6] 1) associations in a collaborative relationship with labor unions; 2) community development associations; 3) income-generating groups, and 4) associations growing out of public institutions or publicly and privately provided social services.

I eventually found five associations that met my criteria. All were recommended by key informants and some were recommended repeatedly. Although I had met some of the membership of several associations in the past, I did not select associations where I had a longterm personal involvement. There were no publicly available lists of grassroots associations, and, as with most women's groups, they remain invisible in institutional settings and documents, fitting the pattern of exclusion of subordinate groups. Community development groups, for example, are not even mentioned in a regional profile and economic development directory for Southwest Virginia

(Burkett 1990; Lacy et al. 1990), although the documents include volunteer organizations.

A sixth association emerged from discussions with respondents in other groups. Because this study is reflexive in method as well as theory, I chose to write about this association because analysis revealed its importance for the collective practices of two respondents, and because it met the criteria stated above.

This study is concerned with marginalization and social change and, on that basis, numerous groups were eliminated from consideration. Women's groups with primarily middle-class membership were excluded; and women's church groups were excluded if they did not address concerns growing out of socio-economic marginalization. Environmental groups were also problematic because they tend to be dominated by outsiders and/or a middle-class membership, they may not have a female majority, and they tend to have a narrow agenda.

INTERVIEWING WOMEN

My next step was to select a small group of women from each of the associations to interview over a period of time long enough to allow for other interactions with them and other women through my role as an "oberserver-as-participant" in their group meetings. The interpretive dimension of this study led me "to seek out subjects who have experienced epiphanies" (Denzin 1989:125). Because I was interested in the "how" questions of social change, I sought out women who could tell me, within the context of their life stories, how their participation had changed them.

My selection of twelve women as "life story interview" respondents followed a strategy combining elements of snowball and purposive sampling techniques. Because the research is concerned with the *process of change* within a *marginalized context*, I asked the members of associations for volunteers or names of women who could speak about both. In requesting that women suggest respondents, I may have been referred to exemplary rather than typical women. But even if this is so, the strategy can contribute to the representativeness of their accounts because these women have been identified by others in their groups as women who can speak *for* their experiences.

Strategies varied only as necessary within the contexts of the associations. For example, in the union auxiliary I asked for volun-

teers at three meetings I attended so that I would reach all members who regularly attended; two women volunteered *and* were
recommended by their colleagues. I purposely sought out the third
respondent from the auxiliary because she had been repeatedly
mentioned as the central person in a break-away faction in the
association. I was careful to fully disclose the purposes of my research and to ask for permission to carry on the study in meetings
both formal and informal with members of the associations. Among
the many gracious women who contributed to this research project,
I was fortunate to find a few women with whom I have maintained
a relationship of solidarity and friendship.

Shared experience deepens understanding and promotes trust,
and I never hid or masked my sympathy with the women's collective efforts. The essence of our relationship was *not* partial disclosure to maintain distance, but engagement to make truth possible.
Since the completion of the research project, I have invited women
to speak during the Virginia Tech Women's Week and Women's
History Month; I have tried to facilitate connections to possible
funding sources for some groups; and I have asked other women to
participate in two international conferences on women.

Forester (1989) has said that "criticism is requisite to objectivity; detachment is not"(16); and Freire (1972) has noted that
"one cannot conceive of objectivity without subjectivity" (35). Yet
this engagement can be problematic particularly when the socio-
economic differences between researcher and respondent create conditions for a relationship of dependency; the researcher must be
sensitive to this possibility. I was careful to establish relationships
outside the research process with respondents who are strong and
autonomous persons, and, in one case, to discourage a relationship
with a person who asked for my counsel in ways that I was not
capable of providing. To discourage, however, is not to dismiss: this
respondent had told me that the *process* of participating in my
research project had opened up possibilities to her for changing her
life, and she wanted counseling. I had a responsibility to respect-
fully refer her to supportive professionals who could give her the
help that she wanted.

One is more likely to be truthful in a situation of trust and
mutuality (Oakley 1981). In hearing about my personal life, women
often expressed their concern for me, and their identification with
my experience. Reinharz (1992) asserts the importance of women
doing research with women, both in the connectedness of women's
experience and in the holistic content of women's communications.

Because I am a woman, a mother of daughters, a divorced head of household, and in the same age cohort as many of the women, we established a common standpoint. If some women felt changed by the research process, so was I.

DATA COLLECTION AND ANALYSIS

Most of the interviews with the twelve respondents were conducted from February to November 1991. Women told me their life stories while we sat in their homes, in restaurants and coffee shops, in a park, a laundromat, or in their places of work. Since that time, we have had additional interactions, sometimes to clarify or expand on the interviews.

I conducted the interviews with each woman in two to four sessions ranging from three to eight hours in length per session. An open-ended interview guide provided the basis for the interviews. Considerable latitude was taken in order to respond to emergent topics of research interest (Anderson et al. 1990) and to encourage the communication of feelings as well as thoughts. As Lofland and Lofland (1984) suggest, the interview was a "guided conversation" using a "list of things to be sure to ask about" rather than a finite and structured set of questions. Care was taken to keep the format of the interviews open to avoid silencing the subjectivity of the respondents.

Feminist research that argues for an engaged position for the researcher provides another source of data in observer comments that are grounded in the observer's experiences as a woman (Acker et al. 1983; Reinharz 1992). DuBois (1983) notes that in feminist research

we are the observer and the observed, subject and object, knower and known. When we take away the lens of androcentrism and patriarchy, what we have left is our own eyes, ourselves, and each other. *We* are the instruments of observation and understanding; *we* are the namers, the interpreters of our lives (DuBois 1983:112).

Observer comments within the transcribed interviews or conversations and field notes are the form of this data. These comments convey settings, describe processes, and reflect on meanings for both the subjects and the researcher. The interview process, including my own role as an observer-as-participant, tried to encourage the highly contextualized and personal narratives central to a feminist standpoint (Harding 1986; Hartsock 1983; Jaggar 1988; Smith 1987) and the values of feminist research practice (Cook and Fonow 1990).

All interviews were recorded, and the verbatim transcription of tapes of these interviews provides data for this study. I transcribed the entire interviews within one week of their occurrence, and included observer comments within the transcription. Although having another person do the transcription would have saved many weeks of work, I have come to realize that it was important to have the person who was involved in the interaction do the actual transcription. Because I came to know the women and their speech patterns, I could be more responsive to expression, intonation, pauses, emotion, and other non-verbal clues.

Field notes were written following other interactions with women in the associations. These field notes, as well as documents, other print materials, videotapes, photographs, and memorabilia provided illustrative materials for the analysis of the data. Analysis was an iterative process of going back over transcripts of each interview numerous times as the analysis progressed.

Following Denzin (1989), I "bracketed" central themes and recurring features in each of the life stories. I then made a chart of these themes and reviewed all of the other respondents' interviews to look for recurring themes. In creating this grid of persons on one axis and themes on another, I contextualized themes, and looked for the contextualized meaning of the negative case. For example, one respondent who was not overtly critical of a project organizer was always interviewed in the group's meeting place. We met there because her husband would not have appreciated my coming to her home; there was evidence that she had much experience limiting her criticisms of others.

Recurring themes were contextualized within each respondent's life story and within the collective stories of communities. My own experiences as an observer-as-participant, other illustrative material, and secondary sources deepened the understanding of the context. It also allowed for the analysis to draw out from women's experiences connections to social structures and processes.

ISSUES OF RELIABILITY AND VALIDITY

Two political criteria influence the knowledge validation process. First, knowledge claims are validated by a community of experts whose members represent the standpoints of the groups from which they originate. Within the Eurocentric masculinist process, this means that a scholar making a knowledge claim must convince a scholarly community controlled by white men that a given claim is justified. Second, each community of experts must maintain its credibility as defined by the larger group in which it is situated and from which it draws its basic, taken-for-granted knowledge. This means that scholarly communities that challenge basic beliefs held in the culture at large will be deemed less credible than those which support popular perspectives. (Collins 1990:203).

At the center of issues of reliability and validity in feminist research are epistemological debates about the construction of knowledge. Rather than fight the criteria for methodological adequacy of the powerful, Collins (1990) calls for feminists to find alternative epistemologies. She acknowledges the validity of concrete knowledge (wisdom), knowledge that seeks connection rather than distance, and knowledge that represents an ethic of caring and an ethic of personal accountability.

Although qualitative methods in general are usually perceived to have a high degree of validity but problems of reliability (Denzin 1978), feminist methods suggest that findings can be replicated through the shared standpoint of the knower and the known (Smith 1987; Reinharz 1992). In this study, the involvement of members of the associations in the selection of respondents created the possibility that similar themes and processes would be described by different respondents. In one association, for example, I have had several opportunities to ask similar questions of other members and to discuss my analysis of their collective experiences with respondents and with others. Other members have described similar processes of change through participation in the group. Individual and group responses to my analyses of gender and class experiences, as well as the association as a context of change, have been positive. Lofland and Lofland (1984) view the decision to trust or not trust the veracity of the subject's account not as a dichotomous choice but as a positioning somewhere on a continuum depending on the circumstances in the field, again allowing for the engaged discretion of the observer is assessing claims of truth. Further, by recognizing that each account is a "fiction of self-representation," we shift our concern from assessing the validity of "something that happens to people" to the "subjective mapping of experience" (Behar 1990:224–225). In doing so, we attempt to go beyond the production of "spectator knowledge" (Mies 1983:123) to what Cook and Fonow (1990) name as a basic epistemological principle of feminist research, an "emphasis on the empowerment of women and transformation of patriarchal institutions through research" (72–73).

REPORTING CONVENTIONS

The conventions for reporting from the interviews are as follows:

1) In order to protect the confidentiality of the women and assure their anonymity, I have chosen not to report data in ways that would create individual profiles, or fictionalized composites of individual women, although I constructed individual profiles during the analysis. Patterns of responses within and across individuals inform the analysis. Each analytical observation required the review of all transcripts for every woman.

2) Each respondent is quoted or summarized at least once in each of the analysis chapters (on family, work, community, and development). In this way, no one woman or group of women controls the discussion. However, recognizing that some women are more organically poetic than others, not all women are given equal voice on the page.

3) Quotations from individuals to illustrate the analysis are divided with asterisk symbols (*). For example, if there are two quotations from the interviews illustrating a particular point, they will be divided by asterisks and will be from two individuals. For the sake of clarity or to maintain anonymity, there are some editorial additions or deletions to the verbatim transcripts; additions appear within parentheses.

"You've got to be grounded"

THE DISCREET AND LESSER SPHERE

Oppression is domesticating. (Freire 1972:36)

The relationship of work, family, and community are central to a feminist understanding of movements for social change. The women I interviewed in Southwest Virginia had, to varying degrees, initiated change in their lives through the labor that they did in association with others. That labor was mostly unpaid and was done in a variety of settings. Women in an educational institution, for example, were engaged in "emotional labor" (Hochschild 1975), creating an effective and communal context for women to succeed in their studies. The labor of strike-supporting union-identified women and the labor of women in community development associations exemplify varieties of community management and integrative work primarily done by women worldwide (March and Taqqu 1982; Moser 1989).

In addition to their participation in domestic production and reproduction as mothers and caregivers, all of these women have worked outside the home as well as within. Their paid work in sewing factories, furniture factories, grocery stores, restaurants, shoe stores, and other secondary labor markets, and their "homework" sewing by the piece, is also work primarily assigned to women (Kessler-Harris 1982). Like all of the work in formal and informal labor markets throughout the world (Joekes 1987; UN 1991), this work is defined within patriarchal structures (Mies 1986) that women first experience within the family.

I begin a discussion of women and the family with the observation that working-class women's labor, inside and outside the labor force, is performed inside and outside the confines of social and biological reproduction. Marxist analytical categories, as well as feminist attempts to correct them, may be inadequate to capture the complexity of the labor of women, its deep embeddedness in

27

familial relationships and community values, its psychological and ideological dimensions, and the possibilities within it for revolutionary politics. How women might envision "collective democratic citizenship" (Dietz 1987:17) is rooted in what women do and whom they care about. The conceptual limits that separate what women do inside and outside the household are both porous and transparent to the women who push at them. As Petchesky notes, " 'production' and 'reproduction,' work and the family, far from separate territories . . . are really intimately related modes that reverberate upon one another and frequently occur in the same social, physical and even psychic spaces" (1979:376).

Much of women's community-based work has been viewed as an extension of the private and domestic sphere where women, ideologically subservient to men, have almost universally been assigned (Rosaldo 1974). In this "discreet and lesser sphere" (Smith 1979), women, especially those outside wage labor work in the third world, have been "invisible" to development planners (World Bank 1980). Even with the substantive efforts of the development industry (Maguire 1984) to include women as both "agents and beneficiaries" of development (USAID 1983), the primary goal has been to increase the economic efficiency of women through "income-generating activities" where women are not defined as workers but as housewives (Mies 1986:118). No matter how well-intentioned, income-generating projects to increase women's purchasing power and personal autonomy in Central Appalachia are also grounded in the logic of the new international division of labor. According to Mies (1986), "(t)he economic logic of this *housewifization* is a tremendous reduction of labour costs" (119).

The logic is extended to the non-traditional job-training and gender equity programs in the public educational institutions serving the region in this study: they are mandated to increase women's economic participation as workers (Vocational Gender Equity 1989), and, in doing so, they increase women's potential as consumers of goods produced often by women in the third world. These "third world products" may also be made by housewives doing industrial homework in the first world, revealing international class complexities for a gendered analysis of work.[1] Neither position of "housewife" challenges the hierarchical dichotomy of women's public and private lives, production and reproduction, or allows for material and ideological connections across the borders of class, race, and political geography.[2]

In the separate spheres model of feminist materialism, the material base of women's oppression is capitalism, and patriarchy is its ideological site (Mitchell 1971). Capitalism assigns the places in society, and patriarchy, as a set of social relations among men, determines who will fill them (Hartmann 1984). "Gender domination thus becomes a resource or capacity of men vis-a-vis women, rather than a characteristic of the larger structure" (Wharton 1991:375). Recent discussions in socialist feminism have tried to resolve the theoretical problem of separating patriarchy and capitalism for purposes of analysis: Wharton proposes that gender is both structure, a property of social organization, *and* agency, a property of social actors. She argues that "feminist accounts have tended to privilege either social identity or social organization, treating the other one as derivative" (1991:384). Chinchilla and Giminez (1991) summarize this argument by stating that "all social relations should be thought of as fundamentally gendered as part of a single system ... but that the processes by which gendered social relations become a source of identity, meaning and action in this single system are historically contingent."

The central Appalachian region of the United States that includes Southwest Virginia "has occupied a peculiar place in the American economy and imagination" (Hall 1986:357), yet women have been subsumed into analytical categories mostly unexamined on the basis of the social relations of gender. Like the women of Hall's historical study of the Elizabethton, Tennessee rayon strike, the women of Southwest Virginia are "neither traditionalists acting on family values nor market-oriented individualists, neither peculiar mountaineers nor familiar modern women. Their irreverence and inventiveness shatter stereotypes and illuminate intricacies of working-class women's lives" (Hall 1986:357).

Similarly, a 1950s account of Chicana women's union activism in a Southwestern United States mining strike and the women's increasing, even if temporary, awareness of their strategic gender interests is presented in the film "Salt of the Earth" (Jarrico, Wilson, Bieberman 1954 (film); Rosenfelt and Wilson 1978.) The film resonates with what respondents told me about the strike in the Virginia coal fields, in the strategies women used, and in the tensions with husbands and other men over their growing militancy and independence.

In the context of this study, we can ask under what historically contingent circumstances in Central Appalachia can structurally gendered positions and gendered identity, in both material and psychic conditions, be both forms of exploitation and oppression *and* sources of strategies of subversion. If "the family is the place where domination and submission are learned," (Hartmann 1984:182), the family may teach women how and why to struggle. Put another way by Scott (1985): "If the exercise of domination depends on a social context for its creation and maintenance, so does the exercise of resistance" (329). This story seeks to clarify this central contradiction.

WHY WOMEN ACT

Recently, "women in development" (WID) literature and African-American feminist theorists have critiqued western or Eurocentric feminist assumptions about the primacy of feminist consciousness for social change (Chinchilla 1991; Collins 1990; hooks 1981; Mohanty 1991; Sen and Grown 1987). WID scholarship, which intentionally addresses the development *planning* issues, is now very interested in women's associations both in terms of development policy implementation and resistance to its inherent inequities. Particularly in Latin America, women mobilize politically not as members of the working class, but as wives and mothers, in recognition of what Molyneux (1986) calls practical gender interests. Participation in new social movements formed for others who are bound to you as "family" does not preclude the development of revolutionary consciousness. Quite the contrary, Safa (1990) argues that "Latin American women think that their roles as wives and mothers legitimize their sense of injustice and outrage, since they are protesting their inability to effectively carry out these roles. . . . In short, they are redefining and transforming their domestic role from one of private nurturance to one of collective, public protest, and in this way challenging the traditional seclusion of women into the private sphere of the family" (355).

Nine of the informants in this study have been politically mobilized in community development and labor support groups; for three women, income-generation and education have been the contexts for their associative practices. The women who define themselves as politically mobilized share with the other informants, as well as with Latin American women, a sense that their activism is rooted in their traditional gender identities as daughters, wives, and mothers. Yet to equate the activism of Latin American and

Appalachian women would unfairly conflate their historical specificity and agency. There are too many dissimilarities: in Latin America, there is a tradition of collective social action; Latin American women tend to present their demands directly to the state as they face the effects of extreme economic crisis; and their jobs tend to be outside the formal wage economy. Safa (1990) sees a distinctively Latin American position: when Latin American women challenge the state, it "differs from contemporary U.S. and Western European experience, in which women seek a gender-neutral participation in the public sphere" (355).

Until recently in Southwest Virginia, class struggle has been waged primarily by men in the union, the United Mineworkers of America. Even though the "rigid division of labor and women's hardships in (coal) company towns have resulted, paradoxically, in the notable militancy of miners' wives" (Hall 1986:372), women's activism has been circumscribed by its supportive role to the union. From this research, it is evident that when women challenge the state in grassroots community groups, they tend, as Safa noted, to present a gender-neutral position. But they also challenge class-based associations, like the union, to meet their "practical" gender interests, which may become "strategic" in the process (Molyneux 1986).[3]

Through collective action, directed to the state, capital, or labor, the women of Southwest Virginia may also be challenging or transforming their domestic roles in ways similar to what Safa discusses. As women find new ways to deconstruct the boundaries between public and private domains, the class-based concerns of women here and abroad may become more similar, as economic crisis, cutbacks in social welfare, and "housewifization" in the gendered international division of labor (Mies 1986) bring women from the two Americas closer.

Varying forms of gendered political consciousness, reflecting the tensions and interactions between public and private spheres and distinctive in their responses to culture, race, and class, emerge in Bookman and Morgen's (1988) edited volume on grassroots community and union activism among working-class women in the U.S. In this volume, Luttrell (1988) argues that although "women's female consciousness" may have been the impetus to collective practice, their experiences "actively refocused and reshaped their political analysis of the situation" (142). Similarly, in her exploration of an Afrocentric feminist epistemology, Collins (1990) discusses the capacity of African-American women to develop oppositional consciousness and strategies of resistance within the familial and community context of the social role of "othermother" and the traditional roles of Black women within the church. Clearly, feminist analysis of marginalized women's activism must take into account the nuances and complexities of women's positions within class and racial hierarchies; it must also attempt to understand how these women are embedded within communities that are both holding them and motivating them as social actors (Scott 1991).

THE INTIMACIES OF PLACE

The informants in this study are situated in communities in the mountainous, rural area of Central Appalachia. The Appalachian Southwest of Virginia has been characterized as a geographic and ideological "place" where loyalty to one's family comes before loyalty to any other group in society or any principle of organization outside of kinship bonds (Photiadis and Schwarzwellwer 1971; Weller 1965). From this "culture of poverty" perspective, the bridge from family to civil society has been weakened by cultural isolation and dependency. Even those who view familialism as a defensive strategy to find refuge from economic exploitation (Lewis, Kobak, and Johnson 1978) acknowledge the centrality of kinship, which can be defined as the blood and marriage networks that provide "cultural values connecting the individual to land, to community, to history, and to identity" (Beaver 1991:299). It is especially important to take culture and community into account, Hall (1986) says, to avoid "thin description" and a "one-dimensional view of labor conflict" (355).

For rural people in Appalachia, "land and family, place and kinship, are intimately interwoven" (Beaver 1991:299). The idiom of kinship has *not* been replaced by the idiom of the market to describe civil society. Kinship, as Beaver (1991) points out, satisfies contemporary economic needs for the women and men of the region. Kinship provides the "expected or ideal patterns or reciprocal activity and mutual aid" (300). Parents provide land to children and kin share labor, including labor associated with agricultural work, child care, building, and household repairs. The kinship idiom acts as a barrier to the commodification of scarce resources in poor places.

The nuclear family as constructed in contemporary capitalism is both the center of the kinship system and the site for its contradictions. Hall (1986) cites the historical importance of kinship in the Appalachian mountains when "high levels of farm ownership sustained cultural independence. Within the internal economies of families, individual fortunes were cushioned by reciprocity; an orientation towards subsistence survived side by side with the desire for cash and store-bought goods" (370). In contemporary Appalachian families, Beaver (1991) acknowledges that "the conflict between nuclear-family independence and the necessity for extended-family economic cooperation creates a structural bind" (304), particularly for women. Wives are expected to provide emotional and material labor to their husband's family, yet are isolated from associations with others in a work environment that would give "means for venting their feelings away from the domestic scene" (306). Even when familial cooperation is both materially and emotionally rewarding, reciprocity is no longer enough to meet the needs of poor families, especially those headed by women.

The activism of women in civil society in this study draws on the kinship idiom to enlarge rather than retreat into the family, as the culture of poverty thesis suggests. However, it is important to recognize the contradictions within the nuclear family under capitalism. The end of the family as a production unit, the isolation and privatization of the nuclear family, the emphasis on individual rights, the "housewifization" of women, and the dependence of children create problems for equating the "family" that women speak of with the nuclear family. When respondents use the family as the metaphor for a just society, they may be resolving the contradictions within the nuclear family and the idealized norms of kinship in order to create new models for communities.

JUST LIKE A FAMILY

Working-class families are contextualized within places; in and around the coal camps and mining towns of Southwest Virginia, family life has been affected for generations by coal and other extractive-based industries. In this historically specific place, the gendered division of labor was intensified and women were prohibited from the mines or perceived to bring "bad luck" when they get too close. This cultural prohibition is also found in the tin mines of the Andes (Nash 1979) and the zinc and copper mines of New Mexico and Arizona (Kingslover 1989). But in all of these regions, women have both mined the earth themselves, and have emerged as leaders in labor struggles (Jarrico, Wilson, Bieberman 1954 (film); Kopple 1976 (film); Kingslover 1989).

In telling the story of women's activism in the 1983 Arizona copper miners' strike, for example, Kingslover (1989) writes that "while everyone seemed attached to the community, it was the women who saw themselves as inseparable from it" (70). The inseparability of women and communities was also expressed by respondents in this study, some of whom also took on a highly visible and mobilizing role in a mining strike (Porter and Ramey 1989 (film); Yancey 1990). Just as work and family resonate for women, so do family and community, as women in this study used the language of familial intimacy to discuss their community work.

(Our first action) brought the people all together; there was such a closeness, a togetherness . . . It was just like a family working together and it was terrific.

******

We did it because we had to. Maybe it's radical to go in there and do something that may be against the law but it's our children, our lives that are at stake.

******

I accepted the position (of president of the association) because there was not a child in that room that I did not know on a first name basis!

******

I had a hard time drawing the line (between my family and my community work). It's hard sometimes saying that I had to separate that part of my life.

During the thirty-two months that I met with women in Southwest Virginia and in interviews with respondents, in almost all cases, women noted that their decision to enter into communities or situations of profound change was grounded in their intense concern for the well-being of their families and communities. They spoke as wives and mothers: in a sense, they domesticized their public work and politicized its connection to their private lives. They spoke of connection and responsibility to husbands, children, parents, grandparents, cousins, ancestors, descendants, and to the communities that bind their lives through time. The timelessness of their commitment was evoked through spiritual language that evoked empathy rather than justice as the basis for action.

I thought, this is what God intended me to do: to come home and do what I am doing now—to try and make people's lives better, to help them help themselves. . . . I understand people here, understand how people feel if they've never seen anything or done anything. . . . It's not that they don't want it. It's intimidating and exciting at the same time. How degrading it can be sometimes when you have to ask for help. . . . That's why I can relate! . . . I know what it's like to be without water, without indoor plumbing, I know what it's like to be without lights, or good things, because I've been there. It's like a remembrance, or God saying: 'Don't forget.'

The work of women in community and union associations began and often remained within the confines of traditional gender roles.[4] A community development leader talked about the activities of her association to build community in its early days.

The majority (who were involved) were women, and they were involved in different ways. We would have cake walks and dances twice a month, and the women would bake the cakes, set up for the dances, and clean up.

Another women spoke of how important her husband and her faith were to her.

(My husband's) the one that instigated all this. . . . I tell everybody that God gave me (my husband) first, and then He gave me my job (in community work). But He gave me my husband first: if I didn't have that, hell, I'd never last three days!

For many of the women in the United Mineworkers of America (UMWA) auxiliary, participation was never picketing, travelling north, blocking roads, taking over buildings or getting arrested: instead, it was cooking food and delivering it to strike supporters in "Camp Solidarity."[5] Other women helped with a phone chain.

> When we came out on strike and wanted people on the picket lines, I could call 14 women and those 14 would call everybody on their lines so it wouldn't be long distance. So if you needed women to come to the picket line, you just put out the word. The first day of the strike we got 300!

Women in another association engaged in class analysis when economic relationships were perceived in human and relational terms.

> We had lost the mining company... and economic depression was really setting in. I could see all over the community people suffering! ... It seemed that every time I turned around something was being taken away from us!

The last thing that was going to be take away was the industrial park. It was land left to the community years earlier by departing industry and was intended to be used for local economic development. The industrial park was a gift to the community, the women said, in recognition of what the people of the community had given of themselves to the industry over several generations. When county government attempted to sell the land, it was a betrayal of a trust, and sparked the women's activism.

> There was talk all over town: at least we could use it as a playground! At least it could stay in the community. ... When we had a meeting, everybody came out.

After stopping the sale, the newly formed community organization formed an economics discussion group.

> I found out that a big grocery store ... (like) Kroger gets their stuff from Kroger factories, so the money stays within Kroger. A small 'mom and pop' grocery store buys ... their cabbage, say, from S&J Cabbage Factory, and Uncle John and Aunt Doris and their kids own that factory or grow that cabbage. ... So now, I try to buy everything I can here in [this town], even if it costs a little bit more.

In this way, individual and collective social action followed women's recognition of practical gender needs (Moser 1989), rooted in the family.

Meeting family needs was paramount, even when to act was to risk disapproval and sometimes violence from those persons having power over them. Seeking work outside the home, or even "homework," could carry the risk of a husband's anger. At the same time, it allowed one respondent the opportunity to give her children the "nice things" of "middle-class kids." Despite her husband's opposition, another homeworker looked forward to the possibility of buying gifts to compensate for not raising the grown children that had been taken from her when they were young.

I always felt a little guilty within myself . . . that my children didn't have their mother. I feel like I owe my children because I took away something. It was something that they couldn't help! It was between me and their dad and not them. I'm not to blame for the divorce, but these children didn't get what they deserved either. They didn't ask to come into the world, and they were innocent victims of it all. That's how I feel. The children always are the ones to suffer. Like I say, I try my best now to give them a little bit.

If families were the reason for women's activism, the reality of material need is a relentless motivator. There were more pressing needs than buying gifts. For an older woman with many health problems, the chance to have her community work partially paid under a VISTA volunteer program meant that she could get the prescription medication she needs. Another woman heard she could get paid to go school in the community center. Both she and her husband were unemployed and living in "the smallest trailer ever made", so she picked up bottles on the roadside to earn enough gas money to get to the center to register. The community college would pay for books, transportation, and tuition, giving the family at least some cash income.

"You've got to be grounded," a woman told me: grounded in the family and the community. And when you are grounded, you recognize that the threat of economic deprivation or violence to you requires you to act not only for the present but for future generations.

My son, 14 years old, got a phone call at 3 o'clock one morning that said when he came to school the next morning they was going to cut his throat. The hardest thing I ever did in my life was put my kid on the bus next morning and send him to school. . . . I decided I was going to quit this stuff . . . and I called my family together. My 14-year-old son said: 'Mamma, if you quit, who's going to do anything? Mamma, if you quit, we have no future.'

Similarly, another respondent was explicit in noting the relation between her actions and her hopes for the community. Finding the time, while working third shift at the sewing factory, to become involved in the community association wasn't easy, but she did so

> because it was improving the community. Bringing people that lived here years ago back . . . it makes everybody feel better. . . . I got into it because of the young people: the thing I like best is working with the young people. . . . I have a teenage daughter and I always like having the young people at my house. . . . A lot of people catch flack if they say they're from (here). Well, the people really do need to be built up, especially the young people, and they are. That's what it's all about! It builds everybody up; it makes them feel better. One of the greatest things that comes out of it is to uplift the people here.

For African-American women, the Black community and especially the Black Church are the enlarged family that sustain women's activism; the idea of uplifting the community is a common theme for African-Americans (Davis 1989; Collins 1990:149).[6] The women of Southwest Virginia express a similar longterm and inclusive vision of their collective work. What connects the motivations of African-American and Appalachian women to become community activists may be in how both communities have been exploited on the basis of class and culture.

> (Our community) was looked down upon . . . The community really started together because we had lost our school, and kids from (outside) made fun of our kids. . . . We got the reputation of being mean out here; that's something the kids had to face!
>
> ******
>
> What I'm trying to preserve is that sense of community. I don't want to recreate it because then it would be mine.

But I want to preserve what's here. . . . I want to preserve some of those things so that (the kids) get an understanding of who they are, and be proud of who they are.

******

(We did it) not just for the women, not just for the men, but for all. . . . I think that women work for the good of all; I think that men work for the good of men, and I don't think that they really realize it.

******

It's like me helping you (the researcher) with your paper: if I help you, and you help someone else, and that someone helps someone else, it goes around and everyone benefits.

OUR KIDS, OUR LIVES, OUR UNION

Travelling the roads of Southwest Virginia during the UMWA's confrontation with Pittston Coal, you could not avoid the green and white bumper sticker signifying the collective commitment to class struggle: "Our kids, our lives, our union." For the women of Southwest Virginia, this form of expression is more than rhetorical. The women in this study and their peers in grassroots associations are working-class women. All of the informants recalled moments in their childhood or young adulthood when they knew that they were different from the children of the managers, that their lives were circumscribed by how they and their families labored.

Significantly, this working-class consciousness was expressed in the empathetic and caregiving language that has been the available speech for women in the ideology of the modern family. In discussing a decision to join a support group for women miners, one women said:

At least I know that there is another woman that's working in the mines and she's having the same problem. I will support her. I can give her a little help in how to handle her problems.

Why women think relationally, or have "women's ways of knowing" (Belenkey et al. 1986), has been the subject of considerable interest especially to contemporary cultural and psychoanalytic feminist scholars who have looked beneath the words and behaviors of women to understand "the reproduction of mothering" in the human psyche. Chodorow's (1978) work in object-relations theory proposed that personality development in the modern world is significantly different for women than men as both genders are almost exclusively "mothered" by women. Because girls are parented[7] by persons of the same gender, the experience of individuation is rooted in empathy for others and "the basic feminine sense of self is connected to the world"(169). Gilligan (1982) looked at how women develop moral reasoning and concluded that for women, "the moral problem arises of conflicting responsibilities rather than competing rights. . . . This conception of morality as concerned with the activity of care centers moral development around the understanding of responsibility and relationships"(19).

Following Chodorow and Gilligan, the research of Belenky, Clinchy, Goldberger, and Tarule (1986) suggests that the "feminine predisposition toward connection and conversation" (18) begins in a gendered epistemological grounding that is related to women's self-concepts, use of imagery, and discursive practices. Ruddick (1980) further explores the relationship of gender, knowledge, and values, and proposes "maternal thinking" as an alternative basis for building political community.

But whose "maternal thinking" does she propose, and what is the material reality of that kind of mothering? Although Ruddick's work emphasizes the social *practice* of mothering (Morgen and Bookman 1988:21–22), critics of the psychoanalytic and cultural strain of feminist theory point out that there is a tendency in it to idealize and valorize middle-class mothering: as a social role constructed in the disequilibrium between white, middle-class women and men, it needs to be more critically examined (Morgen and Bookman 1988). Gilligan's work has been particularly criticized for ignoring the experiences of women of color and working-class women who might find that the processes of moral reasoning occur in the intersection of multiple structures of oppression (Davis 1990; hooks 1989). For Dietz (1987), "(t)here is no reason to think that mothering necessarily induces commitment to democratic practices (15). The maternalists stand in danger of committing precisely the same mistake that they find in the liberal view. They threaten to turn historically distinctive women into ahistorical, universalized entities" (12–13).

Assuming that there can be "gynocentric ways of thinking and acting" is named "the new feminist essentialism" by Morgen and

Bookman: "Social relations of power are so fundamentally structured in contemporary American society by the intersection of gender, race, ethnicity, and class that women's struggles for
empowerment cannot be understood without making these factors
central to the analysis" (Morgen and Bookman 1988:23). A static
and normative concept of gendered consciousness limits the agency
of women as social actors. It is more appropriate to a study of
women and change to ask how women interpret at various times
and under various conditions their own experience of family, the
material reality of connection and caring for others. Collins (1990),
for example, explores the "othermother" tradition in African and
African-American communities as a community model of mothering that pushes the limits of a relational identity to include political communities. Mothering, then, is a strategy to conserve a
heritage and survive oppression, and may be expressed in ways not
at all similar to middle-class and individualistic norms.

Following recent theoretical work in socialist feminism that
rejects the separate spheres model, or the analytical separation of
patriarchy and capitalism, gendered consciousness—what happens
in psychic spaces—emerges from what Eisenstein (1979) calls "ne-
gotiation." Working-class women actively negotiate between dominant and oppositional ideologies (Morgen and Bookman
1988:11–12) in a practice of resistance similar to what Collins
theorizes for African-American women under structural positions
complicated by racism. For the respondents in this study, gendered
consciousness emerges from the structural position of coal miner's
daughter and/or wife, of female industrial or service worker or
working-class wife, of single mother, and of Appalachian woman,
embedded in the economic, social, political, cultural, and religious
institutions of place.

THE DARK SIDE OF FAMILY LIFE

For women, irrespective of class, race, and region, the family can
be a painful place to be (Barry 1979; Dobash and Dobash 1979;
Hartmann 1981; Heise 1991; Martin 1976; Mies 1986; Rubin 1976;
Thorne and Yalom 1982; Yllo 1989). For rural working-class women,
"family structure is basically the nuclear unit, with temporary ex-
pansions to include extra people" in times of disruption like divorce
or the incapacitation of a parent (Fitchen 1991). Women learn how
to be subordinate within the nuclear family (Horkheimer 1972;
Hartmann 1981), and can experience profound isolation, degrada-

tion, abuse, and exploitation based on their position within patriarchal capitalism.

The women in this study have experienced the most intimate of social institutions as "worlds of pain" (Rubin 1976), inscribed in their bodies and minds as working-class people and as women. As working-class people in Southwest Virginia, they have known the historic brutality of the mining industry in its colonization and exploitation of the natural and human resources of Appalachia (Gaventa 1980; Yarrow 1991; Lewis 1970, 1978; Lewis and O'Donnell 1990). The violence waged by the owners and managers of the mines and against the people of the region has been matched in contemporary times by the violence of union men against one another (Gaventa 1980; Yancey 1990).

Shifflett (1991) says of the coal towns even after WWI: "It was an all-male world where coal operators exploited workers and the environment. The workers released their frustrations and aggressions upon themselves and other miners. Since ethnic and racial prejudice prevailed, the confrontations easily involved mixed groups" (52–53). For Shifflett, the coal fields are male domains where the social relations of gender are more polarized than in more heterogeneous communities (81–83). As respondents in this study have observed, men also released their frustrations and aggressions on women, replicating the violence of the social relations of class in the relations of gender.

The women I interviewed had grandfathers, fathers, brothers and husbands who worked coal or zinc or made carbide, all jobs that were dirty and dangerous. A coal miner's daughter recalls the Dickensian qualities of her father's life.

It was really rough. I remember him talking about the mines being so low that you'd have to lay on your belly to load coal. I remember that his knees had sores even with the knee pads that they had then. You had to shovel—they didn't have the machinery that they have today. They had ponies that pulled out carts of coal.

Disability or death were not uncommon. Men went into the mines as teenagers, and spent exhausting and dangerous years underground often to find that by middle age they were gasping for breath or incapacitated by other injuries.[8] The observation that there was an "awesome toll of death, injury, and disease in the bituminous coal industry" (Shifflett 1991:106) was reinforced by women's testimony and my own observations.

I learned of a husband whose chest was crushed, another husband who was mutilated by a beam that drove through his face and destroyed his palate,[9] and two grandfathers who died in explosions, one in a mine and another building the railroad spur to carry coal out of the region. While spending the night as a guest in the home of a respondent and her coal miner husband, I watched him wince in pain from a back injury every time he tried to rise from a chair. All evening and the next morning, I was conscious of the pain he experienced as it was inscribed in his deliberate and slow movements and the expressions on his face. Like other disabled miners I had met or heard about, this man's disability claim was being contested by the company.

Of six informants whose husbands and fathers were employed for most of their lives in deep mines, one has a father dying of black lung, one was left a pregnant teenage widow when her husband was killed in a mining accident, and three have husbands who are permanently disabled from mining injuries. One women told of her father losing a leg in a mining accident at the age of 17 and being put to work cutting the low coal (coal seam 30" or less in height), often lying in water, until mechanization eliminated his job.

CHILDHOOD: NO TIME FOR INNOCENCE

"I never had time to be a girl," said one woman when I asked her to recall her childhood at the beginning of our interview. For most of the respondents, childhood memories were of hard times. Ten of the informants are in their early forties, and recall the deprivations and dislocations they experienced during the recession in the coal industry that began during the 1950s, when mining labor was de-skilled and demand declined with mechanization (Shifflett 1991; Yarrow 1990).[10] Inadequate housing and inadequate food made life "rough" in the coalfields.

I lived here in a little two-room shack, and there were eight of us all together: no running water, no facilities.

******

It was a hard life: if the wind blowed, the rugs flew up off the floor in those little shacks. . . . If it was cold—freezing— you'd put everything in the refrigerator to keep it from freezing.

******

There was times that we didn't have no money... There was a winter pear tree out in the yard and she used to take frozen pears off the tree, bring them in to cook them, and sometimes that was all we had to eat.

Because of the physical environment in the coal camps and company towns, women and children were drawn into the industrial process in a variety of ways. In addition to inadequate housing conditions, there were environmental effects, like the dust that always covered the carbide town:

They would call it firing the furnace and the men would take these real long poles or rods and flames would shoot out, and smoke came out. The grey dust would settle all over the town on people's houses. Even over here we would get dust from it.

With instability in the coal industry, families were separated, forced to migrate, or engaged in subsistence production and the informal economy to survive.

I remember him having to go over to Hazard, Kentucky to work. He would stay over there and come home on the week-ends. He did that for a long time until he could find work closer to home.

******

Back then you just couldn't go out anywhere and find a paying job. Sometimes he'd get to stay in one place for a while. Eventually he gave up moving from here to yonder and we moved back into the family hollow where I still live. He just farmed and cut timber.

******

We were just barely making it because we had to raise food and everything. When he couldn't find a job he would go herbin': mountain tea leaves—he pulled that—sassafras, ginseng, birch. When he didn't have a job, that's what he would do. He would do that to raise his family.

In the gendered hierarchy of the coal towns, it was often the women and their children who suffered, not only through economic deprivation but physically and emotionally within the patriarchal family, where violence has historically been sanctioned as a form of social control (Barry 1979). In this study, women and children became acceptable objects of male working-class frustration and rage. Often the rage followed alcohol or other substance abuse: one of the interview subjects, a coal miner herself and a recovering addict, explained.

I was so angry! I was working in the mines and I'd come home and smoke three or four joints and drink a six pack and sleep for four hours and get up and smoke again. I couldn't sleep. I was so angry one time I ripped a phone off the wall and broke the gear shift on my car.

Nine of the twelve subjects talked of their husbands' problems and three women talked of fathers' problems with alcohol and, for some, other drugs. Several woman saw drinking and mining as inevitable companions.

I guess he drank since he was a young boy, and he spent 30 years in the coal mines. Back in them days, way he tells it, when the men come out of the mines they had so much coal dust in their mouths and dirt, about the only thing that quenched their thirst and got that nasty stuff out was to go and pool their money for a glass of beer... On pay-day, he'd go and drink some moonshine, too.

Shifflett (1991) argues that "mining coal brought greater divisions in gender" than in agricultural areas in the southern Appalachians (101). Men could drink, but women understood the consequences of diverting income to the local pub.

My father drank up a good bit of the money. Mom used to get upset. He'd bring home a pie and try to buy his way back in and he'd be so drunk she'd throw the pie out. Drinking and bringing home a pie when she had bills to take care of and rent! They didn't own their own home. All her life she was just moved from one house to another house. She worried.

******

Sometimes mom would get the money and sometimes she wouldn't. He'd spend the money for drinking and ...

entertaining his friends. He was abusive to my mom and I felt that (if I left) it would just be one less mouth to feed.

Although alcohol is associated with abuse, it does not cause men to act violently towards women: men choose violence because it is available to them, as the structural position of women is both subordinate and vulnerable. The position of working-class men is also subordinate in the context of class, but powerful in relation to women. One women observed of her husband: "The longer we stayed together, the shorter money got, the more violent he got." This also does not mean that domestic violence is caused by class oppression as there is ample evidence that women of every class, ethnicity, and world region are battered (Carbonell et al. 1984; Heise 1991). There is, however, cross-cultural evidence that there is less violence against women in societies where women have the most political, economic and social autonomy (Friedl 1975). Men who use violence against women are behaving more appropriately in the ideology of gender (Barry 1979) than men who might find more pacific or "womanly," and therefore devalued, ways of dealing with their frustration and anger. Women who are their victims are less likely to be autonomous enough to escape their status as "objects."

Shifflett (1991) cites the "ambience of maleness" in mining culture as "one of its salient features" (xxx–ix). In the "macho" culture of coal, the object of a man's rage, rather than a phone or a gear shift, would often be a wife or a child.

I was raised in an alcoholic home. My dad was hard on my mom—almost killed her a couple of times. I witnessed this; even called the police on him one time! Then *I* got beat near to death.

Another woman observed:

Daddy is not an alcoholic but he was very physically abusive. He beat us with his mining belt that had these buckles on it. He was angry a lot. . . . Daddy worked 'hoot owl' shift, and he would come home in the mornings and we would have to be really quiet, and it was really hard with eleven kids. So Mommy would start first thing in the morning setting us on the stairs for any infraction so that by the time that daddy woke up, we would all be sitting on the stairs. And we would sit there and wait for daddy to call our turn. We lived in a two-story company house. He would get up, go into the bathroom, and take out his mining belt, and he would call out our names one at a time. And we would just sit there and wait to get the shit beat out of us!

The father that beat his daughter also sexually abused her at the age of five; the mother that sat her on the stairs was complicit in denying and covering up incest as well as aiding the beatings. Five of the mothers of informants were victims of abuse themselves and alcohol consumption by fathers was volunteered as a contributing factor in three of those cases. This suggests that "in the context of substance abuse, child abuse, and spouse abuse, child sex abuse may be one more component of an environment that accepts violence as normal" (Butler and Burton 1990:79).

THE DANGER OF BEING FEMALE

There are two experiences that unite women across culture and class, those of giving birth to new life and fear of male violence. (Heise 1991:1)

For the women I interviewed, their own and other women's experience of violence often began in childhood and was often sexualized through ideological pressure to become sexually active, to do one's marriage "duty," to being raped as young girls by male relatives. In linking beating women and sexual abuse, it is important not to diminish the *sexual* base of violence against women (MacKinnon 1987). The politicization of the heterosexual family by radical feminists, where "women and girls experience female sexual slavery without ever going out of their homes" (Barry 1979:410), should caution us from concluding that sex crimes are just another expression of male violence rooted in frustration: the women I interviewed communicated their own painful understanding of the constraints and dangers of their womanhood and their sexuality. MacKinnon (1982) makes a powerful argument that "(s)exuality is to feminism what work is to marxism: that which is most one's own, yet most taken away. . . . As the organized expropriation of the work of some for the benefit of others defines a class—workers—the organized expropriation of the sexuality of some for the use of others defines the sex, women. Heterosexuality is its structure,

gender and family its congealed forms, sex roles its qualities gener-
alized to social persona, reproduction a consequence, and control
its issue" (1–2).

Ten of twelve women acknowledged that the most difficult aspect of growing up was the recognition that their sex made them
powerless. Being female marked you for work within the family
that boys were exempt from. Your freedom as a child was limited
not only by gendered boundaries of proper behavior but also by the
inference that stepping out made you physically vulnerable. Puberty meant being humiliated by the jokes of male relatives at the
same time that you were expected to be both seductive and saintly.
For some girls, being female gave male blood relatives the right to
expropriate their sexuality as well as their work.

Of twelve respondents, five spoke of being physically or emotionally battered by parents, usually fathers.[11]

> I got many whippings from my dad, I mean he brought the
> blood! I'd have had welts on me two inches wide.

✳✳✳✳✳✳

> Growing up, girls didn't have any privileges. The boys was
> the ones! . . . I wished many times that I had been born a
> boy!

What was the hardest part of growing up?" I asked another
woman. "Having a vagina." was the reply. "Being female: that made
me different; that made me vulnerable." Two of the twelve respondents volunteered that they had been victims of incest,[12] raped by a
grandfather, father, or possibly other male relatives.[13] As an eight
year old, one woman was introduced to the demand for her sexuality as well as labor within the family.

> When I was a little girl, my grandfather raped me time and
> time again. I knew if I told my dad, it would mean some-
> body getting killed or him not believing in me, mostly not
> believing me. They always expected me to go over to
> mamaws and papaws cause we lived right next door; ex-
> pected me to go over there and see if she needed anything
> done, even if she was home or not. I had to go.

It was not irrational for this woman to conclude that sex was work
reinforced by ideology.

I think sometimes mamma thought that having babies was
her job. . . . a girl was expected to grow up, get married,
have kids, have sex no matter whether she wanted to or
not, that was her duty.

TEACHING THE IDEOLOGY OF GENDER

Emotional abuse sometimes took the form of dependency and an
absolute prohibition against girls establishing a life outside of filial
and wifely bonds. Isolation was enforced by the work requirements
of female children and enhanced by the geography of the coal fields:
the hills and hollows off winding dirt roads, where multi-genera-
tional families lived, allowed little contact with outsiders, especially if you were a girl.

I had friends but they were never allowed in my home.
There were too many of us. And when I got home I didn't
have time to sit and talk and to be a girl.

One woman recalled her longing to ride into town on the rare
occasions that her parents would load children into the truck and
take them along when they went for supplies. The children that got
to go to town were her brothers: as a girl, she was expected to stay
at home to take care of the house and the babies. Another woman
remembers never straying too far from the front porch: her household and child care chores tied her there so that her mother was
free for farm work.
    Girls who took tentative steps towards independence—taking
a job, moving into an apartment with girlfriends—were stopped,
threatened by being cut off from the family.

If you spend the night away from home (with a girlfriend to
see a movie), you can't come back.

******

If you go to Florida (to meet the family of the man she was
dating), never come back.

******

A lady came from the airline school and told me that I
could learn to be a stewardess. . . . And mom and dad

wouldn't let me go! I was eighteen, but still . . . you live with your parents and you did what they said. My parents was the type that you don't move out of the house until you get married if you was a woman.

******

One time I worked with the girl in a supermarket and she said: 'You can come live with me.' . . . Daddy told me that if I ever did, I couldn't come back. . . . Daddy said: 'If you leave, you cannot come back in this house. If (your brothers and sisters) pass you on the street, there better not be a one of them that speaks to you!' . . . Anyway, I was gone about two or three hours and . . . when I got home, every picture (of me) that was set out, they had got already and set away! My senior picture that my mom kept on the TV for a long time, and it was gone! I was nineteen or twenty, but I was raised that if you go out here and find a job, you're automatically going to get into trouble.

Several of the informants recognized that their dependency on family or husbands was a way to assure their compliance. A coal miner and a single parent says of her own parents:

I always lived with them. I was told that I can't make it. I was making more money as a miner than most people and I was told constantly that I couldn't survive!

Several women talked about being raised in large families but being cut off from establishing close relationships with outsiders.

I wasn't allowed to go anywhere! My friend lived eight houses up, and I was never allowed to spend the night.

Education for girls was not only discouraged by the cultural imperative to marry early, girls often missed school in order to help out mothers physically and emotionally stressed by hard work and many pregnancies.[14] Dependency was reinforced by the willingness of schools to accept their absence.

I loved to go to school better than anything, but mom kept having these babies and I kept on having to stay home

from school. How I would cry!... It started when I was
about eleven years old. Even if it was just four or five days
a month, it was still too much for me.... It was in my
junior year that my mommy had her last baby and I was
out it seemed like forever. I was out two or three days a
week, and I cried, it hurt me so bad!

Although half of the women I interviewed finished high school
during their teenage years, it was a struggle to do so.

They understood at school that if you have to be off, you
have to be off. But I kept up with the work. I was a C
student. If I didn't have to stay out I probably would have
been an A student, but that's what girls were expected to do.

******

(From a woman who missed school because of a nervous
breakdown:) I later found out that the high school had offered to pay for a tutor for the last three months of my
junior year but (my parents) said: 'No, she'll repeat her
junior year.' That was their way of keeping me one more
year.

******

I had to quit school here in my twelfth year. My mom knew
of a friend that knew of a woman that needed a live-in
baby-sitter, so I went down to (the city) and lived with this
family.... Mom just couldn't afford to send me through
school.... I did graduate (in the city)... but it was hard,
real hard.

For those who didn't finish high school, the reasons vary but
are related to both class and gender positions. With frequent lay-
offs in the coal industry, the children of miners often moved with
their fathers to follow employment.

I'd go to one school and then to another school and then
back to a school and then another school. My dad was going
to where the jobs were, anywhere he could make a living.
The we moved to Tennessee so he could take care of his
mother. We were living on a farm, and I just gave up.

Pregnancy interrupted the education of two women. One woman did not marry the father of her child and recalls that the school "forced you to quit." For the other woman, newly married and entering her senior year, it was her husband who refused to let her finish.

(He) wouldn't let me. I had a baby in seven months. Oh, I cried! I wanted to go back to school, but it wasn't that important to him. He had dropped out of school himself.

For several women, the humiliation of being marked at school as someone from a poor or "rough" community made the struggle to resist the gender stereotype that girls don't need school not worth the effort.

I never liked school. I didn't do bad, I just didn't like going. . . . After I got out of grade school, you'd tell them that your from (here) and it's an automatic block what comes next.

******

(Daddy) didn't believe in a woman going to work. And I didn't like school. I started dating my husband when he was 15 and I was 10, so one thing led to another and I just didn't want to go.

If you escaped abuse as a child, survived the domestic work, and did not suffer too many humiliations at school, reaching puberty might find you feeling trapped by the expectations of womanhood. As in other cultures of machismo, young girls were taught little about their own or boys' sexuality; they often felt that they couldn't escape from sexual involvement and that the only life open to them was through early marriage.

I just can't imagine me talking about stuff like this! We were raised so we weren't even allowed to say the word 'pregnant' in front of a man or boy; we wouldn't say the word 'sex' even in front of women.

******

My dad, he's the type of person that thinks a women should be at home, like the old saying, 'barefoot and pregnant' all the time.

******

My parents didn't believe in dating.

******

I don't think I knew what love was when I got married.
. . . I never dated nobody! Mom and dad would never let
me. I went out with (him) six months before we got married
and one night I was out until 11 o'clock, and honey, I wasn't
nothing but trash!

Pressured by parents to marry and by boys to become sexually
active, girls were caught in the classic contradiction of the virgin
and the whore.[15]

Back then, people talked about you. They gossiped, and if
you did something like that, you were trash, you know?
They treated you awful. . . . Abortion never occurred to me.
That just wasn't something that you could do. I just married him. We were young.

Six of the informants dropped out of school, eleven were
married, and ten had children in their teenage years. In a study
of young rural mothers who had been pregnant as teenagers,
Butler and Burton (1990) note that more than half of their subjects had been sexually abused by the age of 18. Although only
two of the women in this study volunteered that they were victims of incest, the high incidence of all forms of domestic violence in birth families was associated by the women with their
move into motherhood and marriage. Some women thought of
marriage as a way to escape the deprivations or degradations of
both poverty and being female.

I would never have left if I hadn't gotten married and I
know now that I married to get out. But I went into the
same situation. A body to wait on him hand and foot, that's
what he expected.

******

Mistake, mistake, mistake! (Getting married.) But it was a
way to leave, to get out.

******

I guess I didn't think about the marriage part of it. . . . He worked, brought home the money, and handed it to me. I never had stuff like that, and it was a new adventure for me.

For all of them, *not* to marry was not a choice.

I met my husband while I was working at this diner. I didn't like him but he wanted me to go out with him. I just wanted to be his friend.

The structural complexities of interlocking gender and class positions, and the ideologies that support them, can be drawn out of the decision to marry for the second time by a young woman with two small children. She had run away with her babies from a brutal husband by getting money from a Red Feather agency to pay for the cross-country train ride. The young woman went to live with her mother, who counseled her to marry again even though the second prospective husband showed signs that he, too, would be abusive.

I didn't want to get married because I knew he drank. We had scheduled a blood test and I canceled it. I didn't want to get married! But mom got kind of upset with me and said: 'There ain't no other man that's going to love someone else's kids. You ain't living here then!' And I thought: Oh lord! Here I go. I don't even have a place to live. Where am I going to go? Here I am pushed into the same predicament again. Lord, what have I done? I felt like I was pushed into a corner, so I called him and told him that I had reconsidered and to schedule the blood test so we could get married.

The ideology of gender enforces dependency and a fear of the loss of family connection that goes beyond economic necessity. She continues:

Instead of listening to myself, which I knew was right, I ended up being intimidated by my mamma. She wouldn't have thrown me out! But back then, I didn't know that.

The majority of respondents later had strong and conflicted feelings towards their mothers for failing to communicate to them the harsher realities of marriage.

I think some of it was my mom's fault. . . . I don't think she did what she should have done because I didn't understand a lot.

She never talked to me about sex. . . . When I was seventeen, I had this idea that you got married and you lived happily ever after! . . . That's what my friends were doing and that's what you do. So I got married when I was seventeen.

******

She never did tell me anything . . . about what to expect! But that's something I always told myself, that with my daughters I would tell them things . . . I remember how I felt so I would talk to them woman to woman. She really should have told me.

MARRIAGE: NOBODY TO LOVE ME

Q: What did you expect from marriage?

A: A little bit of heaven.

For ten of the twelve women, marriage brought not a heaven but an environment of physical and emotional abuse ranging from being "slapped around" in early marriage to extreme examples of dehumanizing and brutal treatment from husbands.

Like I said, I didn't have any confidence in myself: it was the verbal abuse. He would put me down and say things and he would resent it, I guess, that I got pregnant!

******

I've had all kinds of sex in my life but I never had nobody just to make love to me. Never. Just to care about how I feel.

Enforced isolation was a dimension of abuse for several of the women.

At that time I had no friends. I was just in that apartment; that was it and it was pretty rough! I never thought of it that way, though, (that I had) no friends.

******

I didn't have a driver's license at the time. I couldn't go anywhere! . . . I'd have to get my dad to come and get me, or some other relative. But, I don't know, it seemed like I just expected things the way they were.

******

I couldn't go out. I couldn't go anywhere or do anything because he was jealous.

******

(Even though I was working), he controlled where else I went. . . . I was at work on the day shift and I knew that the kids got home at 3:30. I got off at 3:15, and if I didn't get home by 3:30, I wasn't so sure he would be there to let them in, and that he would be OK taking care of them.

For the wives of workers in an uncertain and vulnerable industry, dependency was enforced economically as well as physically:

If I had to list a major fault, that would be it: I don't see his paycheck.

******

I don't know why, but I always get these guys with such a possessive attitude. . . . You know, it seems like an 'always no' attitude. If it's something he wants, we get it or we do it, but if it's something I want, it's always 'no.'

******

He never did agree for a woman to go out and work, he don't believe in that. . . . It broke my heart when my brother died in (another state), and I couldn't afford to go!

******

He wouldn't let me have clothes. He didn't think I deserved anything.

WITH EVERY BLOW

When women are isolated and dependent, they find it difficult to disclose their oppression because they have been socialized to accept it as a "natural" condition. Even when they do not accept this ideology and devise strategies of resistance, they still do not have sanctioned forms for politicizing their problems.

I was alone quite a bit. I still had . . . a high school friend
that I could talk to, but I wouldn't even talk to her about
some things because I didn't want her to know.

What she didn't want her friend to know was what is conserva-
tively estimated to occur in 25 percent of marriages or cohabiting
relationships between women and men in the United States, the
battering of women. According to Heise (1993), an estimated 3 to 4
million women are battered each year in the United States (See
Koop 1989).[16] Battering includes acts of beating, bullying, slapping,
and verbally harassing and degrading women by husbands and
partners (Carbonell et. al. 1984).

Battering is part of the full range of gender violence against
women, defined by Heise (1993) as "any act of force or coercion that
gravely jeopardizes the life, body, psychological integrity or freedom
of women in service of perpetuating male power and control. . . . A
more expansive definition would move beyond individual acts of violence to include forms of institutionalized sexism that severely com-
promises the health and well-being of women. This wider framework
includes discrimination against girl children in food and medical
care, female feticide, lack of access to safe contraception and abortion, and laws and social policy that perpetuate female subordination" (171). Gender violence cuts across all class, race, age, ethnic,
national and regional boundaries, and "is perhaps the most pervasive yet least recognized human rights issue in the world" (ibid).

When the battering of women by their intimate partners is
considered as part of the sexually based disequilibrium of power
rather than as individual pathology, domestic violence, in all of its
sexual, emotional, and physical dimensions, can be understood as a
structural and political issue. A United Nations (1991) publication
defines domestic violence as "the dark side of family life, (which) is
inflicted on a family's weakest members—women, children, the very
old, and the disabled" (19).

Respondents informed me of their own and other women's experiences of emotional abuse, physical battery, and rape in marriage. They reported that children were physically and emotionally
abused, and in two cases abducted by fathers. One women refused
to discuss the details of her abusive relationship with a former
husband. Another woman made no direct statements about her
own marriage but openly discussed the abuse of a family member.
Seven women directly talked of being slapped, four women of being
beaten, and one woman of being raped by her husband.

The most common form of abuse mentioned directly by nine women was verbal abuse, being "put down" or told that they "weren't worth anything", that their capacities and potential were limited, or accused, unjustly, of infidelities.

Despite the invisibility of words on the body, both verbal and physical abuse are emotionally inscribed in the victim.[17] For respondents in this study, verbal abuse was not interpreted as less emotionally destructive that physical abuse in a hierarchy of oppression.

The thing I suffered most from was verbal abuse, and I think that's the worst kind.

******

A lot of women are emotionally abused and the don't even realize it—men are always right and you're always wrong. I've seen a whole lot of that. The emotional abuse is worse than the physical abuse.

******

Every blow knocked that much more of the feelings out of me. And men can do that.

The cases of physical battering in marriage reported by re-spondents could not easily be related to individual or familial char-acteristics. Some of the husbands were almost always employed, some were almost always unemployed, some were substance abus-ers, some not. The number of children varied from none to six.[18] Half the women were employed and half not, although two of the three women who directly discussed extremely violent incidents of battery were highly dependent and isolated within the home. Of eight women who mentioned varying degrees of physical abuse, three were still married to those husbands and all three claimed that the slapping or beating had stopped years before.

Of the respondents who acknowledged that they were severely beaten, only one was still married to the man and she was not sure of the longevity of her commitment. The stories of physical batter-ing, compelling as they are on their own, contained within them the subtext of how the women had found the voice to speak about it.

I'd be so tired and wore out I'd be in bed. If things didn't go right with him, he'd come home and grab me out of bed and start slapping, choking, punching, things like that. I had busted ear drums.

******

He put me in the hospital three times.[19]

******

He beat me one time so bad I couldn't brush my hair for a week.

This brutality was also sexualized: women were both attacked sexually, or they were beaten because their husbands had unfounded suspicions that some other man may have gained sexual control over them.

He accused me of flirting with that man. He called me names. He started making threats—he acted like he was going to kill me!

******

I stayed out longer (at a PTA meeting) than I should have and he got home from work before me. He was standing behind a tree in the driveway. He ran out and grabbed me in the crotch and yelled: 'Where was you at?' Checked me out to see where I been! He was cruel. He'd say I was out with other men.

One women told of being raped by her husband, and two women were beaten during pregnancy.[20]

We went out to dinner and he didn't have any change for the tip, so I reached in my purse and said: 'Here honey' and laid the change down. As we got outside the door he said: 'You won't belittle me like that!' I didn't understand what he was talking about! And then with that, he pushed me against the car. I was seven months pregnant and the buttons popped off the front of my coat. It wasn't the first time.

******

He knocked me around, knocked me up against the wall, and in January I lost the baby . . . I think it was his fault.[21]

Two of the women who spoke of extreme physical battery had been victims of incest. They spoke of the isolation in their marriages and how they blamed themselves for their abuse.

I though I'd done something wrong: I looked the wrong way, I dressed the wrong way. It was my fault; I deserved what I was getting.

******

I let him beat me up because I had no self-worth, and it was my history that I should be abused by men. I deserved it.

Women were beaten by their husbands because their husbands had ideological and often institutional license to do so: churches preached for the submission of women, schools looked the other way, and the medical establishment trivialized women's pain. In this way, families that included the abuse of women can be seen not as dysfunctional but as hyper-functional, replicating through gender relations the power relations of class in a highly personal and politicized space. *It is not that all men have the potential for violence but that all men have the position that allows for that potential, if there, to be realized.*

In reflecting on their life experiences of family, some informants theorized that their exploitation was the result of a volatile combination of personal dependency, the economic insecurity of boom and (mostly) bust cycles in the mining industry since the 1950s, a tradition of Christian religious fundamentalism outside of the liberal influence of mainstream Protestantism, the geographic isolation of families on marginal and mountainous land held for generations, and the distinctive male working-class machismo of the coalfields.

I stayed with him . . . and I made a mistake . . . But I didn't have a GED. I didn't have any self-confidence. I had low self-esteem.

******

Marriage was set up more like slavery, and sometimes when women see themselves changing, working outside the home, that sometimes makes it worse because the men can't handle the women not being slaves. . . . But the whole system is

just not right! . . . It's getting to where if you don't have two
incomes, you can't run a household, and even then it's hard!

******

It was just like he exploded. . . . There were so many
frustrations. . . . It was hard getting used to going from a
very good paying job to nothing!

******

I think a lot of it has to do with the isolation that women
are in—isolation in the hollows. And then the whole idea
that women aren't really human—that they're property.
. . . And a lot of it was propagated by the churches—that
females are inferior.

MARRIAGE: A GOOD CALM LIFE

It was like we was two different people in two different
places seeing two different things!

The chasm that separates men and women in families (Bernard 1972) seemed to be bridged for some respondents only by
abusive interactions and some women ended the marriages that
provided the structural supports for that abuse. Six of the women
have been divorced and one has been divorced twice.[22] Although the
normative experience of marriage for most informants was at least
oppressive and often violent, the women still perceive a primary
relationship of equity and mutuality as their ideal, if not their
experience, of marriage. This contradiction is at the center of
women's lives within families.

You don't raise a family and live with someone to be
abused. . . . There's nothing bad enough that you have to hit
a woman! . . . If you're a wife and a mother, a homemaker,
you're going to want the love that goes with it.

******

In a relationship, I wouldn't want to boss (him). I wouldn't
want to run all over him, tell him what to do, tell him who
his friends are, because I wouldn't want to take advantage

of him. Unfortunately, it just doesn't work out that way. You hardly ever see a marriage where the two can be that way with each other. I know there are some, but you're lucky if you found one.

Yet half of the women are now married, one is living with a man, and two have significant relationships with a man. For those unmarried yet heterosexually connected women, the differences between women and men do not necessarily require domination, and bridging those differences through good communication is not only possible but necessary:

> I guess it works because we were friends before we were lovers. . . . Now he and I are living together, and . . . I've had a big readjustment to make. But anyhow, you're going to have conflict and disagreement, but it's like I tell him: 'Hey, it's OK to disagree! We've got a right! We're different people.'

> ******

> He treats me different. . . . He has never tried to touch me. . . . We can sit and talk for hours! I didn't know that they had that kind of man in this world. . . . Right now I'm just glad I got somebody to talk to: we're real good friends! I never been this close to anybody.

> ******

> We became good friends. I began to understand that you don't have to have that pushing and shoving and 'I'm the man!' kind of stuff.

For one of the informants, a second marriage was an unusual, if not unique, opportunity to develop personal autonomy within a highly contradictory institutional framework. Marriage also gave her the family foundation for her to work in the community.

> You know, I can get way out there—way out in left field! He's just the foundation of my life and that's all there is to it. . . . He keeps me kind of on track. He thinks a lot of stuff out, you know. He's real broad-minded, real solid.

Although financial problems are a strain and his personal habits "get on (her) nerves so bad (she) could die," their relationship is based on communication and mutuality.

> We got a real good calm life here. He says: 'I ain't fussing. If you want to talk, we'll talk, but I ain't fussing.' That's a good life for me.

This marriage avoids the disequilibrium of power between men and women without denying the centrality of their primary bond and the domestic sphere. "What does he expect from you as a wife?" I asked her. Her reply: "It's just the superest thing! He just expects me to love him."

> Like I cook when I got the time to cook and I can cook, and he appreciates it and he tells me. When I can't cook, he goes and fixes whatever. He just expects me to love him and all I expect of him is to love me, and to calm me down when I get too hyper!

CHILDREN

Another dimension of the contradiction of family life centered around mothers and children. Women found the strength to endure and sometimes to resist abusive relationships with husbands because of their children. All of the women spoke of their love for and joy in their children despite difficult material circumstances. Motherhood changed their lives: one respondent claimed that the "real change of life is when you have a baby," not at the end of your reproductive years. Despite the confinement of caring for young children, respondents who were economically secure enough to stay at home remembered their years as young mothers fondly.

> I loved it! I really thought that was the highlight of my life. Taking care of her was all I needed to make me happy. I didn't work very long; I didn't like leaving her at babysitters at all! (My husband) was working in the mines at the time and it was a secure job.

For four of the twelve respondents, the possibility of "a good calm life" for themselves and their children was unthinkable without leaving their husbands and the fathers of their children.

He hit me in the head. Then he took a gun and threatened to kill me and (my child).

******

My kids were whipped with belts.

******

My kids, his stepchildren, he beat.

Five of the respondents spoke directly about emotional and physical abuse of their children by fathers and stepfathers.[23] By the time of this study, either the marriages had been dissolved or the abuse had stopped. Of the six women who divorced, four women initiated separations to protect their children if not themselves.

If I didn't have (my son) I wouldn't have left. I probably would be dead by now because he would have killed me. One time (my son) came between us and said: 'Don't hit mommy!' Just old enough to talk, and he had to say that! It just come to the point where I realized that, not for my sake but for his sake, I had to leave.

If resistance to domination is inherent in the operation of power (Foucault 1980; Mohanty 1991), some women turned resistance into action when they "talked back" or "took the blows" for their children.

The boys . . . started in Little League baseball. If they would strike out or anything, he'd get real mad and he'd start beating them up when they got home. He'd pin them up against the wall and say: 'Why did you strike out?' And I would step in and say: 'Leave them alone! You don't have to beat them up like that!' He had a habit of kicking. A lot of times I'd get the kicks, I'd take the blows because I didn't want my kids suffering.

In another case, a young mother confronted her husband in a more dramatic way. Like women who fight oppressive political and economic structures to protect their families, her stance of combative motherhood motivated her to fight patriarchal oppression.

He was abusive to his own children. He'd take a stick out of a window shade and take my son (age two) and set him in the middle of the floor. He'd dare him to move and then hit him with a stick. . . . My nine-month-old had black and blue marks on her. Then I took a knife after him and said if he hurt my kids I'd kill him.

For one woman, staying in the marriage to give her child financial, if not emotional, security was her own form of resistance.

The only reason that I stayed with him was because of (my son). . . . It was me! If it weren't for me, our family wouldn't have held together, wouldn't have had some good times in the bad times. . . . We separated once when (my son) was a baby and I filed for divorce when he was 15 months old . . . but I'm a really committed person.

Two of the twelve women in this study had their children abducted by fathers *while they were still married to them.*

One day he said he was going to go visit his mother and he took (my son) and never brought him back. . . . He never came home and he left me there without any food or anything. Nothing.

******

I had my next to the oldest son with me and he had the other children at the time. When I came home, I couldn't figure out why the house was locked up. I couldn't get in, couldn't get no answer. And I went around to the back and you could just see through the curtain on the kitchen door. . . . The cupboard doors was open and they was empty! . . . Later I found out that he went to work and asked for a transfer, . . . re-mortgaged the house for the full amount, . . . pulled up with a camper and told the kids that they was going on vacation with him. . . . When they got to (another state), he let (the kids) think that I run off with another man, that I didn't love them no more, that I didn't want no part of them.

For the women as well as the children, these were especially severe instances of emotional abuse because women in this study were socialized to avoid at all costs being cut off from family and its extension in kinship (Beaver 1991). Threats of abandonment and shunning by family members, and fears about life outside the extended family network were recurring themes in the interviews.

> I considered going back to him because of being afraid of not being able to make it. I think that's the reason I didn't leave before. There's a fear that a women on her own cannot make it. . . . It's a big fear that society puts in women.

******

> I couldn't stand the thought of mommy crying and all the kids crying because I couldn't see them no more.

Although the strong kinship bonds of Appalachia may be idealized or contradicted in the nuclear family, the taking of children from mothers by fathers seems particularly compelling in this context. Yet, despite their suffering within families and their fears of losing families, the women in this study found the emotional space within them to develop bonds of caring and connection that would form the basis for their community and political work.

CHAPTER FOUR: WORK

"She provided for the family"

REVERBERATING SPHERES

Just as an analysis of women's lives within the family begins with a discussion of work, understanding work begins in the family, for it is within this "lesser" sphere that the respondents in this study began their working lives. A very young girl could be expected to wake up before dawn to stoke the fire, to do the chores after school rather than play, and to stay home from school to mind the children when her mother gave birth to yet another one. A feminist perspective allows us to politicize the personal lives of women in families and to read filial and wifely interpersonal relationships as structurally engendered; it also allows us to re-evaluate the work that women do within and without families. In women's lives, work and the family "reverberate . . . in the same . . . spaces" (Petchesky 1979:376).

The work that women do outside of formal wage labor has historically been undervalued or misrepresented. Feminist scholars have challenged both liberals and Marxists over the division of labor by gender but more fundamentally for the representation of domestic labor as nonwork. Beginning with Boserup (1970), the policy implications of how work is gendered have been central to the WID critique of mainstream development planning; when mainstream policy does not recognize what women do as work, strategies that target women to increase their "productive," i.e. income-generating capacity, also increase and intensify women's labor burden (Rogers 1979; Maguire 1984).

Women's participation in paid labor markets is also open to a gendered reading. Sinclair (1991) states that "it cannot be understood in isolation from their position in kinship and family structures and their relationship to childbearing and reproduction. Their positions in paid and unpaid work are mutually determining. The significance of women's unwaged labour continues to have a crucial effect on their identity as waged workers, in spite of their integral

67

role within the paid labour force" (2). The devaluation of domestic
and unpaid work also intensifies the gendered division of labor and
reproduces overall class inequities at regional, national, and global
levels (Mies 1986; Mies et al. 1988; Sen and Grown 1987; Young et
al. 1981; Young 1988).

Although Marxist theory has helped us to understand how
the institution of the family is related to capitalism (Engels 1972),
feminists have challenged Marxist orthodoxy about exactly what
it is that women do in the family. Central to the feminist critique
is how Marxist theory has slighted the work of reproducing human life in the conceptual division of production and reproduction. Yet even feminist Marxists contain their analysis of
reproduction to its relationship to the mode of production: the
richness of the radical feminist analysis of sexuality and gender
ideology is subsumed in class analysis. For feminist Marxists,
contemporary patriarchy is an ideological dimension of the mode
of production; they tend towards an essentially economistic account of women's oppression by re-casting analytical concepts in
Marxist theory to account for the labor of women. Kelly-Gadol
(1987) observed that "(w)omen constitute part of the means of
production in the private family's mode of work" (24). DallaCosta
and James (1972) assert that domestic work of housewives creates not only use value but surplus value, as no other labor is
possible without it. Hartmann (1987), whose work is difficult to
pigeon-hole, states that "the creation and perpetuation of hierar-
chal gender relations depends not only on family life but crucially
on the organization of economic production" (114).

Socialist feminists reject the representation of women as a
class because 1) some women are oppressed by other women, 2)
forms of patriarchy are prior to capitalism, and 3) because constructing women as a class assigns to men a secondary role as
oppressors of women (Jaggar 1988). Because socialist feminists are
concerned with radical and psychoanalytical insights as well as an
analysis of capitalism, they are able to account for the oppression
of women based on sex, a salient feature of the informants' narratives concerning their families.

In the end, it is a question of emphasis: feminist Marxists
privilege class struggle, Marxist feminists (Hartmann 1979; Barrett
1980; Davis 1987; Rowbowtham 1973; Sacks 1975) see class struggle
as essential to the end of patriarchy; socialist feminists see the
need to analytically disassociate class and gender oppression with-

out losing the importance of their intersection in movements for social change (Eisenstein 1979; Hartmann 1981; Hartsock 1985; Jaggar 1983). For example, both patriarchy and capitalism can viewed as structural systems that need each other to survive (Eisenstein 1979). There are, however, inherent contradictions when interests collide, such as those found when women enter wage labor and possibly challenge gender ideology. Other socialist feminists examine the articulation of patriarchy and capital in the current restructuring of the global economy. Sassen-Koob (1988) is concerned with the relationship of female migration and integration into export production as the "feminization" of labor supply. Mies (1986) describes the trend toward insecure, low-wage, and unorganized jobs in the new international division of labor and the growth of female employment in both the South[1] and the North as the "housewifizaton of labor."

Socialist feminists also remind us that Marxists have no historical evidence that class struggle alone can accomplish the liberation of women. The socialization of domestic labor leads to women doing the same kind of work outside the home as within (Sargent 1981); the entry of women into social production has certainly not ended the oppression of women within the proletarian family, as Marx and Engels had envisioned. Consequently, we cannot assume that for women "social production is the key to the determination of collective consciousness" (Sinclair 1991:3).

Since collective consciousness can only be achieved by people, socialists feminism also allows for an analysis of human agency. It is *women* who learn how to negotiate and resist within the structural constraints of capitalism and patriarchy, and women's lives are shaped outside the boundaries of productive work and inside the family. The family, then, is a good place to begin to understand both how work is gendered and how women might challenge their condition as working-class women.[2] Part of that challenge may be to develop alternative forms of paid labor *and* alternative forms of political and social community, including the family. Despite differences in economic, political, and cultural contexts, there is growing evidence that women in both the North and South are doing just that.

Marginalized women in the third world countries of the South are driven, by macroeconomic structural adjustment policies played out at national and regional levels, into informal urban sectors and also into wage labor in the production of export industrial goods formerly manufactured in the U.S. As in the South, the conditions of the expropriation of women's labor in the coal counties of Appalachia are also directly related to the marginalization of the population as a whole. In the coal counties, the latter half of the twentieth-century has brought cyclical economic crises, the end of labor shortages, the decline of unions, the flight of manufacturing industries, and the end of the welfare state (Gaventa 1990; Yarrow 1990).[3] In a socio-economic study of the seven coal-producing counties of southwest Virginia, Kraybill, Johnson, and Deaton (1987) conclude that "the unique economic structure of the coal-mining region creates a system of opportunities, constraints, and incentives which leads to a quality of life that is below the state average in most respects. The pattern of income resulting from the economic structure of the region explains much of the deficiency in quality of life" (1). Higher rates of poverty, infant mortality, disability, and dependency on transfer income are some of the indicators of a deficient quality of life in the coal counties. Other indicators are lower rates of labor force participation, lower average income, lower quality of housing, lower performance on standardized tests by students, and a lower percentage of residents with a high school education (2–3). The forces that "placed labor into a more vulnerable position than ever before" (Shifflett 1991:199) affect both primary and secondary labor markets, and the paid and unpaid work of women. Although acknowledging the complexity of social change, Shifflett (1991) looks to cultural continuities and adaptions rather than structural forces in discussing coal towns, emphasizing the themes of paternalism and culture (xiv). Yet it is painfully clear from the narratives of informants in this study that culture does not exist outside of the economic and ideological organization of society: class and gender, like work and family, "reverberate" in women's lives, and are heard when women theorize about their position in society.

The decline of the coal counties since the 1950s, the period roughly approximating the lives of the informants in this study, has driven men and women into "additive labor" or "multiple jobs, tasks or economic activities carried out to make a living" (Shifflett 1991:16). Additive labor is "one of the most characteristic and perhaps formative experiences of mountain people down through their history" (16). For women, this "piecemeal way of making a living,"(Shifflett 1991:16) can both reinforce and be at odds with the ideology of gender as it is interpreted in the culture. Shifflett also states that the "gender differences . . . in rural society . . . seem to have intensified in the coal town" (xv). Until the 1970s women were excluded from working under ground,[4] the domain that "dominated every aspect of life," creating a "workingman's culture" (xiii-xiv). But women have been required by economic necessity more than by tradition to look for additional streams of income in addition to the overwhelming majority of unpaid work in domestic production. If that is the case, women's paid and unpaid work in the coal counties may be even more "invisible" to planners because it intersects less obviously with male employment. To make that work visible and to understand how it relates to class and gender consciousness is the purpose of this chapter.

THE LABOR OF MOTHERS AS DAUGHTERS

The exploitation of girls' labor in impoverished households reflects not only assumptions about gender but structural characteristics of the economy. The respondents in this study are working-class women who have all worked for wages at some time during their lives, although only the three coal miners could be considered to be in a primary labor market. Entering wage-labor, however, did not necessarily create the conditions for their emancipation: they work not only for capitalists but for working-class men and for parents who appropriate their labor power in marginalized families. Thus, wage-working women not only remain domestic laborers, their unwaged-labor is formed in the social relations of production.

Just as capitalism shapes families, patriarchy shapes work. Girls become working-class women long before they realize a liberating potential in wage labor. All of the respondents recognized that their childhood labor was required for the household to survive and that the work they did was defined by gender. This recognition was not unique to women in this study. Their stories are similar to those of Hall's (1986) historical subjects who led a textile strike in Appalachia sixty years ago, and who shifted between paid and unpaid domestic labor depending on family circumstances: "I'd come back when Mamma had a baby and wait on her, and help if she needed me in any way. . . . The girls were supposed to do the housework and work in the fields. They were supposed to be slaves" (362).[5]

The social role of childhood, available to the young of the middle-class since capitalism reconstructed the family with the industrial revolution (Zaretsky 1986), was not available to children in vulnerable working-class households, and especially not available to girls.

There wasn't much difference (between my brother and me), but dad got *me* up to build the fires, to make sure that I had coffee ready. . . . I can remember having to get up at four o'clock in the morning.

******

If my mom and dad had to go (to town), they would take the boys with them and leave my sister and I at home. And I don't know why, but I can remember that I wanted to go! But we needed to stay home and wash the dishes and sweep and clean the house. And she took the boys with her.

Young girls were required to fully contribute to the household through the labor of their bodies: taking care of the home, the other children, and, at times, the sexual "needs" of male relatives. Girls learned about the wages of women's work from the example of their mothers who supplemented family income in subsistence activities. Their mothers grew food in large gardens and raised animals for milk and meat.[6] Sometimes they sold their produce and animals, or the cured meat. At other times they took on informal domestic work, but none of their efforts could guarantee that a family would be kept together.

Mamma chops wood, hoes the garden, worked for people, raised pigs. She'd sew a dress for somebody . . . My mamma slaved from daylight in the morning until almost daylight the next morning. She got very little sleep, but she provided for the family.

******

She was the one that had to feed them (her twelve children). She would take in ironing and washing, plus all of the other things she had to do. I don't know how she ever did it! She still had to give the first four away to other members of the family to raise because she couldn't.

Three of the respondents discussed their mothers' physical and mental illness caused by too little income, too much work, and too many pregnancies. The burden of child-care and housework fell to their daughters, even if it interfered with school or isolated them from the community.

My senior year, she had her last baby and a hysterectomy.
She come home before she was supposed to, and she busted
open and started bleeding. So here I was again, *out* (of
school)!

******

She got so weak in her body she just couldn't cope . . . I'd
feel that I had work to do—housework, dishes, all that
stuff. When I was a teenager, I'd sometimes resent it.

Opportunities for girls to prepare for labor force participation
were limited by requirements for their household labor: girls
"missed" school, dropped out of school, and felt alienated from
school culture.

A third of the respondents volunteered that they did not have
the security as teenagers of knowing that their family could care
for them. At times they were put into the care of relatives or
neighbors, and one woman knew that she was set aside for the
church, that at some time she could be "given" into the care of the
Roman Catholic "sisters." Another respondent worked while a student in high school through the Neighborhood Youth Corps (NYC)
Program.

I worked outside of the home from the time I was eight. . . . I
worked in school in the NYC . . . cleaning or whatever they
told me to do. . . . You'd work at home and you'd work at
other places.

As in so many development projects for women, participation in the
NYC only increased the work burden on a girl who was already
expected to do "motherwork" for her ten siblings. A girl who was
sent away from home her senior year to become a live-in maid and
nanny in an un-related urban household, "a family that had money,"
was forced to do so because her mother would then have "one less
mouth to feed." The work she was sent to do replicated the confining labor of young girls and women in families.

I moved in with the baby, in his room, and I'd get up and
feed him at night just like it was my own. . . . I felt just like
a prisoner! It was go to school, take care of the kids, clean
house. On week-ends, I never dated; my week-ends were

booked for me: baby-sitting someone *else's* kids, or all of the kids together!

Girls recognized that the household needed their additive and remunerative labor to support the family during periods of crisis. They worked in part-time minimum-wage service jobs, or informally by sweeping up hair in the local "beauty parlor" and picking blackberries for sale on the side of the road.

It seems like we never had enough money, but we made it: we had a big garden. But we never had anything extra. I know my mom would worry a lot about how we were going to pay bills. I guess it was on my mind too. I knew that they were having a hard time when I was a teenager and I got a part-time job after school.

******

Maybe you would do an odd job for somebody. . . . You'd get wood for people. I cleaned house some. . . . I picked up pop bottles. I remember when they was half a penny a piece, and I thought it was just the grandest thing in the world to find a party-pack of ginger ale bottles cause you could get a nickel out of it.

The hardest part about growing up, one respondent told me, was coming to "realize that you really did have to *work* for a living." By the age of fifteen, she was expected to baby-sit, clean houses, and do odd jobs in order to have an income for the household.

GOING OUT TO WORK

The gendered division of labor assigns women into secondary labor markets where they work in what are perceived to be unskilled jobs without income security, opportunities for advancement, benefits, or the protection of unions (Hartmann 1979; Luck 1991). Respondent's paid labor outside the home was ideologically obscured or made less visible because husbands resented wives both for taking time away from home and for making obvious their own inability to provide for the family. A typical employment history for a woman who considers herself a homemaker included "work at the sewing factory, the dry cleaners, as a cashier, and even managing a small grocery store."

Although three of the women were union miners, they have been laid off since the mid-1980s: since women were not employed underground until the 1970s, they are the most vulnerable group in recessionary contractions in the coal industry (Hall 1990). One respondent had migrated out of state where she found steady employment as a factory worker and supported three children. With the recession of the mid-1970s she lost her job, then her car, and finally her house: "I came back to the mountains for the same reason I left," she explained. Another respondent also returned home to the mountains, with her husband. She had been employed in the Northeast as a nursing-home aide, but without two incomes— her husband couldn't keep a job—the family couldn't survive.

Four of the respondents had worked in the garment industry in sewing factories and cotton mills,[7] two had been employed in the furniture industry, two did industrial homework in sewing, and one woman survived by cleaning houses and baby-sitting. All but one respondent had held part-time or full-time service jobs at one time or another: as a cashier in the grocery store, a waitress, a deli clerk, or as a cleaner for a small business. Sewing clothes, preparing, selling, and serving food, cleaning houses and caring for the elderly and incapacitated are jobs that mimic segments of women's reproductive work without its more independent and integrative aspects.

The most difficult work I've ever done was working as a cashier in a supermarket. I worked on my feet, sometimes thirteen hours a day, sometimes seven days a week, for 75 cents an hour.

Because women's work is devalued, women do these jobs. In *Out to Work*, a history of women wage laborers in the United States, Kessler-Harris (1982) observed that "(t)he inequality of the job market was rooted in the inequality of the home, which in turn was rooted in fundamental assumptions about women's biology, psyche, and social roles (316). The wage differential between the paid work of women and men is also based on this gender ideology: Employers could pay women less money because of "the *belief* that they are less skilled than men, irrespective of their actual skill levels" (Sinclair 1991:12).

SCHOOLED TO SEW

In Southwest Virginia, wage-earning women can be easily found in the garment industry, and four respondents have worked in at least one sewing factory. Kessler-Harris (1982) observes that "the garment factories that dotted the Appalachian Mountains" beginning in the first quarter of the century were the product of the industry's attempt to "find cheaper and less militant labor sources" by escaping the unions in the North. Moving to the southern Appalachians presented an environment where the mutually determining structural inequalities of class and gender provided opportunities to exploit both men's and women's labor more effectively. Kessler-Harris noted that "(m)iners' high rates of injury and death forced many women into the labor market. And, except for occasional domestic work, the garment trade provided the only other employment available. . . . Soon every mine had its (sewing) factory" (241–242).

The women in this study who worked in the sewing factories of the last quarter of the century responded to similar push factors and gendered conditions of employment. Although there were now possibilities for other low-wage service jobs, in the fast-food restaurants, grocery and sundry stores, and the furniture factories, the garment trade was still the most commonly perceived employment option for women. Women went out to work in the sewing factories because their wage labor was required by the insecurity of their husbands' earnings (Kraybill, Johnson, and Deaton 1987).

> We were having a hard time, really. He had gotten laid off . . . and then he was working where they built the tunnel. He broke a leg and was out of work, so I just went to the factory. That was the easiest way to get a job and I needed the money.

Not only were there few alternatives for employment, women felt they were incapable as wage earners. As girls, they were taught to devalue their productive potential because of the necessity of their reproductive present. Eight of the twelve respondents took wage jobs before they completed their high school education. Significantly, all of the women identified themselves during that period as daughters and wives rather than as workers. They entered the labor market not only undereducated, but with the feeling that they did not have the skills that could take them farther than the sewing factory: in a sense, they were schooled to sew.

When you fill out an application for a job and you haven't finished high school, you really don't have anything to offer anybody. You just take what you can. . . . The majority of the women around here worked in the sewing factories, and I knew that you didn't need a high school education for that.

The isolation of women within their extended families also diminished their opportunities as workers. In a rural area, you need a driver's license and a car, or someone to drive you to work. Not only were women less likely to drive cars on their own, they needed the permission of husbands and male relatives to travel with non-related men. These constituted both practical and ideological barriers to women's employment.

Everywhere I worked, I never had a car: didn't have my driver's license. So it was more or less you worked where you could get a ride. When I went job hunting, I didn't look at places where I would *want* to work, I went looking places where I could have a ride.

After the woman who swept up in the beauty shop as a teenager dropped out of school, she went to work in a sewing factory, then a furniture factory, and finally, after marriage gave her limited freedom,[8] she enrolled in "beauty school." It seemed the best she could do: she had no education and was afraid to aspire beyond the kind of job that was acceptable for a *woman* of her *class*. Messages of subordination came not only from men, but from the school system that tracked girls from the "rough" and poor town into serving other people's physical needs, like washing and cutting hair.

THEY WENT OVER TO VENDING

Income insecurity sent women out to work whether they were wives or single household heads. But jobs available to women in Southwest Virginia and surrounding states offered women little security and a lot of stress, particularly as an already marginalized region began experiencing the transition from an industrial to a service-based economy. The employment history of one respondent's family illustrates the micro-level effects of global economic processes on women, men and families.

She was the daughter of a maker of carbide, once a major extractive-based industrial product based in Southwest Virginia until the 1960s. Her mother supplemented her father's income with subsistence production: gardening, canning food for winter, and milking the cow. The respondent quit school at thirteen, married in her late teens, and began having babies. It was a good marriage, even though the changes in the rural economy and the flight of industry were bearing down on her family. Her husband, a Korean War veteran, got a job at the carbide plant only a few years before it closed. She remembers vividly the presence of the carbide company and how the production of carbide, the primary source of jobs, dominated her physical and social environment.

> There was so much smoke that came out of the furnaces! They had these real hot furnaces and the front of them was open. They had cranes that men ran that came in there to make the carbide. It was real hot! You could feel the intense heat on the road.

After the carbide plant closed, the family moved to the city of Richmond so her husband could find work, but the urban environment was hostile and the cost of living high: "We didn't like it down there! So we came back to the mountains and he went to work at the cotton mill." The cost of living had also increased back home, and what one could produce to supplement income no longer seemed enough. Her husband looked for higher wages by going underground in the zinc mines still operating in the area; she went to work in a family-owned deli that would eventually find it impossible to compete with fast-food chains.

> And then both my husband and I lost our jobs within a couple of weeks of each other. They told him sometime in November (1981) that the mines would close, and then they told me that the store would close on Christmas eve.

The husband returned to the cotton mill until he was laid off in the mid-1980s: by now, capital moved more smoothly across national borders and the textile industry had gone further south.

Since then, he has worked in furniture factories and as a laborer digging ditches for the sewer and power lines needed to fuel rapid development along the service corridor of the interstate. The respondent still needed wage work just to keep up with living expenses: the food, heat, phone, and especially medical bills. She was thankful that housing costs were minimal. Like so many other families in Southwest Virginia, their housing was sub-standard but unencumbered (Beaver 1991; Fitchen 1991): the house and the land had been in the family for generations and long since paid for. But her husband's income was uncertain, and she needed a job.

I went to work in the cafeteria at the (community) college but it was only for nine months! I guess I was the last one hired and the first fired. They went over to vending (machines).

SO GOOD AT DOING YOU THAT WAY

Even if you kept your job, your income was uncertain, and women spoke of terms of employment that were without benefits or the advocacy of unions. "The only thing you can count on is the salary: we don't have any benefits or health insurance," a factory owner told one of the respondents; she soon found that she couldn't even count on the salary. Such "income uncertainty" is associated with a lower quality of life for the citizens of Southwest Virginia (Kraybill, Johnson and Deaton 1987), and respondents in this study reported that they could not count on a regular income over a long period of time because the company could change the number of hours that they worked each week or lay them off periodically to decrease costs.[9]

I went to work in the sewing factory making children's clothes. And I didn't like the way they'd do it. . . . If you run out of work they would lay you off for a week or two, not enough time to collect unemployment. I got a job at a furniture factory but it didn't pay enough. You'd work two days this week and three days the next, and maybe six days the next week. But you couldn't *depend* on getting more than one or two days a week.

Management could decrease labor costs not only by changing the number of hours worked each week, but also by manipulating quotas and using state-funded programs to generate corporate revenue. One respondent reported that the sewing factory that employed her would receive a placement fee for accepting women who were in a state-funded, job skills program. The company would lay-off their current workers in order to hire women in the program. They continued periodic lay-offs to replenish their work force with fee-paid workers, keeping other women on lay-off just long enough to prevent them from collecting unemployment benefits. Another respondent told how management utilized the quota system to decrease their pay.

> We were working at the garment factory. You work forty hours a week and you work piece work. You'd get to doing pretty good work and making your quota and then they'd come up and try you out on something new. You could be making 75 cents and hour and maintaining it, and then on the last day you made a quarter an hour, you had to take away from *all* that you made. They'd take off for all of the days in the pay period, and they was the ones that switched you! It was really a struggle because they were so good at doing you that way.

Exploitative conditions for female labor in the factories had both class and gender dimensions. Jobs were dirty, dangerous, or boring. Some women labored under physically unsafe conditions and others reported psychically unsafe environments.

> I was standing there one day at the band-saw working on a chair. I put the wood in there and the band broke. And that thing was flopping from side to side right by my head. It scratched me a little bit right here (on my forehead). I knew that if I moved just a little bit that I would be killed. It got me to thinking. . . . If I get killed or if I get crippled so I can't work, my kids will have nothing to live on. So I said to myself: I'm going into the mines. Even if the work is hard, even if I can't take it, I'm in no worse shape than now.
>
> ******
>
> I didn't like the part like in the sewing factory and the furniture factory where you're doing one specific thing for eight hours except for lunch time and break time. If I ever go back to the factory to do hard labor, it will be because I

absolutely have to. I know about that: by the time my day
has ended, I am tired! I am wore out, and I don't want to do
anything else. I don't want that feeling.

Respondents spoke of being trivialized by male coworkers, being
given the easiest jobs, or, in the case of coal-mining women, being
given the most physically demanding yet lowest paid jobs underground. Management, male workers, and female workers in traditional jobs formed cross-class and cross-gender alliances to maintain
the gender ideology that women did not belong, that women were
weak, that women, not management, were to be opposed.

The first job I had at the furniture factory I was the only
woman in the cabinet room, and I know that they did not
want me there. I was putting glue on pieces of wood for
men to glue together. I think that they were a little bit
afraid I would be hurt or something, so the easiest thing
they had in there, I did.

******

We were working at the (sewing) factory when we heard
the news that they passed a law that women could go into
the mines. . . . So we went in and told them we wanted an
application for mining, and they gave us an *office*
application. . . . They called me in there and they said: 'You
don't work in mining! . . . You don't *want* to work in mining.'

******

I wasn't accepted as a woman in the mines: 'You need to be
at home in the kitchen. You're taking a man's job. *Why* are
you doing this? . . . You don't belong here!'

Security of person is both physical and psychological, and for
women, it almost always involves sex (MacKinnon 1987; Kelly 1988).
Sexual harassment is a form of sex discrimination that is "any
unwanted sexual attention" (Carbonell et al. 1984) through "men's
use of gesture and language" (Kelly 1988). Four of the respondents
talked of sexual harassment by employers and other workers; the
women felt both objectifed and threatened as workers.

I had a friend (that) I worked with and we were sharing an
apartment together. . . . One afternoon, (the boss) called us

upstairs and he said that if we both didn't put out for him together he would fire us on the spot.

******

You know, I heard some *horror* stories at the beginning (when women first went into the mines). Things that happened to women just because they were women . . . sometimes they grabbed at you. . . . I know of a woman that was raped underground.

When sexual harassment is viewed on a continuum of gender violence against women, the line between sexual harassment and sexual assault is not very clear. What is clear is that women perceive a range of behaviors from "physical assaults . . . to what on the surface appear to be innocuous remarks" (Kelly 1988:106) as sex-based coercion. Sexual harassment then "gravely jeopardizes . . . (the) psychological integrity or freedom of women in service of perpetuating male power and control" (Heise 1991:1). Like the majority of women in the United States who will at some time in their working lives experience sexual harassment (Carbonell et al. 1984), the women of Southwest Virginia understood that being female made them vulnerable at work as well as at home.[10]

COALMINER DAUGHTERS

Caught in the intersection of class and gender relations, some women looked to unionized industrial employment and non-traditional jobs for income security despite male opposition. Some women moved out of the state to the factories and cities of the midwest and north, but the decline of industrial jobs in the United States since the recession of the mid-1970s (Sassen-Koob 1988) meant that all forms of wage work were uncertain.[11]

I was working in a factory and I had a good job. I bought myself a home and I had a nice car. My kids didn't have the best of everything, but they wasn't hurting. . . . And then, in a job that I thought was really secure, I lost it because I got laid off and they sold the company. . . . And my unemployment benefits run out and they were about to foreclose on the mortgage on me.

For a woman who stayed in the coal fields and was willing to contradict gender ideology, becoming a coalmining woman was her chance at security.

Women have labored in the mines long before they pressed for paid employment and despite the historic prohibition against them across cultures and regions. From the Appalachians to the Andes, the "exclusion of women from mines is a tradition as old as mining itself," evident in pre-colonial times in the gender ideology of the Incas (Kingslover 1989:2). Just as contemporary Bolivian women have picked the slag heaps of copper ore to earn a subsistence wage (Nash 1979), Appalachian women have gone underground to fuel the subsistence economy. Two respondents remembered their mothers going into the mines to get "house coal" from what was left by male wage workers.

Despite their labor underground, women's visibility as miners and status as wage workers reflect the intersection of their class and gender positions: when their labor was needed as wage workers in times of labor shortage, women were allowed to work underground as they did during World War II (Shifflett 1991:81). As jobs decrease, women are pushed out, usually on the basis of protecting them from unsafe labor conditions and returning them back to where they are really needed, in the home (Kessler-Harris 1982). One respondent noted that with the decline in union jobs in Appalachian coal fields, women miners would never again have the opportunities they did in the 1970s.

> I don't consider that I had a real good job, that I was making a *living*, until I started working in the mines. Then I had what I consider a middle-class life style. But then the coal company started laying off in 1982.

Like the women who worked and endured great suffering in the British collieries of the nineteenth-century, Southwest Virginia women "would prefer not to work in mines, but would rather have that work than none at all" (Walby 1986:121). One respondent talked of personal decision to become a miner:

> In this area, either you work in the mines or you don't have anything. It's still true today as it was then. I was twenty-one years old and had two children. I needed the money and I knew that I could do the job.

To break out of the secondary labor market, three of the respondents went into the coal mines to work underground after the industry opened up in the 1970s[12] and coal companies started hiring women for the best-paying jobs underground. Two of the women were single household heads, one the mother of two children and the other the mother of six. The third woman entered the mines with her mother both to improve her family income—her husband was already a miner and they wanted to build a house—and to escape the monotony and low pay of the sewing factories.[13]

The most difficult time for me was working in the factory. . . . I'd rather do the mining than factory work because at the factory you do the same thing over and over and over and you didn't make that much. . . . I was looking forward to getting paid for one week because one week in the mines was more money than one month in the (sewing factory).

Mining coal is a dangerous, dirty, and physically demanding job. "If war is hell," Kingslover (1989) wrote, "so is mining: underground shafts collapse, smelter furnaces explode, lung disease is endemic. In few other professions are the odds so stacked against living long enough to retire" (4). Yet mining is perceived as the only possible entry into a middle-class way of life in the coal fields, despite the insecurity of employment in an industry sensitive to economic downturns, and the bitterness and violence of an intensely adversarial relationship between company and labor (Shifflett 1991).

When women entered the mines, this adversarial relationship was complicated and contradicted by gender: efforts to exclude women from mining included deliberate attempts by working-class men to protect their position at the expense of working-class women (Hartmann 1979). The contradictions of class alliances were not lost on a woman who spoke of her entry into this male domain.

When we started in the mines, they (the miners) were *not* for women! They didn't *like* women, and they didn't want them working there. They didn't like women taking a man's job. And we didn't have any union backing.

Worker barriers to female employment, like worker barriers on the basis of race, serve the interests of the company, and management united with labor in efforts to discourage women from going and staying underground.

And you fought with the company constantly! They had the attitude that you should shovel belt and shut up; that you shouldn't advance. It was a constant fight to get trained on equipment. It was always: 'We're afraid that you're going to get hurt.' . . . Shoveling belt is the lowest pay and the *hardest* job that you can do.

******

I went to work in the mines in January 1975. . . . I had a hard time being accepted. The superintendent told them that I had been sent in to spy on the guys.

One respondent believed that the coal company created medical barriers to her employment after she had completed a training course to be certified for underground work.[14] All of the respondents with families in mining reported stories of harassment over medical claims or the complicity of the medical establishment with the industry to deny claims and benefits. In this situation, the respondent believed that the company hoped to stall or discourage her from working underground by suggesting that there were medical reasons to keep her from employment. Fortunately, she found one physician who was her advocate.

I finished the (mining) course and they sent me for a physical and turned me down. They wouldn't tell me why! So I went to two doctors in Bluefield, and then they sent me on up to Charlottesville because they couldn't find anything wrong with me. The one in Charlottesville sent me to one in Richlands. And did I have tests! I gave more blood during that time!

Q: Did you have to pay for the doctors?

Oh yeah, I had to pay for them. Think about it: Here I am with six kids, and something's the matter with me that I can't hold a job? I *had* to find out what was the matter so I could get it corrected.

Q: Did the coal company give you your records?

Nope. . . . The doctor in Richlands had dealt with the coal companies, and he had this form that he filled out to take back over there to get the x-rays. I called (the company) to set up an appointment and said that I had these papers and that all these doctors couldn't find anything wrong with me. So they told me to come in the next day; I did, and they said to report to work on Monday! $500 worth of doctor bills to find out I was healthy.

The opportunity for health insurance was a strong inducement for women and men to enter union mines when the jobs were available. One respondent who was not in a coal mining family spoke of the consequences of losing your health insurance.

We had real good insurance because my husband worked for a union company. But he lost his job and the insurance ran out. . . . We worked so hard! We didn't have no warning that the company would shut down! You could keep the insurance for a while but you had to buy it and you had to pay $300 or $400 a month. Hell, you didn't even get that on unemployment! . . . Anyway, I found this lump on my breast and we didn't have no insurance. So I went a few months before I even told anybody about it because I kept on thinking he'd find another job. . . . Every day, it seemed like it would grow that big. . . . I finally had to go to the doctor because I was not feeling well, and he said that I had high blood pressure, the stress of all this had given me high blood pressure! The lump continued to grow for a year before I could afford to have it operated on. It was a tumor but it was not malignant. But in the period of time that we knew I had a tumor, it was real hard, real stressful on me and him knowing that we was facing something that might be real bad. That was a real turning point for me. Here I had something growing inside me and I couldn't do nothing about it.

Health-related issues, including mine safety and parental leave, were central concerns for the group that emerged in the coalfields of Appalachia in 1977 to become a national association of women coal miners, the Coal Employment Project (CEP) (Hall 1990); two respondents in this study were original members. Health care benefits to miners was also a major issue in the 1989–1990 strike against the Pittston Coal Company by UMWA District #28. "At the conclusion of its 1984 contract, the Pittston Company ceased providing health care benefits to its retirees, suddenly depriving some 1500 Pittston miners of benefits" (Erickson et al. 1989).

What really set everything off and keyed everybody up and put the fight in them was when they took away the health care. I remember when I was a little girl, my dad would always say that even though he may be poor, even though he may not always have a job, at least he's got his health card. And sure enough, they knew that when they got old and retired they would have their health care and could have their medicines. Taking that away—that was the biggest mistake that the company ever could make.

For the women of Southwest Virginia, the company's betrayal of the miners who had given their lives to the company was an affront to their sense of corporate responsibility, connection to community, and concern for the wellbeing of past and future generations. When the UMWA looked for support for the impending strike, it was women, like the miner above, who rallied other women and their families over this issue.

MAKING ENDS MEET

Wage work was difficult for respondents who were household heads, especially for those in low-wage jobs without benefits or union protection. The full burden of raising children fell on these working but impoverished mothers. This was not what they had expected: the comments of seven respondents reveal the power of mass culture, even among the daughters of impoverished and sometimes abusive families, to create the expectation that marriage would bring them a comfortable middle-class family life.[15]

My whole idea of marriage, like from TV, was that the man went off to work and the wife stayed home and took care of the kids, and then when the man came home, she took care of him. The kids went to bed, and it was time for love. And it was a lie! It sounds ridiculous, now.

More often than not, marriages didn't work out, and women were left as primary care-givers and providers. None of the six respondents who had children by absent partners had any help from them in raising children and only one received child support and for only one of her children.[16] One respondent never pursued child support to avoid being controlled by her ex-husband.

> I did not expect any child support. I agreed to let him see her but I did not want him telling me what to do. . . . Everybody said that if I ended up leaving the state that I couldn't leave without him consenting, and I didn't want that hanging over me. That might not be true because I never asked a lawyer, but that kind of stuck in my mind.

For another woman, the amount of child support required under state guidelines at the time her children were growing up was worth less than the cost of collecting it.

> He was only supposed to pay $60 or something like that. $10 for each child! If I had tried to make him pay it, I would have had to hire a lawyer and went into court every month and everything else.

Even when child support is enforced under the more generous terms of the current guidelines, men who are not regularly employed and who do not earn very much money cannot be forced to provide resources they don't have.

Poverty is not the only constraint: since women were not socialized to engage the world outside the family, they were doubly unprepared for the possibilities of advocacy or protection within judicial and political institutions. Echoing the statement of the respondent above, a woman told me of her sense of powerlessness in dealing with police, courts, and legal aid: the barriers were so great in her case that she could not see any way to get help in getting her children back from an abusive father who "kidnapped" them and took them to California.

> The law said it was not in their jurisdiction. They said in order to fight him that I would have to go out there to the district that they were in. They wouldn't do nothing. . . . My kids were whipped with belts. They had all kinds of buckle marks on them. . . . When my son went to the police depart-

ment out there, this lieutenant helped him call me. I said to her: 'Can you help me?'. I thought that maybe through the police they could send them back here. But she said that they couldn't. The only way that I could get them back would be to come out to (the west coast) and file charges in the court. It might take months before I could get a court hearing. How could I get there? How could I stay that long a time, hire an attorney to fight the case? I didn't have any money and I had one son who was sick with me. Welfare sees that they're being abused! Why couldn't they step in and take care of them?

Single mothers earned low wages because they were under-educated and assigned to gender-specific and insecure secondary labor markets. Although some women found freedom in paid work, entering social production did not provide others the opportunity to break out of the relationships of dependency created by their class and gender positions; instead, it sometimes intensified them. A single mother of two children lived at home with parents and brothers and their wives: they needed her income and she needed them to care for her children. Even after she went to work as a coal miner, she felt trapped in her parents home and resentful of how they usurped her role as a parent. The alternating shifts of a coal miner made it impossible for her to live anywhere without other adults in the household. All her life she had been told that she could not make it alone, and she still believed it, even though she was earning good money in a what was considered a man's job. For a while, she turned to alcohol and drugs to escape the contradictions.

For women who could not rely on family for child care and who had minimal self-esteem and job skills, the only alternative was trying to survive on public assistance or entering the informal sector: cleaning other people's homes, taking care of other people's children, and hoping that no one would find out.

Right now I'm on ADC: $207 a month. HUD pays my rent and I don't ever buy anything extra. . . . Right now my sister stays here with me and she does help me, but she's not supposed to. If she didn't, I couldn't make it! I have a lot of jobs. I will do anything to make ends meet! I baby-sit, clean house for a woman, but it's not like I can advertise. I can't report it.

Living with the father of your children did not necessarily lessen the burden on mothers to provide for their children. The male "living wage" and the "father-as-provider" persist more in the collective imagination than in the reality of Southwest Virginia. As the security of industrial employment disappears along with ideal of the welfare state, the new service jobs created become more like the labor of housewives, and housewives and mothers must do "anything to make ends meet."

I've done just about everything, Well, I haven't sold my body for food, but I've stolen food to feed the kids.

Another respondent was forced to move her family back home to the community she associated with poverty and the disdain of outsiders after her husband was injured in a mining industry accident. At least there she could work in the sewing factory.

Q: Why did you decide to leave?

The biggest reason was so that I could go back to work. There weren't any jobs there unless you went into the mines which I didn't think I had the nerve to do. Maybe in the grocery store or something, but the pay is low. Matter of fact, they only hire part-time, so I never even went and applied there.

HOMEWORK

Other women could not venture far for wage work because of domestic responsibilities and the watchful eye of their husbands: for these women, industrial homework was a way to "make ends meet." Two of the twelve respondents were involved in an income-generating cooperative that could more accurately be described as a form of industrial homework, closely related to informal domestic wage labor. Both of these women had intensive caregiving responsibilities and intensely controlling husbands. The work that they do, sewing clothing in their homes for sale in a specialty catalogue, threatens neither the traditional division of labor nor the isolation of women within the private sphere.

The shift from going out to work as an employee of the garment industry to sewing at home illustrates the shift to more flexible forms of capital accumulation. On a global scale, industrial homework, like contract farming, frees capital from the political and ideological as well as the economic costs of production. Gone are the costs of building and maintaining the factories and the labor force. The "flexibilization of labour" (Mies 1986:126) in the international reorganization of capitalism in the late twentieth century turns those costs over to the worker, and in the third world here and abroad, she is more likely to be a woman. "The housewife is the optimal labour force for capital at this juncture and not the 'free proletarian', both in the underdeveloped and overdeveloped countries" (von Werlhof 1983; Mies 1986:126).

The most purely manipulated forms of consumption are based not on needs but on wants constructed within the realm of fantasy (Leiss 1976; Illich 1978): thus it may be more profitable to sell costumes than clothes. The company that subcontracts to these homeworkers markets specialty products, "authentic arms and armor replicas plus period clothing at the most reasonable prices possible." According to the company catalogue, potential customers include participants in "Renaissance Faires, SCA (Society for Creative Anachronisms) Tourneys and Revels, Scottish Highlands Games, Medieval Feasts, and Science Fiction and Fantasy Conventions." In addition, the catalogue copy continues, "they're entirely appropriate for theatrical productions, costume parties or as part of your Royal Court Garb. . . . Make yourself the most dashing warrior in the realm." (research document—company catalogue).

The "dashing warrior" who chooses the "Viking Tunic" or the "Renaissance Shirt", both at $49 plus $3.50 for shipping and handling, will wear "clothing" made in the homes of Southwest Virginia. The women who made the patterns and carefully cut and sewed the shirts in their kitchens and sewing rooms, while performing the simultaneous and multiple tasks of their domestic work, are paid $10 for their labor plus direct costs.

It's not a whole lot. I try myself to take in four or five pieces a week: That's $50 a week. But you don't always get $10 a piece. There are some pieces that you only get $8 for, some things you get $9 for. You have to work that much harder to get more money.

Working at home allows this respondent to care for a husband who is ill and has always carefully controlled her access to persons and places outside the home. Making money not only helps pay bills, it gives her "peace of mind." She can buy presents for her children and grandchildren. The income literally means freedom of movement and association: instead of always being told by her husband that they can't go out because there is no money, she can now pay the cost of a going to a restaurant for family celebrations.[17]

> I just don't like to hear 'no' all the time if something comes up. Like when my brother died in (another state) and I couldn't go because I couldn't afford it. It broke my heart and I still haven't gotten over that.

Sewing at home allows women to buy their teenage daughters the kind of clothes that will erase their class position at school. But the benefits of doing homework are questionable: in providing the temporal and spatial opportunities for women to do the unpaid labor of caring for the sick and elderly in their homes, women's labor compensates for the failure of capital and the state to provide longterm health care. Without insurance and benefits to cover home nursing care, women who must earn money often must work more than the double-day.

> I had been working at the sewing factory and I had to quit my job. My mother got real sick and I had to stay at home with her. But we had a lot of bills to pay at the time and I had to do *something*! . . . I was just reading the want ads and I ran across an ad . . . "Wanted: Experienced Sewers." . . . It sounded like a good deal to me. I could be at home with my mother and still make money.

The radicalizing potential of homework as wage work is both partial and contradictory. Respondents often recognize the power of men over them and sometimes resist men's authority through their homework, but they also fail to connect homework to class exploitation or to why it is *women* who must do it all.

> When I first said I wanted to sew, he said: 'You want to work? Good! Then I'll quit and *you* pay the bills.' He said that in an attitude. He never did agree for a woman to go out and work: he didn't believe in that.

> Q: If the sewing cooperative failed, would you look for a job?

Not something that would take me away from home because he wouldn't want me to work.

******

I was sewing night and day trying to get this order out. But he got tired of hearing the sewing machine and got kind of cantankerous about it . . . and I just quit. After a while I thought about it and it was real important to me. And I said I'm not going to do it, not going to quit! . . . I usually try to sew when he's not there. Maybe sometimes I have to put the finishing touches on something, but most of the times he's so busy he don't pay any attention to what I'm doing. . . . It's given me more confidence in myself and what I can do. I can go ahead and do something on my own.

Although the group that these women belong to is described by the outside organizer[18] as an income-generating "cooperative," it has not to date provided the participants a framework for collective self-mobilization; this lack may limit the longevity and potential of the group for further development.

MOTHERWORK

I was supposed to be a *servant*! I wasn't supposed to feel! . . . I mean how can you walk with a kid stuck to your leg?

Servants who do not freely sell their labor are slaves, and more than one respondent acknowledged that marriage "was set up more like slavery," confirming Mies, Bennholdt-Thompson, and von Werlhof's (1988) assertion that women are "the last colony." In the old international division of labor under capitalism, housewives[19] were needed for consumption and reproduction. "The bourgeoisie first withdrew 'their' women from . . . (the) public sphere and shut them up in their cozy 'homes' from where they could not interfere in the war-mongering, moneymaking and the politicking of the men" (Mies 1986:104). The housewife, Mies says, is the "non-free worker" who allows the wage earner to freely sell his labor power: "Proletarianization of men is based on the housewifization of women . . . Thus the Little White Man also got his 'colony', namely the family and the domesticated housewife" (p.110).

The justification for the colonization of women can be found in the social role of the mother which constructs and is constructed by work. In mothering children, husbands, parents, and communities, women are tied by ideological apron strings to the capitalist mode of production: their work, the fundamental work, is motherwork.

> I've been a mother all my life. From the time I was old enough to carry a baby in my arms, like seven or eight, it's been like that.

It was not the joy of nurturing a younger sibling that the respondent recalls but the labor which limited all other dimensions of her life: as a girl, she had no vacations or free time to visit with other children; she wasn't allowed to have friends in her place of work, her home; and the requirements of her job limited her educational opportunities.

> If the washing or something had to be done, . . . then I had to stay home from school.

Wage work, performed in addition to her motherwork, was set aside as soon as she was able to realize her productive potential by getting married and having a baby; it was part of the job.

> To get married, to have kids, have sex no matter whether she wanted it or not, that was (a girl's) duty.

But when the marriage ended, the job didn't. She was alone with a baby. She was an abused wife with no self-esteem or wage employment skills, but her motherwork was required to support the wage labor of extended family members. Through motherwork, women are exploited by capital, the state, and the family. The necessity of two incomes to achieve an adequate living standard and the lack of affordable child care meant that some women in families exploit the labor of others who are left at home. In this way, motherwork is integrated into the process of housewifization in the new international division of labor.

> Every member of my family, every one of them that's got children, I took care of them (the children). . . . Even if it wasn't the children, they was wanting me to do something. They'd say: 'Take the kids over to (her). She'll watch them.' And they'd be gone all day! Sometimes all night! . . . They

would call at five o'clock in the morning and say: 'We need some potato salad and we don't have time to make it. Can you make it?' I'd say: 'What time do you need it?' I guess I been a mother all my life and I felt it was my duty to do it.

Another respondent, abandoned by her husband and left with only one of her children, the sickly child, first did motherwork as informal labor. With references from this employment situation, she was "hired" to be mother to the family of a single father by marrying him.

I done housework and I baby-sat for this lady and my son and I lived with her. . . . She told me about him (my future husband) and the children he was raising. . . . He worked at the fire-department and sometimes he had night shift. . . . He asked if I would be interested in working then for him. So between working for (the lady) and working for him, it kept me and my son. . . . When I married my husband, I was always there for (his children). I cooked for them, cleaned for them, washed clothes after them, took them places where they wanted to go. My poor kids! . . . I wasn't there when they needed attention.

IT'S NOT THE FACTORY

Motherwork is extended into communities through the volunteer labor of women. In describing the work she did in the ladies aid society of the church and the Parent Teacher Association (PTA), one respondent called herself "the former Betty Crocker of the mountains." She now refers to this work as "conformist-type stuff," recognizing its exploitative aspects even though the volunteer work she does now in a grassroots association is much more demanding of her time and energy. The women in this study have done both conformist and tranformational community work, with the latter more possible within their own grassroots associations where they have both the ideological and political space to strategically benefit from their labor.

Community work is both volunteer and paid, and each has aspects of the other. Moser (1989) uses the concept of the triple role of women—in production, reproduction, and community management—to explore the relevance of women's subordination in the gendered division of labor to the field of development planning, or, more specifically, to what she terms 'gender planning.' She contrasts women's community management role to men's community politics role: women's community management role is an extension of their reproductive role, "in order to ensure the provision and maintenance of scarce resources of collective consumption. . . . It is voluntary unpaid work, undertaken in 'free time'" (34). In Latin America, there have been numerous examples of women's community work to provide for basic necessities like housing, food, education, and health care in response to the decline of government services as a result of stabilization and structural adjustment policies imposed by international lending agencies (Beneria and Feldman 1992; Safa 1990). Moser (1989) describes the deliberate inclusion of community management as women's contribution to economic development as the "efficiency" approach to women in development. As a strategy to compensate for declining social services, this approach depends on the "elasticity of women's time" and does not facilitate women's capacity to act on their strategic interests (Moser 1993:57). For the women in this study, community management work was done in the context of traditional organizations, like the Parent Teacher Association, or in grassroots groups, like community development associations.

Men's community politics role, in contrast, "comprises activities undertaken by men at the community level organizing at the formal political level. It is usually paid work, either directly or indirectly, through wages or increases in status and power" (Moser 1993:34). This division of labor in Southwest Virginia was evident from the respondents in this study: community development organizers tended to interact with men who were paid in some way for their community work, like their allies who were ministers, *and* like their adversaries who were often local politicians and public administrative professionals. This gendered division of labor was not always stable when one took into account class: educated local women activists were almost always paid professionals. However, it was the women's professional rather than community credentials that were the basis of their employment.

As with examples from Latin America, the importance of women's community management work in the U.S. is magnified within the context of economic restructuring: marginalized women's labor compensates for the decline of public commitment to the provision of social services. In communities where those persons who do not qualify for mortgage loans also do not have access to public housing, alternative access to housing may be provided in the partnership of community associations and private and voluntary organizations, through the community management work of women.

Volunteer work for women in Southwest Virginia also reflects the inability of marginalized communities to socialize production of support services or to provide women with significant purchasing power through wage jobs. While a middle-class professional may drop her child at the day-care center, the marginalized woman who is employed will look to women who are kin or community for motherwork. The women who fix the food and do other tasks for community events do so because the cost of hiring labor is prohibitive and the work is perceived as an extension of their domestic roles.

For some women, the emotional wages of volunteer work are as important to survival as money. For example, the PTA provided one respondent a way to get away from a violently abusive husband who isolated her from other women.

I became the treasurer (of the PTA) and I felt like I was worth something, I was somebody.

When women feel that they have some control over the decision-making process within the community and its institutions, volunteer work has non-material rewards that may contribute to their capacity to change their material reality.

The material rewards for community work may be more direct. All but one of the five women who work at community development associations now receive some income for their work. The other woman, a strong and charismatic leader, does not want to take a salary: she believes it would diminish her effectiveness, although she works hard to find grant money to support others in her association. All of these women began as volunteers and still work many more hours than are paid. The possibility of getting free community college classes and a minimum stipend drew one respondent into her association, and another woman stays with her group partly for the health insurance she receives through a federal grant.

Respondents who participate in other kinds of groups also receive some benefits such as opportunities to travel to workshops, conferences or other events, including speaking at a nearby university. All of the women who volunteer or are paid, except the women in the income-generating cooperative, claim they will continue as volunteers if the funds ran out.

> If I ever go back to the factory to do hard labor it will be because I absolutely have to . . . but I would never drop out completely. . . . After you get in there and find out it's something to be enjoyed, you just want to grab it and run with it.

Non-conformist or transformational community work is done by women who not only believe that what they are doing is personally rewarding, but that it will change the power relationships that created the need for their labor in the first place. At a meeting of a community development association, the difficulty of doing this kind of work was played out in a sharp exchange at a staff meeting. One member complained when a staff person requested time off for her family. The group had just been discussing how they were going to administer a program for teenagers and how they were going to keep the teenagers from "slacking off." One of the respondents, a leader in the community, slammed the table with her fist and said:

> This is community work, not some factory! How many of you could take off for your families if you were working in some factory? Remember when (member A) had to go to court? Remember when (member B) had to take care of (her grandchild)? Remember when (member C) had to go home to cook for her husband?

She continued to remind them that if they expected to be treated with dignity and to have their domestic responsibilities integrated rather than separated from the working lives, they also needed to assist teenagers to motivate themselves rather than focus their concerns on policing them. Helping the next generation to become subjects rather than objects was a central goal for the women who worked in grassroots associations to better their communities. In accomplishing that end for themselves, they may also be demonstrating the radicalizing potential of women's community work.

CHAPTER FIVE: COMMUNITY

"That Place is My Home"

THE INESSENTIAL APPALACHIAN

The failure to support (the goals and benefits of industrial society) . . . is rooted in the values of agrarian society. (Ford 1991:101)

Fatalism in the guise of docility is the fruit of an historical and sociological situation, not an essential characteristic of people's behavior. (Freire 1972:48)

The central Appalachian communities that are homes to the women in this study have been characterized as repositories of a unique folk culture.[1] Some authors have affirmed the strengths of a humanistic tradition in Appalachian communities (Coles 1971; Kahn 1973), while others have acknowledged a distinctive rural culture as important to the historical process of class struggle in the region (Clavel 1983). The most pervasive representation of Appalachian communities, however, is that there exists within them a unique *sub*culture, with internal deficiencies that explain the poverty of the region (Weller 1965; Loof 1971). Conventional wisdom since the 1960s has argued that Appalachian people are poor because they have reproduced behaviors and attitudes that work against the creation of metropolitan community, inhibiting their integration into the modern and subsequently prosperous world (Ford 1991; Caudill 1962; Weller 1965; Loof 1971).

Emphasizing traditionalism, familialism, fundamentalism, and fatalism, a negative stereotypical image was created of Appalachian "hillbillies" as victims of their own cultural inadequacy. It grew out of the same intellectual milieu that produced "culture of poverty" explanations (Lewis 1961, 1966) for the relative deprivation of other communities in the U.S. (Moynihan 1965)[2] and in the "third world" of the economic South (Foster 1973; Inkeles 1969; McClelland 1966). The root cause of poverty in Appalachia and elsewhere[3] from this perspective is not the political and economic position of Appalachian communities within an historical moment, but certain unacceptable cultural traits that are always contrasted with middle-class, metropolitan cultural values and practices (See discussion in Lewis 1991.) Ethnic stereotyping of Appalachian communities—as poor, white, and homogeneously Anglo-Saxon—justifies the exploitation of Appalachian people and resources as conveniently as racism and Eurocentrism has justified the exploitation of the economic South.

Fisher (1991) has summarized this "blaming the victim" (Ryan 1971) approach and its emphasis on the collective expression of individual characteristics: the "culture of poverty" in Appalachia is rooted in an individualism that prevents an understanding of the "public good," a traditionalism that is resistant to progress, and a fatalism that leads to passive acceptance. The rugged mountaineer or hillbilly is action-seeking rather than routine-seeking, person-oriented rather than goal-oriented, isolated from contemporary urban values, overly loyal to family, and enslaved by a locally autonomous religious fundamentalism (Weller 1965 discussed in Fisher 1991).

Austin (1966) and Best (1973) point out the contradictions within subculture models and reveal class bias in the interpretation of cultural meanings (Fisher 1991:190). Lewis (1978 with Johnson and Askins, 1991), Fisher (1991), Walls and Billings (1991), and Gaventa (1980) reject the cultural assumptions that have so distorted both popular and academic writing on Appalachia in favor of a structural approach to understanding the region's underdevelopment: "Poverty is not a consequence of insufficient modernization but the result of a particular kind of economic development and its political consequences" (Billings 1976:135). Lewis presents Appalachia as an internal colony, while Billings (1974, 1976) and Walls (1976) view it as an internal periphery where underdevelopment is an outcome of class domination. Lewis, Kobak, and Johnson (1978) discuss the cultural insularity of Appalachian communities as a defensive stance in the process of colonization: they "became defensive and reverted inward to protect members from the sudden influence which came with the development of industrialization" (In Walls and Billings 1991:55). Gaventa (1980) explores the power of elites and their corporate sponsors over Appalachian people and communities.

Although the "culture of poverty" model has been convincingly challenged by contemporary Appalachian scholars, both subcultural and structural models ignore gender in their analysis. In a gendered reading of the subculture model, the essential Appalachian, like the essential human, is a man, the "mountaineer," and women's experiences are invisible.[4] At the same time, those behaviors and values discredited in a "culture of poverty" are also associated with women: a connection to the past that is deeply rooted in family life and the tendency to personalize public interaction. The Appalachian's "passive resignation and tolerance of undesirable conditions" (Fisher 1991:187) could be read as a realistic and non-combative survival strategy associated with women as a group as well as Appalachians.

When Appalachian people show no allegiance to the work place, for example, they are criticized for excessive personalism and individualism, marking them as unreliable workers. One respondent spoke of her pattern of moving from one sewing factory job to another without giving notice.

I just come home one day and didn't go back, and that's true with every job I had.

Understanding her sense of alienation derived from the class and gender conditions of this work, her response may have been the only form of resistance available to her.

Internal colonial and class analyses tend to focus on the expropriation of resources and relationships of production in an industry that excludes women; the absence of women in structural analyses is fundamental since reproductive labor is fundamentally excluded from work. Even for Gaventa (1980), whose interest is an analysis of power, gender is absent: Gaventa ignores how the operation of power within Appalachian communities may be related to the relative positions and power between women and men. Such an analysis would explore how the ideological dimensions of gender relationships reinforce the power of capitalists and their surrogates through the gendered division of labor and through cross-class alliances of men; it would also examine how local institutions fail to represent not only working-class but women's interests.

Gaventa argues that the indirect operation of power in a "third dimension," as proposed by Lukes (1974), takes place "behind the social construction of meanings and patterns" (Gaventa 1980:15). It is within this dimension that we can examine the response of the respondents in this study to their community institutions, their sense of communal identity, and their acquiescence to the interpretations of the powerful. Whether the "powerlessness" of these women leads to quiescence or political non-action is a subject for following chapters.

THE FAILURE OF LOCAL INSTITUTIONS

It is within the context of community institutions and community participation that the pervasiveness of the subculture model in Appalachia becomes relevant to planners: Fisher states that "the debate over the Appalachian subculture would not be of much significance except that the persons and agencies concerned with fighting the conditions of poverty in the mountains have accepted this view of Appalachia. . . . There has been little questioning of the manner in which the institutions of the region serve and affect the people because there has been agreement that the values of the people are at fault" (Fisher 1991:191).

The institutions of community have failed the people of Southwest Virginia: churches, schools, community organizations, the union (UMWA),[5] local government, law enforcement, the courts, health care providers, and social service agencies have been described by the women in this study as inaccessible, degrading, oppressive, or, at best, irrelevant to their daily lives and struggles. While subcultural explanations may interpret these attitudes as evidence of cultural dysfunction and structural explanations may ignore them in an analysis of a regional political economy, the alienation of these women from conventional community institutions may reveal the deeper estrangement of administrative structures from political community.

TROUBLE WITH THE DOCTOR

In coal-mining communities there are high rates of injury, long term illness, and an "exceptionally high level of reported disability" (Kraybill, Johnson, and Deaton 1987:27–33). The region has fewer physicians in proportion to the population of the state as a whole (ibid:33), and respondents reported few opportunities for health insurance outside of unionized mining benefits. Yet health-related issues are fundamental for the respondents and their families.

In addition to their adversarial relationship with the coal companies over safety issues and the provision of health benefits, respondents reported deep resentment towards health care providers, often characterized as representatives of capital rather than as

estimable members of their communities. Of the twelve respondents, five women had no husband or father who was directly employed in the coal industry, although two of those women have been
miners themselves. Of the remaining seven respondents, there are
three women with husbands permanently disabled from mining
injuries, one with a father dying of pneumoconiosis, commonly called
"black lung," and one whose husband died in a mining accident.[6,7]

In both formal and informal settings of women's associations,
especially in the union-based associations, women's conversations
eventually got around to mining-related injury and health problems, and how these problems create other problems for their families. A common theme was the adversarial relationship with the
medical establishment to get rightful compensation for their family
member's injury. Since physicians are involved in the decisionmaking process to determine disability, company physicians are
held in low esteem because they are perceived to be plotting with
management to deny miners' claims.

You can be walking around dragging an oxygen tent and
the doctors will say that you don't have a black lung.

After reports by three respondents and several other women in
their associations of miners' health claims being routinely contested
by management, I asked a respondent if her disabled husband had
to fight for his pension. She replied:

So far, we've had more trouble with the doctor. The doctor
says he's able to do light duty work, and he can't hardly do
nothing even for a thirty minute period of time!

Another respondent said that her husband's chest was crushed
in a mining accident; company physicians declared him recovered
even though he continued to experience symptoms of pain and
fatigue. He initiated a disability claim which is being contested by
the company, and their physicians have now referred him to an
affiliated psychologist for evaluation and therapy.

A respondent spoke of a surgeon who would not remove her
tumor without cash payment because she was uninsured. Other
women told of their resistance to client relationships with mental
health professionals working in publicly-funded programs; the

problem was not their attitudes about therapy but the class bias they perceived in the attitudes of professionals.

LISTEN TO MY PAIN

The pain of women who suffered gender-based violence was denied within their families and within the institutions of their communities. Two women who were beaten along with their children by their husbands could not find help within administrative and legal structures. Another woman told of the reaction of emergency room physicians when she sought help after a beating by her husband.

> Oh, they were as sensitive as can be! One time he knocked my teeth out in front and this male doctor said: 'Well, at least he can't knock your teeth out any more.' Basically they didn't care; there was no counseling or anything.

Gender oppression disguised as therapy was prescribed for one respondent who was abused as a child. A victim of incest and abuse from the age of five, she "fell apart" emotionally in high school.

> I had a breakdown when I was seventeen. I was at school one day and I couldn't stop crying . . . In front of the principle I said my life is falling apart and he said I better get some counseling. I don't know if you know about the infamous Dr. (names him). He's the company psychiatrist, the one all the miners and the miners' wives went to. He was the only option, so I went to see him, well not him, but another doctor he was over. I guess I was really depressed and I tried to kill myself so they put me in St. Albans. I don't think I was really trying to kill myself because I would have done it. But he put me on shock treatment. Now I'm angry as hell! I had twelve shock treatments. They came in series of six, and I also know that my father had signed me up for another six. I stuttered for a year after that, and I still have trouble with my memory . . . He treated a lot of young people with shock treatments! He had an EST treatment in his office, and he'd do them on a daily basis. He did outpatient shock. All I wanted was for somebody to listen to my pain.

In a barely controlled voice, she spoke of what happened when she attempted to speak about her abuse in counseling session following the shock therapy. The therapist had consulted with her mother who has never admitted to the abuse.

And this counselor, this man, crossed his arms and said: 'Now, is this a mountain or a molehill?' And I, of course, said it was a molehill. I couldn't trust him.

The medical establishment participated not only in class oppression but in perpetuating her powerlessness. The respondent was doubly caught in a bond between men who abused her body sexually and treated physical abuse with emotional abuse.[8]

THEY DON'T HAVE TO LIVE IT

False charity constrains the fearful and subdued, the 'rejects of life,' to extend their trembling hands. True generosity lies in striving so that these hands—whether of individuals or of entire peoples—need be extended less and less in supplication, so that more and more they become human hands which work, and, working, transform the world. (Freire 1972:29)

Professionals in caregiving and social welfare bureaucrats were often described as persons who are "outsiders," persons who "think they're better." Women from several communities talked about how either they or their mothers had refused "welfare" because they wanted neither the humiliation nor dependency associated with public assistance. As Tickamyer and Tickamyer (1991) observed: "the experience with the welfare bureaucracy disempowers poor people" (309). Within one of the associations in this study, a community development program sent women from the community to the homes of local pregnant teenagers. Local development workers, including a respondent, found this extremely difficult in the beginning because people thought they were representing the welfare department, and "people hated the welfare so much they didn't want to open the door."

A woman receiving Aid to Families with Dependent Children (AFDC) and a housing subsidy commented on the seemingly endless administrative requirements of public assistance.

Why do they always make you fill out so many forms? Is it so that you will feel like you're nothing, that you're not even a person? . . . You know, some of us have no vehicle, and you don't have any way back and forth if you don't have no vehicle.

Primarily male welfare programs, like unemployment compensation and social security, do not carry the stigma of poverty. If the respondent was a widow rather than a women who left her husband, she would be eligible for social security, a welfare program that does *not* make you "feel like you're nothing."

Ryan (1981) and Tickamyer and Tickamyer (1991) have observed the inherent bias against the poor in entitlement programs, and Funiciello (1990) reveals the gender ideology: "The message: the needs and rights of women and children are determined by the nature of their prior relationship to a man; the only difference between the 'survivor' families and 'welfare' families is the imprimatur of the father" (36).

Weiss (1990) argues that "without jobs, or decent-paying jobs above a poverty wage, women and their children are left to the not-so-tender-mercies of the social welfare system" (65). Historically, social welfare policy promoted disruption in marital or parental partnerships. This was confirmed by a couple who left a northern city because of the cost of living and the lack of secure jobs. Returning home to the mountains where housing and food were less costly, a respondent recalled the days when she was penalized for keeping her family together.

Neither of us was working, and we were collecting food stamps, that's all. At that time in Virginia there was no AFDC, only ADC. So with him in the household there was no way I could get anything!

Weiss (1990) also faults the social welfare system for perpetuating gender stereotypes in current regulations for Aid to Families with Dependent Children (AFDC), which "reinforce occupational segregation and prevent social service programs from taking bold steps to encourage non-traditional occupations or small-business development as a way out of poverty" (65). Key elements are regulations that prohibit recipients, unlike all other business persons, from separating business and personal income. *"(A)ny return* to the business is considered personal income, regardless of the business expenses incurred, and, however small, is deducted from the welfare check" (ibid).

Discouraging entrepreneurial activity among women is only part of the problem. Because a respondent cannot support her family on what she can earn *or* on what she receives as public assistance, she is forced into lying about her informal income.

> It's not like I can advertise. I can't say that I'll do babysitting because then I have to turn it in. And if I turn it in, they would take my HUD, they would take my food stamps, and I just couldn't *live*!

The problems go beyond the social welfare system that directs aid to individuals. Another respondent angrily recalled an incident with the director of an economic development center that is administered out of a large state university: the behavior of the director towards her was evidence for her not only of his individual bias but the true class interests of the center.[9]

> Remember I met you in the parking lot . . . and I was in tears? . . . Over a man that treated me like I wasn't as good as something off the floor! . . . I just thought (the economic development center) was the most wonderful thing when I first heard about it. . . . They got educated people and I can go and tell them what our problem is and they can help me figure out how to do it! . . . Like they can help you write down a feasibility study—that was their job, I thought! . . . I took everything, every piece of paper down there. We had set up here and we had planned and planned and planned, and we knew exactly what we wanted! And we went down there and asked: 'Can you figure out a way to help us to do this? Can you get it down on paper and get it right? . . . And I went down there and I was made to feel like I was the worst thing to hit Southwest Virginia, that I was completely uneducated, completely inadequate, and should go home and die because I was completely worthless! But these people down there is *supposed* to be *helping* people like me in Southwest Virginia to do economic development. God knows how much they make! They're probably all making about $50,000 a year or more! So here you got all these experts

making big money and they ain't helping *nobody*! The . . . economic development center is *not* about economic development, it's some way for some rich cats to stay rich. . . . I look at all the state money that's being spent down there! . . . And God help the people of Southwest Virginia if they depend on that place for economic development. . . . I'm going to be honest with you and this can be printed anywhere in the world: that economic development center—I would not spit on it if it was on fire.

The insecurity of life in the coal counties based on income instability and associated socioeconomic problems often produces extreme change: a person who is relatively secure one year may lose everything the next. One respondent reported that she had lost everything that she owned three times in her life.

When my house burned down I lost everything again! And when I left (the city) everything I owned was repossessed because I didn't have any work: my house, my car, the whole nine yards. But I've gotten stronger because of it, and I know how people feel in this community: how degrading it is to have to ask for help.

In communities where people are poor, people are both treated and humiliated by outsiders and professionals. Wariness of administrative structures and those who enforce them is a survival strategy, and healthy disdain is good medicine for self-esteem.

IT'S HARD TO KNOW

The material and ideological resources of the coal companies give them the power to destroy a sense of trust and well-being in one's home and community and to limit opportunities for creating a community base for resistance. The disability claim of a respondent's husband remains unresolved after at least two years, and the company has gone to great lengths to gather evidence that the miner is capable of work. There was one incident that the respondent described as a typical intimidation tactic: during a hearing on the claim, the couple were shown an aerial photograph of their home with wood-cutting tools on the property. The photographs were taken by private investigators hired by the company. The respondent also reported that helicopters have flown over their property and swooped down for a closer look.

> They offered him $1500 to settle, and after all that he has been through! They really did him dirty, spying on him and all like that. They act like even if you're able to do something simple like taking care of your place, which isn't the same thing as working in the mines, just little things like mowing the lawn . . . They showed us these photographs of our place and our apple trees are in bloom, and the cherry trees—it's so pretty! . . . In the field there was his brother's wood splitter—his brother and his nephew was getting trees out of there all winter, and they claimed it must be him that can do that work.

This mining family had been living on a $78 per week check until his unemployment benefits ran out. Other women reported that it was typical for the coal industry to use time and the desperation of mining families without an income to wear down miners to settle compensation claims in the company's favor. In these situations, the power of capital is exercised in its ability to amass resources to contest a health claim and to wait out their more vulnerable opponent.

The power of capital is also exercised in its ability to create an environment of intimidation and insecurity that goes beyond an individual worker and his family's relationship to the company.

> They're really after (him). I think it's because of the work he did on the picket line—he was really active in the union. I was too! I wonder if they've seen us in the paper; I've been on TV, and I've been going out speaking and talking. I know they got pictures of me when I was arrested, It's hard to know how much they know.

If people in Appalachian communities are suspicious of those outside of their kinship networks and hesitant to participate in local civic and administrative structures, it may also be because capital has been successful in incorporating other interests in the community into their service. Not only are the healthcare professionals and social welfare bureaucrats implicated, but local people—the company managers and clerical employees, those who rent and fly the helicopters, and those who hide in the woods and take photographs—are accomplices in surveillance and control (Foucault 1979). The power of corporate capital in the coal fields splits families and friendships. There were those people in communities who did not support the United Mineworkers strike: clerical workers in coal company offices, those miners who move into quasi-management positions, miners who work in non-union coal operations often owned by Pittston, and miners forced by economic necessity to break the strike and to go to work as a "scab" for the company. The divisions within families and the larger community were deep and bitter: for union-affiliated women, strike-breakers were "scabs" who betrayed them in a life and death situation.

The company also has the power to limit opportunities for community connections that could become subversive. I spent an evening in the home of a miner who was a union activist and who was being "punished," according to his wife, with a particularly difficult schedule. By limiting possibilities for time commitments outside of work, the "swing shift"[10] is another mechanism of control.

> The way they started doing these swing shifts, the person doing the work really can't plan to go to church or go to meetings or anything! Because of the way they got their schedules set up. And they got it set counter-clockwise: like if you work this week on evening shift, next week you work day shift. Clockwise would be easier on them, but Pittston's got it set up to go backward. These men don't really have any social life! All they got is a little time at home.

The shift to centralized services such as regional schools, and the decline of locally controlled business also distances institutions from their base in the community. As more stores are owned by larger firms and outside capital, community solidarity is threatened. During the strike against Pittston Coal (1989–1990), some merchants, particularly those with stores owned by outside chains, refused to support the UMWA. One respondent characterized the difference between two grocery chains as evidence of the motivations of big business versus local business.

> If I walk into this place and they say they wouldn't put up a sign and they say right out: "We don't support the UMWA, all we want is to do business", I know that all they want is

money. . . . Piggly-Wiggly put their sign up and I suspect they lost a few customers because of it. But Food Lion said that they would shut their doors before they would support the UMWA. . . . They're a really big company and they're anti-union.

Other women expressed their sense that "things were OK" in the coal communities before local coal companies were taken over by large firms with multinational interests. Despite the actual owner-ship of the companies in question, the perception of at least two coal companies in the area is that they have lost their sense of corporate responsibility to the community because they are too big, too diversified, and too distant.

It's been bad ever since. Clinchfield used to be a local company. . . . The men worked hard. Everything was fine. That's why we had a false sense of security, I guess. Then the operators sold out to Pittston. Pittston owns Brinks, and Burlington, a well-known freight company. They're such a huge outfit they're insensitive. They don't care! It's not like it used to be.

TRYING TO BE WITH THE LAW

I always tried to be with the law not against it. But it seemed like I never got any protection or any help.

Civil authorities didn't help two women get back the children that were taken from them by estranged husbands. For one respon-dent, there was no justice in giving legal rights to a parent who beat his baby with a stick from the window shade: "the law that said he was just as much his as he was mine." For another respon-dent, the law was harsh and intimidating, and the risks of break-ing the law too great: after the father of her children kidnapped them and took them across country, one child phoned his mother but feared his father's violence if the father found out. Legal aid and the police could not help the mother get her children, although she had filed a complaint. Social welfare agencies had told her the problem was beyond their jurisdiction, and the cost of getting across country to file a complaint in court was beyond her comprehension of the possible.

My son went in an talked to this woman officer and told the police that his daddy had put them in a car and taken them away from me and that his mommy didn't even know where they was at. The police officer helped him call me and said: 'Your son must love you very much to try and file charges against his daddy." I said: 'We're three thousand miles apart and I don't have any money. Can't you get the welfare to get me some money so I can get my children back?', and she said: 'You'll have to come out here to the courthouse and file charges against him.'

The respondent had a friend with another friend in the state where her children had been taken; she asked this person to go to her children's new school posing as a relative to check on their well-being, but she never informed Virginia authorities with whom she had filed a complaint. When I asked her why, she replied:

Because of the situation with the prosecuting attorney. I sent a man in there that wasn't a relative to lie. I couldn't say nothing because that would get my son into trouble and I had to keep him (her son's violent and abusive father) away from him. I couldn't take chances with his life.

The law and those who enforce it also failed to address the needs of single mothers. The adequacy of income-based child support guidelines is a contested issue for middle-class families. In an area where fathers' incomes are unstable and often low, even court-enforced child support is clearly inadequate for poor women. Women who were household heads with absent husbands sometimes deferred filing for maintenance and divorce because they felt they could neither understand the legal process nor afford to hire a lawyer; another respondent stayed married to keep her husband's union health insurance even though he provided no other support to the family. For those women who did divorce, the amount of child support was not necessarily worth the material and emotional cost of collection. For the mother of five children who unwillingly lost four of them when her husband kidnapped them, the contradictions within the legal system were both alienating and absurd.

Through the courthouse, he put a reciprocal order through. He went to court and had the money (for his child support) lowered out there and they ordered him to pay me $21 a month in two payments of $10.50. And that's all I ever got from him.

The estrangement of people within the coal counties from civil authority based on institutional procedures is part of a "mobilization of bias" (Bachrach and Baratz 1970) that Gaventa (1980) attributes to the hegemony of capital within the region. Coal-based communities also experienced the coercive power of the police and the courts in situations of labor conflict (Gaventa 1980; Shifflett 1991), and for respondents, the 1989–1990 strike of the United Mineworkers against the Pittston Coal Company is a particularly severe example. One respondent described the behavior of police arresting striking miners practicing civil disobedience.

They dragged them, pulled their ears, tore quite a few people's ears. The broke arms. One woman miner, they slammed her up against a door and caused some kind of damage to her head: she's got double vision—never be good again!

In addition to the three respondents who were directly involved in the strike through the union auxiliary, two other women spoke of their solidarity with the strikers in going to the picket lines and shopping in stores that identified their support for the union. Three other respondents volunteered that they believed the miners' cause was just, and that the governor, police and courts were unfair. Women in the auxiliary spoke of an emotionally charged environment where law enforcement and the courts were perceived as agents of an enemy.

The people were really getting angry with the company and Vance Security.[11] They were also getting angry with the State Police: They were going to bring the miners they arrested to the courthouse but so many people showed up, they were afraid to do it. So they drove them around for about seven or eight hours, and it was a really hot day, too.

Women told stories of how local knowledge of the back roads and dirt roads allowed them to escape the police or avert their road blocks. They also told of listening to police radio to learn official plans, then switching rural route number signs to trick the police on their way to intervene in a strike action.

The epitome of the lack of justice within the legal system, to all of the women who talked about the coal strike, were the steep fines imposed on the United Mineworkers by state Circuit Court Judge Donald McGlothlin, Jr. of Lebanon.[12] Several women also spoke of their personal experience of engaging in civil disobedience, of being arrested and sent to jail.[13] "I've always thought of myself as a law-abiding citizen," one woman said to me, "but being in the strike, getting on a bus and being taken to a jail, it's hard not to see that the law can be used against you, against what's right."

POLITICS AS USUAL

"The sins of the son were visited on the father" (Yancey 1990:8) was the way a newspaper reporter described the defeat of Judge McGlothlin's father, the incumbent Democrat, by United Mineworkers District #28 President Jackie Stump in the Virginia House of Delegates election of November 1989. The solidarity of union efforts to get out the vote in Stump's last minute bid and the solid defeat of Delegate Don McGlothlin, Sr. contradict the pejorative assumption that Appalachian people do not participate in government because of their clannishness, fatalism, and inability to relate to the state beyond the local level (Photiadis and Schwarzweller 1970).

In the 1989 election for the House of Delegates, working-class interests were clearly represented by Stump and people responded with enthusiasm to the opportunity to have a voice in Richmond, to tell the Judge what they thought of his interpretation of law, and to give a message to the governor's office about the role of the state police in protecting the interests of the coal companies during the strike. "It was a classic populist pitch," and "strikers, their wives and sometimes their children came from neighboring counties to help . . . Jackie Stump . . . (go) from the jailhouse to the statehouse" (Yancey 1990:15).

The high turnout for a write-in union candidate suggests that non-participation in the usual politics cannot be attributed to the cultural deficiency of people in Appalachian communities as both pluralists and subculturalists claim: when working-class people had an opportunity to use the political system, they did so successfully. Gaventa (1980) argues that the failure to contest elites through

statist politics is neither evidence of the legitimacy of political structures nor evidence of the apathy of working-class people. Why people
are quiescent or inactive in conventional forms of politics is more
likely evidence of the power of capital to quiet them.[14] "Powerless,"
a respondent said to describe her feelings about facing a county
authority: "People just felt real powerless."

Power in the coal counties can be examined at a second level
where a "mobilization of bias" prevents issues and actors from gaining access to the political process. This is accomplished through the
institutional procedures discussed above, or consensus values about
what issues are important and how they should be addressed. Both
the quiescence of working-class people *and* their exceptional participation in the 1989 election could be accommodated in this analysis of power: the candidacy of Jackie Stump was a rare opportunity
for working-class interests to be represented, even if only as a
protest.

> If you study it as a voter and if you got to figure out which
> is the lesser of two evils, which is going to cause you less
> harm, that's no basis to have to elect somebody, but that's
> politics as usual!

The irrelevancy of political options at all levels, the union of
politicians and capitalists, and their manipulation of political symbols was discussed by one respondent.

> Where is the Democrat that would speak for the working
> people right now? . . . I mean we go to the polls and George
> Bush was elected by something like 27 percent of the people.
> Is that enough? . . . Just because somebody wraps the flag
> around themselves and says they're all-American, that don't
> mean they're all-American the way *I* look at being all-
> American! That flag has done wonders for George Bush and
> Ronald Reagan, Lee Iacocca. People are so used to thinking
> that if somebody has money, then they're right.

Politics as usual was the way women in a community development group interpreted the decision of the county industrial development authority to sell a large tract of land given to the community
twenty years earlier.[15] Not only were the women infuriated that
the authority was selling their land to generate revenues to be

transferred to the country seat, their anger was based on grounds that to do so would break a covenant, would betray past and future generations. "(R)esidents were angered and insulted both by the enormity of the politicians' decision and the casual way it was communicated, buried in the back pages of a newspaper, to those whose lives it would affect" (Lewis and O'Donnell 1990 A:197).

Gaventa (1980) takes his analysis of power deeper into the ideological domain of the psyche: power may not only limit access but the formation of political consciousness. Like Fanon (1966) and Freire (1972), Gaventa is interested in the relationship of the powerful and the powerless, and how powerlessness and quiescence are internalized until the power field is altered. The process of becoming quiescent was discussed by a respondent.

> If you just *accept*, it's easier. You don't have to think and you don't make no enemies. . . . You go to work, somebody tells you what to do all day long, you punch a clock. You come home, watch television. Everything is controlled. Your whole life is controlled. . . . You just program your life and your life is programmed.

GO HOME AND MAKE COOKIES

This analysis takes on different dimensions when gender is introduced because women experience powerlessness both on the basis of class and gender. Politics as usual was also the way respondents described the political process of the unions. Not only were miners hostile to women working underground, the unions were "still the good ole' boys" who have the power and use it in ways that contradict their class interests.

> The union is a business . . . and that's all there is to it! . . . In the union, they have board meetings and stuff. Things have to filter *down* to the rank and file. It takes maybe three or four months until they get something decided and then they can say: "Yeah, we're gonna have a bake sale."

When women reject or fail to participate in statist politics or in union politics, they may also be reacting to forms of political expression that have historically excluded them. A respondent described the difference between the meetings of predominantly male union miners and a support group for women miners.

We decided that we (the women) were going to have a conference. We didn't want a *convention*, we wanted a *conference*, because conference meant that we could meet together and think and find a solution, and convention meant a bunch of dirty slobs partying!

The pervasiveness of gender ideology that teaches quiescence as "natural" for women operates to limit women's autonomy and opportunities for political expression in ways that are different than quiescence for men.

I'd go to political meetings and they'd call me 'that woman.' You know, planning commissions, industrial development authority meetings, government meetings. They'd go: 'Oh honey.' You know the word 'honey' never bothered me before in my life cause I used to like to hear: 'How'you honey?' But, you know, I can't hardly stand to hear a man use it now to me. Cause when they use it they belittle me, make fun of me. They patted me on the back and they told me to go home and make cookies. 'Go home,' they said, 'we'll take care of everything, honey.' I left meetings and just throwed up.

"Was there any similarity," I asked her, "in the way you were treated by the planning commission and other public authorities or development agencies?"
"Oh sure! It's the same thing, just because I'm a woman."

TO BE AN OUTSIDER INSIDE THE SCHOOL

School systems are not set up for people. School systems are set up by the state and by the education department—from outside the community. It used to not be that way; today it is.

The association that successfully blocked the sale of industrial development land formed an economics discussion group that shortly led to an alternative and successful community-based education program. For the respondents, an education that would prepare you to be an autonomous, productive, and active participant within your community was not something that you could expect to get in the public schools. According to Fisher (1991), in many areas of the region in the past, a majority of Appalachian students dropped out of school before graduation and had a consistently higher than elsewhere failure rate on selective service entrance tests (192). In the coal counties of Southwest Virginia, the high school drop out rate had decreased to 5.2 percent by 1985, but was still higher than the rest of the state (Kraybill, Johnson and Deaton 1987:35). The proportion of adults age 25 and over with a high school education in the coal counties rose from 11.1 percent in 1950, the approximate birth year of most respondents, to 38.3 percent in 1980 (ibid:34).

Public education in general in Southwest Virginia may have improved, but is still below the standards of other areas of the state: the gap between the state as a whole and the coal counties in standardized reading test scores remained constant from 1975 to 1985, and increased in math and language arts scores (ibid:37–38). Educational funding measured by per pupil expenditure in the coal counties has also remained well below the state average (ibid:39).[16] While subculturalists look inside the homes of Southwest Virginia to find reasons for the reproduction of educational failure, Kraybill, Johnson and Deaton (1987) suggest that the poverty of the region and economic instability lead to reduced investment in education, a lack of long-range planning, and the flight of "talented, educated, and productive members of the community out of the area in search of better opportunities" (67).

Both structural and cultural accounts do not look for the failure of education within the dimension of consciousness. They do not ask in what ways the economic and political base of educational institutions reproduces through ideology the powerless position of rural, working-class communities, and especially working-class women; they also do not ask in what ways working-class people resist these messages.

Rather than looking to working-class people for values that reproduce poverty, it may be helpful to look at middle-class institutional culture for its gender and class bias. A woman who "loved to go to school better than anything" realized that the school teachers and administrators *also* believed that if you are a girl who is needed at home, "you have to be off"—if you're a girl, you really belong at home. Half of the respondents completed high school in their teens, and it was a difficult accomplishment: their labor was required outside of school, and gender ideology, inside as well as outside the home, worked against their academic success. As girls, they were discouraged from scholarly interests or the hope that an education might lead to social roles outside of the domestic and degraded sphere.

I quit school when I was 13. Daddy said: 'Don't worry about it. It don't take an education to pin diapers on.'

One respondent's comments suggest that an increase in a educational performance suggested by the decline of the high school drop out rate may instead be an indicator of decreased standards and expectations of working-class students.[17] When her children came home with passing grades and she felt they were "not learning anything," she would go to the school and complain; she felt sure that expectations of her children were low, and not much effort was put into giving them the educational skills to improve or challenge their condition.

There was an overwhelming sense among respondents that educational institutions perpetuated demeaning stereotypes about working-class Appalachian people, and that they perpetuated underdevelopment by tracking children from these communities, already alienated from the academic and social environment of the schools, into low-wage service jobs.

if you're from (this community), they tell you not to take the college courses but to take cosmetology or shop or flower-arranging![18]

Alienation from public education was most often expressed as a feeling that institutions were not controlled by their communities nor responsive to their interests.

One thing that hurts us is that the school is not in the community, so you don't have ownership of it. It's like you're an outsider when you're there.

******

I knew that there were lines that you didn't cross, but when I got to high school, it was the kids whose fathers weren't in the mines, weren't working underground, who were the ones who had nice clothes and money for lunch every day, who were president of the clubs and stuff. The rest of us, the poor kids, I mean the ones whose fathers worked underground, we didn't get to get on the forensics team, we didn't get the rewards.

Increasing centralization and consolidation of schools is represented in the mainstream as a sign of modernization and improvement in education (Ford 1991:100). Yet once communities lost control of their own schools, children lost their points of reference, their sense of belonging that validated who they were. As working-class children were integrated into the "better" schools with middle-class children, they were constructed as "the poor" in ways they had never experienced before.[19] Not only did teachers and other children look down on them, respondents internalized the messages of their inadequacy in the larger culture which assigns value in relation to your ability to consume.[20]

When I was growing up, the kids around here—even the kids you might call rich—really didn't have much more than that we did; So you never really felt separated from the community because you didn't have something.

******

I didn't know I was poor white trash until I went to school and somebody told me. If I had never gone to school, I never would have known I was poor! I just thought we was all alike! But you got all of those pretty little youngins there and they had all the latest fashions and all the toys and things. Then I knew I was poor, and I had a rough time. Mamma made my clothes out of chopsacks—feed sacks. *I* thought I had pretty little clothes, but I got to school and they weren't pretty.

******

The other kids made me feel like I wasn't worth nothing because I was from (here).

Women who dropped out also paid a price in the labor market. One respondent spoke of her fear of being unable to make change when she got a job at the grocery store as a married adult.

I was at home and I was afraid to try, because, like I said, I didn't have an education. After I got a job as a cashier . . . I thought: O my God! How am I ever going to be able to do this? Make change. A lot of people take that for granted.

Even if the lack of a high school education did not keep women from getting the low-wage jobs available in the sewing factories, furniture factories, or service sector, it did keep them from expecting that they could ever do any better.

When you fill out an application for a job and you haven't finished high school, you really don't have anything to offer anybody. You just take what you can. You can't *expect* anything else.

A student who excelled *might* be able to go to college, but it was a community college, not the university in the region or a degree-granting college. After hearing several women refer to their own plans to go to "college," I came to realize that they meant the community college, which offers them employment training. The community college system is a contradictory institution: it appears to channel working-class people into training for more skilled jobs in labor markets that are often absent or highly competitive in the mountains. It also appears that it is institutionalized to deflect working-class aspirations from the state university system. Yet the community college is seen as a positive institution for the most part. Not only does the community college hold out the possibility of a better job, attendance is a source of status in the community, and the colleges in the region have made deliberate attempts to develop community-based education programs.[21]

If you were an outsider in the schools, you could also be an outsider in community organizations associated with the schools, such as the Parent Teachers Association (PTA) and the Girl Scouts: there were material and ideological barriers to participation.

I went to a girl scout meeting, once! It was run by a bunch of middle-class women and it was just horrible. I didn't have a uniform, and I couldn't get a uniform.

Only three of the respondents participation in the PTA. One women, a single parent who had a factory job in the midwest when her children were young, was active in both her union and the PTA. A second women got involved for the opportunity to connect with other women, to have some relief from her suspicious and violent husband. The third woman, "the former Betty Crocker of the mountains," is a strong leader who has been involved in community organizations all of her married life, and church organizations since her childhood.

> I worked in the PTA a lot—did a lot of fund-raisers. I worked a lot in the school, a lot of volunteer work.

THE SAME GOD OF LOVE

Since religion is a central source of meaning and values, the distinctive regional churches of Appalachia—"shouting and charismatic" churches and fundamentalist churches—have been blamed as powerful and primary barriers to progress. For Ford (1991), fundamentalism, or contemporary sectarianism, "tends to draw its adherents predominantly from the low economic strata. Their orientation is other-worldly, since they seek and are promised divine compensation, contingent upon salvation, for their earthly sufferings" (Ford 1991:93). The churches of Appalachia, outside of the mainstream of national Protestant denominations, "still (operate) as a restraining force among depressed classes who continue to use religion as an escape from unpleasant reality. . . . (Religion) can scarcely be considered a strong influence in the promotion of social and economic development" (ibid:95).

Lewis, Kobak, and Johnson (1978) offer another possibility that the Appalachian church, like the Appalachian family, provided an institutional setting for people to escape to some degree the onslaught of capitalist values and metropolitan control that sought to destroy their ethnic identity in the rush for coal. The differences between the positions may be in part how positively one views integration into the normative systems of the modern capitalist state.

Religious experience as expressed by the respondents in this study is contradictory, complex, and not easy to represent within either of the above positions. For the purposes of analysis, it is important to draw a distinction between religions faith as a primary source of meaning and values and the churches as social institutions. Faith is important to the women who struggle for social change, but the church is not necessarily the place where faith is experienced or nurtured (Cardenal 1982).[22] Yet the church, even the fundamentalist church described by Ford, can be the local institution in working class communities that is *the* source of affirmation for people who are not affirmed in their jobs or in their interactions with other institutions in the public sphere.[23] The majority of respondents mentioned their churches as important to their social and community lives, especially during childhood. It provided social outlets for people who had neither the resources nor opportunities to find them elsewhere. It was a place to gather, to meet friends outside your familial circle; this was especially important to women and girls who tended to be confined to the domestic sphere.

It was pretty good back then. The fathers were coal miners. The mothers stayed home back then, but everybody went to church on Sunday and on other days. I was taken to the Freewill Baptist Church. My mom was the treasurer of the Sunday school, and I can remember going to Sunday school and revivals.

If the church was the place where one learned class consciousness, it was because of the disparity between social reality and the message of Christian love and community.

I always had a lot of anger at the church. You would go to church on Sunday and you would be preached to about God, love, and a brotherhood of man. And you sat in the pews with the company bosses who came to your house on Monday and kicked you out of your house because there was a wildcat strike!

The privileged position and hypocrisy of the priest[24] in a poor coal camp was more evidence of the dissonance between theology and institutional power. As an authority in a contemporary public institution, he could be intentionally blind to the subordination of women within the private sphere.

The priest would come up (to our house) on Sunday. Why in the hell would a priest come and have Sunday dinner with a coal miner's family that had eleven kids? That's when we had fried chicken, and we got the leftovers. And that happened every Sunday! Where was this man's sensitivity? With kids being hungry! . . . And he *had* to have seen the bruises because there were a *lot* of bruises! And never once did he counsel my parents or come and ask what was happening!

The church may have been a source of collective strength, but it was also a source of personal oppression, especially for women. Half of the respondents spoke of churches teaching "that women aren't really human," that "women are property."

It was the women who cleaned up and baked all the cookies. It was the men who sat around and made all the decisions. The women were just subjects.

******

I had a friend who was starting to grow, starting to step out of her house and be a community leader, but every Sunday she would go to church and the preacher would say 'the man is the head of the household' and 'cleave unto him' and all that bullshit. It finally beat her down to the point where she stepped away from doing things in the community.

The most intense recollection of the failure of the church and its minister to understand her pain as a young girl came from a woman who was sexually abused and battered by her family.

And then the same God-of-love that loved my mommy and daddy and loved me—how could a God-of-love love them and then me, and I went home and all these things happened? And I knew in my heart that he (the minister) was buying into it.

But the message of subordination was not always being heard by everyone. Just as African-American slaves used the idealized language of the bible, the text of their oppressor, to convey messages of resistance in the spiritual (Cone 1972), one respondent talked of how she used the Christian model of the family taught to her in her church to resist her abusive husband. If God's ideal family was both patriarchal *and* good, she became the "good" wife to combat the patriarch in her home.

The woman had referred several times in our conversations to a time in the past when her husband's behavior was physically and verbally abusive. I asked her why it had stopped and she said: "Because I started fighting back." When I asked her how she fought back she replied.

> Let me think. How did I fight back? Well, standing in with him, when I started going to church with him. They told me at church: 'Don't nag your husband.' Well, I had been nagging and it didn't help. So I quit, like they said. And once I quit—when I quit saying things and jumping on to him and saying things when he come home from a beer joint—well, gradually, it worked. He quit!

> Q: You mean you were ignoring him?

> Yes, I guess. I mean I tried to make a *point* of being good. I was good to him even if he wasn't good to me. And it worked. Over a period of time he gradually quit.

She continued to refer to this as "fighting back" and talked about how her disengagement from the struggle with her husband made her less dependent on him.

> When I started fighting back I showed him that I could do things on my own, like I could manage money. And gradually I took over paying the bills and buying the food, and he wouldn't say anything! . . . I was standing up for myself and thinking that *I* can do things.

This husband had controlled her contacts outside the family including not allowing her to do the grocery shopping without him. After "fighting back," she would "just remind him of what the preacher said—what a good Christian family should be" when he showed signs of reverting to his old and abusive ways.

The respondent's reading of subversion into apparently compliant behavior is an "every day form of resistance" that Scott (1985) argues negates Marxist assumptions about false consciousness. The analysis of women's "every day forms of resistance" has primarily come from Black feminists who have explored the subversive content of quiescence among African-American women within the context of domestic slavery and servitude (Collins 1990). In a similar way, what appears to be quiescence—stopping the fight against her husband's domination—was for her an action in the sphere where women, especially women who are marginalized beyond gender, are most free, their consciousness.

STRATEGIC ESSENTIALISM: NOBODY WAS DIFFERENT

Appalachia is the best known and the prototypical peripheral region in the United States. . . . Appalachia is also a subculture: rural, certainly distinct from metropolitan culture. . . . On the one hand, there has been penetration of Appalachia by commercial and governmental agencies. . . . On the other hand, there is evidence of reaction to these developments. Conscious regionalism was at least as strong in the 1970s as, say, a decade or two earlier.   (Clavel 1983:116–117)

******

Whether urbane or harsh, cultural invasion is thus always an act of violence against the persons of the invaded culture, who lose their originality or face the threat of losing it. . . . All domination involves invasion, . . . at times camouflaged, with the invader assuming the role of a helping friend.   (Freire 1972:150)

******

The struggle between rich and poor . . . is also a struggle over the appropriation of symbols, a struggle over how the past and present shall be understood and labeled, a struggle to identify causes and assess blame, a continuous effort to give partisan meaning to local history.   (Scott 1985:xvii)

******

Industrialization, as we know, changed the nature of work, the meaning of time. . . . At issue, too, were more intimate matters of fantasy, culture, and style.   (Hall 1986:376)

Collective "every day forms of resistance" (Scott 1985) occur when symbols are appropriated and repressive messages are used differently than they were intended for a group. What Clavel (1983) calls "conscious regionalism" may also be interpreted as a form of "strategic essentialism." In part, it is the use of negative cultural stereotypes in a positive way to resist power and domination. An example of essentialism as resistance was the adoption of African styles of clothing and hair during the 1960s by Black Americans who turned them from symbols of shame into badges of glory, despite their historical distance from these cultural symbols.

In this study, there is a tendency to conflate differences and contradictions within working-class Appalachia, to speak as if there were an "essential" and universal Appalachian heritage, an Appalachian ethnicity that is in danger of being lost to the dominant culture of outsiders.[25, 26] One respondent lyrically recalled that "the grandest time" of her life "was hog killing time," an annual ritual that was both celebration of the harvest (of meat)—"I knew that if that hog was killed, that we would not go hungry"—and an initiation into Appalachian culture.

> Here come the men and you know that they're going to kill the hogs that day and you know that you're going to have plenty to eat. And everybody had a job to do, and from the time I was just a tiny little girl, mamma gave me a dull knife, and you start working on the meat. You'd cut lard: that was your first job. . . . And you growed up to jobs. . . . As you came up, you was able to cut and trim the hams, you was able to do tenderloin. Every year you grew to jobs that you could do. But you started with those little dull knives, crawled up to the table. And today up on my mamma's cabinet is all those little chopping blocks—it's just little pieces of wood that we gathered—and the knives are there— some of them are just plain wore out! Today, I hanker for that time, I really want to experience it. . . . If the hog wasn't killed we'd go hungry. And there was times that we didn't have no hog to kill and there was times that as soon as the hog was killed some rich person came along and took it off the pole because mamma had to sell it. And we didn't get nothing, and that was real hard. . . . Vegetarians—you're probably one and that's fine if you are—but to me, the grandest thing is to kill a hog and to cut him up. . . . My husband told my mamma: 'Don't nothin' leaves here but the squeal.' There was no part of the hog that my mamma didn't do. The grandkids will fight over hog ears—to say

that in the world today! People go: ugh! But it was the way
I was brought up. To me, it's a delicacy.

Women both claimed and idealized cultural values and behaviors that have been used to degrade them, including traditionalism,
self-reliance, religious fundamentalism,[27] and fatalism (Ford 1991).
These barriers to modernization, from Ford's perspective, center
around kinship as the "basis for reciprocal exchange, assistance, . . .
the formation of groups, shared values, and identity" (Beaver
1991:299). Although the value of kinship may be common in other
groups, such as third world people, rural people, or African-
Americans, the convergence of these defining characteristics in discussing Appalachian kinship systems is the basis for an Appalachian
cultural essentialism.

In these transformed remembrances of family life, kinship is
the model for community cohesion and mutuality, fatalism is a
practical knowledge of limits, religion is validation and an integration of spirituality and society, self-reliance is freedom from dependence, and knowledge is constructed outside of metropolitan
institutions.

I had some aunts, and they were good, loving people. They
worked hard and didn't expect to get a whole lot out of life,
and didn't do a whole lot of complaining. My cousins and I
were all real close. I think all the hard work brought us
close when we were growing up. They'd walk for miles to
come down and sometimes they'd spend the night with us.
We had this big old porch and my dad and mother would sit
out with us and tell tales about how it was in the old days.
We didn't have to have a TV; the children were entertained
by (the stories) and they loved it!

******

I grew up in a small community with a lot of relatives close
by. . . . We didn't have much, but we had this sense of family unity. . . . We all grew up together—aunts, uncles, cousins—we were all together. . . . We never had extra money
but we made it. We had a big garden that we all worked,
and we'd go to church and revivals for our social life. . . . And
if we had a problem, we'd talk to each other. We'd help if
there was some sickness. I guess that was the strength of

the family. Even if you didn't agree or if you weren't getting along, you still had this unity. . . . I talked a lot to my cousins because my first cousins were close to me: first cousins are almost like sisters. . . . We still have a family reunion every year.

******

My parents relationship was strong, it was good. They were real close. They did things together, they went to church together. My parents believed that if you didn't go to church and Sunday school, don't ask for nothing else the rest of the week. I'm glad that they were like that. You see when I left home and got married, the man I married was not raised up in a church, didn't believe in nothing! My first eighteen years were *in* church, and my next eighteen years were out of church, married to him. . . . One of the best things about being married to my present husband is that I get to be in the church again.

******

When I was young, I was always involved in the church, . . . and it's a shouting, charismatic church.

******

They never collected a dime social security or anything.

******

Every weekend, people came in (to my parents house), and they would sit around talking about what was going on. I learned what I did from those union people just sitting around a table.

In a region where outsiders have taken the resources and the land, and powerlessness is an often observed condition of the working class, family is your protection and kinship establishes your right to reclaim your community.

I think Appalachian people are real clannish about families. . . . It doesn't matter what your brother or sister does, what matters is that they're your brother or sister. . . . I've always said we're kind of mountain Italians. (She had explained that she identified with "The Godfather" films.) You can go to one of our family get-togethers and everybody is standing up in the middle of the floor talking like crazy and fighting. But even though I don't like my sister's opinion, as an outsider, *you* better not say anything like you don't like it or I'll get real mad at you! It has to do with our heritage. I've seen this all my life and I've come to understand in my later years that Appalachian heritage is a big force in our lives. . . . Today, it gives me a real good feeling to know that I came from where I did. I think it gives me my strength and a lot of good feelings. I really appreciate my Appalachian heritage, and I'm scared to death that my children will lose it! They won't know it. It really bothers me that our heritage won't be there with the internationalization of society. You see, like MTV and all that kind of stuff that kids are exposed to. In my little hollow, there wasn't nobody that was different. . . . My mother's family and my father's family had lived there for three generations! So it wasn't company land, it was home. To me, that place is my home.

A gendered reading of the assault on kinship by metropolitan culture is to recognize it as also an attack on women.[28] Appalachian women experience the centrality of kinship as a rural, regional, and economic[29, 30] phenomenon, *and* as women. Respondents came to act in society when they understood the social world in the terms of kinship, through "women's ways of knowing" (Belenky et al., 1986), a constructed knowledge outside of the frames of reference of patriarchal capitalist authority. Celebrating Appalachian values, rooted in kinship, may be a political act from both class and gender positions.

Respondents took the "controlling images" (Collins 1990) of Appalachian women as hillbilly women—plain, simple, and strong mountain women—or "tall women"[31] and used them to describe their own mothers as cultural ideals, sometimes despite the contradictions of their own experience of childhood. Hall (1986) observed that this is not to suggest that opposing these "stylized accounts" of Appalachian women is to replace them with "examples of mountain folk who conformed quite nicely to outlanders' middle-class norms" (377).

My mother would get us around in a group and she could always make up these stories. Even when my mother worked she always had time for us. She worked the farm, too, but Sunday was the one day that you did nothing. She fixed a special meal and we would always have Sunday all together.

******

My mother is a real traditional Appalachian women: real heart of the family. My mother done anything and everything that needed to be done. Today at the age of 84, she still gets out and chops wood.

Claiming your mother as a powerful figure of great influence in your own success contradicts the " 'Daisy Mae' image of mountain women as ignorant, barefoot, and pregnant. . . . A variation of this image informs a ridiculing attack of Appalachian mothers by those social scientists who posit faulty child-rearing as the root cause of the region's persistent poverty (Loof 1971; Weller 1965)" (Maggard 1986:101–102).

My mother was the type of person that would have hit him back; I wish I had gotten a little bit of that from her.

******

The strength in my family was my mother: she was strict and she had pride to no end!

******

My mamma is the source of my strength.

Claiming your mother as a powerful figure is also a way to construct the role of "combative motherhood" as a model for women's struggles. Those women who recognized the accomplishments of their mothers in combatting the limitations of their poverty and subordination, their efforts to create something strong and beautiful within the bleak material reality of their lives, were also claiming that possibility for themselves. As mothers, respondents stood up to husbands, local officials, and company officials. They planned alone to run away from abuse and poverty, and strategized in groups to confront powerful people in their communities.[32]

SHE WAS A HERO TO ME

The women who formed the auxiliary association to the United Mineworkers and led, by many accounts (Yancey 1990),[33] a popular movement against the coal company and the state during the 1989–1990 Pittston strike named themselves "The Daughters of Mother

Jones,"[34] a mother sanctioned in the public sphere only for her exceptionalism. Mary Harris "Mother" Jones, called "the most dangerous woman in America" in 1902, was a founder of the Industrial Workers of the World, fought against child labor, and is best remembered for her work organizing coal miners (Jones 1972). "One of her most-used tactics was to mobilize a 'bucket and broom brigade' of miners' wives to help win strikes" (UMWA 1990:23).

The image of Mother Jones casts her shadow on contemporary Appalachian scholarship in what Maggard (1986) calls "an attempt to recover Appalachian women as historical actors, but which misrepresents their history as a collection of biographies of a few-great-women-of-courage" (100). These are women "more revered than explained" (Hall 1986:355).[35] As in other liberal strategies for the inclusion of a few exceptional women in history, it does nothing to affirm the ordinary women's place in the history of social change.[36]

When women in Southwest Virginia used the name of Mother Jones in the first act of civil disobedience during the Pittston strike—taking over the lobby of company headquarters and refusing to identify themselves by name—they used this image in subversive ways. First, using one name contributed to group solidarity. It helped create a common bond among women who had little experience of themselves as subjects, little experience in women's groups, no experience in civil disobedience, and who were fearful as individuals.

> If I went in there myself, I would have been scared to death! But when there's a whole group, I knew that everybody was there, that what happened to one was going to happen to another.

Their fear of breaking laws and the fear of retribution by the company against family members was lessened because they did not identify themselves by name.

Mary Harris Jones' [37] life and work became a source of knowledge and critique both of the power of capital and the power of the male dominated union.

> Mother Jones was someone that I had studied and she was a hero to me. When we got ready to go in (to occupy the company building), we started throwing out how we was going to handle it and what we were going to call ourselves; 'children of John L. Lewis' was one, and I threw out Mother

Jones and they decided on it. Funny thing was, when we got into the building and started using it, we had to explain to the news people who Mother Jones was! So that gave us a chance again to help people to help people to learn their history, and this was one of the best media attention-getters that we had during the strike.

******

We thought as a group that we would be a good follower to Mother Jones. . . . I've always said if I could do a little thing like Mother Jones, I'd be happy.

One respondent used the example of Mother Jones to contest the UMWA's power over their association: fearing that the union wanted control of the women's group (and the credit for their actions during the strike), she spoke of Mother Jones problems with union leadership.

We're not set up as a *union*, we're set up to be with *whoever* is in need, whoever in struggle. You see, Mother Jones fell out with the international president about this when she started. So you look back, and you see what you're going to have to deal with. And then you do just what you feel is right.

NEVER AMOUNT TO A DAMN

The power of an Appalachian ethnicity was used to create the conditions for community mobilization and to sanction a community development group. For a declining community that had lost its major industry years before, civic pride and self-esteem were caught in the perception of outsiders that it was a "rough" place. Young people told their mothers they hated the town and wanted to leave, and people talked of a "curse" on the town from the last century. A circuit-riding preacher, "upset either over the riotous behavior or lack of interest in his sermon" (Lewis and O'Donnell 1990A:36) turned to look at the town as he rode off and said: "(It) will never amount to a damn" (ibid).

The year before the community development group got organized to fight a land sale, the Ladies Aid Society had a special ceremony the week before Easter. A traditional women's charitable and social group associated with one of the churches, the Ladies Aid had several of the yet-to-be-formed community association participants as members. These women turned the interpretation of the "fatalism" and "fundamentalism" of Appalachian people upside down by invoking and then cleansing the town of "the curse" put on it in years past. One participant remembered the event in the town's history book. She spoke of going up the hill to the place the preacher had spoken his damning words: "It was a lot of members of the Ladies Aid and our church there," she said. "It was probably three o'clock, . . . the same time in the evening that Jesus was crucified. It got dark like they said it did in the Bible, and the wind was blowing, and it was just like you were there when Jesus was crucified."

The ground was anointed, the town blessed, and the Ladies prayed that "the curse be released and let some good come out of (the town)" (Lewis and O'Donnell 1990A:196–197). The woman who reported the event later said that she believed it was the beginning of the new spirit of change in the community; the following year, the community association was formed.

The newly formed association also appealed to family unity and a sense of place, not as a romantic evocation of the past, but as a way to energize their culture for the future. The group used the strong and traditional kinship ties of Appalachian families, ties that bind those who move away and ties that bind the present generation to the past (Beaver 1991), to raise money for the association and to establish its validity within the community.

Families contacted relatives who had moved away, even those who left in generations past. People were asked to join "Hands Across" the community to make a human line across the town, and to pledge three dollars to the community group for a place in the line. If you couldn't come back for the event, you could mail in your pledge, and you could buy honorary places for deceased relatives. For those who couldn't be there that day, a place in the line was represented by a star or a banner, and a rope bound them to family members and neighbors who were there in body as well as spirit.

We had two miles of unbroken hands. The stars represented the deceased. . . . We had a lot of people, and we raised over $3,000! That gave us the funds to start doing things. . . . Each one of us had something to do. It brought the people together: there was such a closeness, a togetherness.

BEING SOMETHING DIFFERENT

When the idealized middle-class norms of metropolitan culture name Appalachian people as "different", they are constructed as powerless; when respondents construct their own position of "difference," it becomes a source of power. Part of identifying difference as strength is recognizing and valorizing your common identity in a group: from that "standpoint" (Smith 1987; Hartsock 1983; Collins 1990) you can build a way of knowing and acting on the world. Another part of using difference as power is to construct the position of "outsider" so that the more powerful outsider cannot define or diminish you.[38]

Outsiders are more than people who come from outside the area or outside the social context: outsiders are those people, from inside the working-class of Appalachia and without, who no longer are one with the community, who perceive themselves as more metropolitan, and hence better, or who have established themselves in positions of "power over" the community.

The use of "outsider" by respondents in this study conveyed more than a cultural distance; it conveyed a lack of working-class consciousness, and it is a pejorative term.

> She's an outsider even though she will tell you that she's a community person. But she's not *perceived* as a community person! She's a (professional) and she set herself up as being something different. And I understand part of the reason for that, having to struggle over being a little hillbilly girl. . . . But there are healthier ways to deal with it that setting yourself up above the community.

******

> She is from a middle-class family and she really has a hard time relating. She tries not to show it, but body language tells a lot—her classism really shows. . . . She has these gatherings and she puts a lot of work into it. She has Christmas parties and she goes out and buys toys for the kids and has baskets for the families and all that. And hardly anybody would show up.

******

> He seemed to have all this knowledge, but . . . it was not going to be (our project) it was going to be (his). . . . It was

like a savior kind of thing: he was real paternalistic. I remember him going around in the first meeting—I could
have killed him! He was saying: 'Hi, I'm Father (first and
last name of individual), but you can call me uncle Father
(first name).' Why not come in and say: 'Hi, I'm (first and
last name). I have some knowledge and can help out here,
so what do *you* want to do?'

THE APPROPRIATION OF SYMBOLS:
WE ALL LOVE THE flAG OVER HERE

A strategic use of dominant cultural symbols and colonizing language was a strategy used again by the community development
association that created "hands across" their town. In a protracted
battle with local government and planning agencies, one respondent spoke of arriving at public meetings "with a dictionary in one
hand and a bible in the other." Rather than fear bureaucratic authority and control of public discourse, she took a tool for understanding officials' language and a higher authority they could not
refute. The community group used the words of county government
to subvert them.

I don't know if it was rubbing their noses in it, but we took
words that really mean something and we really said something with them! . . . We took the word 'enhance' that we
got out of some papers from them that said that *they* had
done all this stuff to 'enhance' (our town)! We put that word
in *our* bylaws: it says we're here to 'enhance the lifestyle of
the people' . . . Little things like that! Little jabs and stuff!

Respondents also spoke of their patriotism and their use of the
United States flag as a symbol of how consistent their actions were
with "true" American values.[39] The union women "sang hymns and
strike songs and waved small American flags" (Yancey 1990:4) when
they went in to occupy coal company headquarters. A member of
the community development association explained why the flag is
always present.

It's like any time we do anything, we put on the flag. We all
love the flag over here, and it's because we *really are doing*
what the flag stands for, and that's real neat.

During the strike against the Pittston coal company, union supporters identified themselves by wearing military camouflage. This was particularly ironic because this strike was both more militant and less violent than other strikes in the area: there was widespread involvement by women and other supporters, but the primary oppositional tactic was non-violent civil disobedience. Women in the Auxiliary enthusiastically adopted camouflage T-shirts with blue jeans as their signifying dress, and sold T-shirts printed with strike slogans as a fund-raiser. Fully accessorized with political buttons worn on vests, sashes and blue-jean jackets, the women also wore jewelry made from jackrocks, two nails welded together so that one point is always sticking up and the union's weapon against "scab" coal trucks.

Women created a distinctive style of dress and home furnishings with a political message, as popular women's crafts became a vehicle for spreading support for the strike. For local people and for the thousands of visitors every week in the union "Camp Solidarity," women sewed and decorated household items, like wedding album covers covered in camouflage material and trimmed in lace, and sold them at rallies and benefits.[40]

Just as women appropriated symbols of power, they also resisted being labeled as powerless. Partly this was accomplished by paying careful attention to dress and hair styles. Mothers were committed to having enough money to buy their daughters designer jeans and other currently fashionable clothes, and on maintaining hairstyles that required frequent care. In informal conversations with women over eighteen months, both those I was part of and those overheard, women spoke about the importance of clothes, and made comments of how poorly professionals and outsiders were dressed. Rather than reading this form of consumption as an example of their ideological manipulation by mass culture, it can be read as a survival strategy. Respondents were conscious of the power of "controlling images" to shape their life chances, like assigning children identified with poor communities into vocational training in the public schools; dressing well might improve not only their image but their economic condition.

RESISTING RUTABAGAS AND RIGHTS

The condition of poverty could also be read in traditional foods. One respondent spoke about why she no longer eats certain foods that were an integral part of her childhood. This example complicates the stance of strategic essentialism and appears to contradict it, but in this case, the essential experiences of childhood poverty can be conquered by resisting symbolic foods of your culture.

> Picked a *lot* of berries, and I *hate* them to this day! Won't put one in my mouth for love nor money—just picked too many of them! . . . Blackberries was always sour and sugar was a luxury; it wasn't something we could buy . . . My husband's grandmother, before she died, used to tell me: 'One of these days you'll be glad to have a rutabaga and a turnip.' My husband loves them but I won't cook them in my house. If he gets a rutabaga and a turnip, he goes somewhere else to get it! I told her: 'When we get to the world where there ain't nothing but a rutabaga and a turnip left, then I'll eat it, but as long as there's something else in this world to eat, I ain't putting them suckers in my mouth!'

Actively constructing an Appalachian ethnicity is the self-definition that resists the controlling images of women and ethnic groups by the dominant culture. Resisting the oppositional dichotomies that are the basis of oppression (Collins 1990) is at once a personal and collective struggle, and involves both women and their communities.

Collins (1990) notes two distinct models of community that African-Americans have experienced in American life: the dominant model of the white society defined by the individual as a rational actor in the market, and the alternative model of the Black community that resists domination "by treating community as family, and seeing dealings with whites as elements of public discourse and dealings with Blacks as part of family business endured" (Collins 1990:53). The "penetration of Appalachia" by "metropolitan culture" through "commercial and government agencies" (Clavel 1983) has brought with it the dominant model of community.

The community that has failed respondents in this study is the collection of public and private institutions that are "(f)irmly rooted in an exchange-based marketplace with its accompanying assumptions of rational economic decisionmaking and white male control . . . (and stressing) the rights of individuals to make decisions in their own self-interest, regardless of the impact of the larger society. . . . (T)his model of community legitimates relations of domination either by denying they exist or by treating them as inevitable but unimportant" (Collins 1990:52).

Resistance to this model in Appalachia may be more than an attempt to construct what Clavel (1983) calls "conscious regionalism" or a geographic or ethnic identity. It implies, as Collins notes of Black[41] and white models of community, "a different version of the connections between work and family" (ibid). The model of community proposed by respondents in this study is not based on "the individual as the 'bearer of formal rights'... in his political guise as citizen" (Dietz 1987:4). It is based instead on democratic practice: "The community may be the neighborhood, the city, the state, the region, or the nation itself. What counts is that all matters relating to the community are undertaken as 'the people's affair'" (Dietz 1987:14).

Flora (1990) discusses how "social and cultural dynamics in traditional agricultural communities" in third world settings, including non-market land transfers, the Year of Jubilee, labor exchanges, and physical and social isolation,[42] work as "barriers to increased dependency and exploitation" (33). In fully proletarianized communities such as those in Central Appalachia, the traditional social and cultural dynamics of Appalachian communities offer similar mechanisms and may be the basis of what Clavel calls "conscious regionalism."

Engaging one's traditional Appalachian ethnicity or the gendered identity within the family is not a retreat but the beginning of empowerment. The process of self-definition that leads to empowerment allows one woman to resist rather than celebrate the rutabagas of her childhood. Hall (1986) observes: "What needs emphasis here is the dynamic quality of working-class women's culture—a quality that is sometimes lost in static oppositions between modernism and traditionalism, individualism and family values, consumer and producer mentalities. This is especially important where regional history has been so thoroughly mythologized. Appalachian culture, like all living cultures, embraced continuity and discontinuity, indigenous and borrowed elements" (379).

The respondents in this study look to the family in all of its material and symbolic complexity to establish community as "family business." This does not mean, however, that the communities women seek to create are replications of the family: respondents were well aware of the contradictions and limitations of families. Participation in grassroots associations can give women the opportunity to politicize their responsibilities *for* families and, perhaps, their positions *within* families as well.

CHAPTER SIX

Creating Communities for
Development and Change

INTRODUCTION

I don't know how to explain this, I really don't, but within myself, I felt like I really lost something. Now I feel like I'm gaining it back.

Although family, work, and community are the spheres of women's lives, they contain within them structural limitations to empowerment. The women in this study have both acknowledged and challenged oppression within their reproductive, productive, and community management roles. Yet, they cannot accomplish change alone: empowerment has collective as well as personal dimensions, and requires social and political as well as economic development. Also, as Moser (1989) has argued, women have *strategic* as well as practical gender interests: *both* must be addressed if empowerment is a process of change leading to the end of women's subordination and an alternative vision of development (Sen and Grown 1987). Consequently, there is need for *women's* groups because strategic gender needs tend to be unsupported by more traditional vehicles for collective action.[1]

We can define these associations as women's groups, as noted in Chapter One, if they are shaped by women's experience and if the majority of participants are women: they need not be exclusive of men. Similarly, even if these groups facilitate the recognition of strategic goals, the path to them may be more familiar and familial, contradicting assumptions about feminist and revolutionary politics.

Grassroots associations are usually underestimated as potential intermediaries for development and social change,[2] although this is more true of associations that emerge *from* poor communities than those organized by others *for* poor communities. The potential for empowerment through them is influenced by the purpose

141

of the association, its relationship to the local state and nongovernmental organizations, to other representatives of working-class or women's interests, and to the internal organization and dynamics of the association. Whether members can move beyond recovery to acting on their strategic interests depends in part on their capacity to move beyond the limitations of the groups described in this chapter.

The tension for development scholars, planners, workers, activists, and others who identify with grassroots women's struggles is to what extent *they* can and should be part of the process. The concept of "grassroots" shifts on a continuum partially delimited by the extent that those usually without power have it, and how collectively that power is shared. A further concern about grassroots associations is how effectively they address women's needs through attention to the "triple role" of women. The potential for groups to make the transition from practical to strategic gender interests is thwarted when their purpose neglects to take into account one or more of these roles (Moser 1989). This becomes increasingly difficult as productive work takes on more of the characteristics of reproductive work, and as we rely more on unpaid community work for the provision of collective goods.

The challenge of *creating* communities for development and change provides a reference point in this chapter for exploring women's participation in three different "grassroots" groups: a support group within a grant-funded community college program; an income-generating cooperative; and a women's labor organization within a specific industry.

THE GENDER EQUITY SUPPORT GROUP

She Voiced What I Felt

During the time the research was being conducted, the community college Gender Equity support group had approximately fifty participants during an academic year.[3] The program works with women in both traditional and nontraditional job training and degree programs through direct financial assistance, Pell Grants, academic and career counseling, referral and help with social service agencies, and most important, the emotional support of the director and of other participants.[4] A participant support group was initiated by the program's director and implemented through a required job skills class and through a peer counseling program. As an example of a planned intervention,[5] this group can be classified within Moser's (1989) "Equity Policy Approach" to Women in Development (WID) planning. Strategic gender needs, based on the interest of women gaining equity with men in labor markets, can me met through the delivery of programs within a state educational institution. An underlying liberal feminist assumption is that job training and the potential for women's economic autonomy will reduce the inequality between women and men in all areas of society. Despite a sensitive and caring director, the program is institutionally a top-down strategy towards women's empowerment.

Gender Equity programs can be extremely effective in providing supportive environments for women.[6] Women in this group reported that they and their peers had experienced a significant improvement in their individual self-esteem, including a recognition that their inadequacies as productive workers were based on structural inequities. "We're *kept* dependent," one respondent observed. Women in the program spoke about struggling to come to voice, to "break the culture of silence" (Freire 1972) about their oppression by men, and to understand that their problems were shared by other women. One important method was a required class where the pedagogy was consciousness-raising.

> The class was really great. . . . You could say whatever you wanted to say. Everybody was sharing, nobody talking outside of class about what went on inside of class. I was really surprised at what a lot of people said, of how they felt, (of) some of the things that happened to the women. Like one lady, she was 50 and her husband had dumped her after her kids were grown. And she was a really intelligent person. You could sit and listen to her for hours . . . but she just couldn't go on! . . . Here she was so afraid of everything . . . and I say nobody would know that she was afraid unless she was telling it. And one day I said: 'I'm just as afraid as you are.' And she said that you would never know it! She voiced what I felt. She would talk about her stomach being in knots and mine was too.

******

> It wasn't like a class, I mean you had a book . . . but being there, being able to talk to each other, there's a lot of things

that come out. . . . In this program, you're dealing with women that don't have the confidence, situations where women just got a divorce, they've got children, many of them are not married. And you need self-confidence whether you've got good jobs, like in the mines, or whether you're a teenage single mother.

The importance of building self-esteem within a group of *women* should not be underestimated because women's groups validate gendered experience and women's culture. "We are," Tong (1989) observes, "fundamentally the selves our communities have created, a fact that challenges the U.S. myth of the self-sufficient individual" (36). In that line of argument, finding one's voice to speak as a woman in society is a necessary part of the process of empowerment. The "self" Collins (1990) claims "is not defined as the increased autonomy gained by separating oneself from others. Instead, it is found in the context of family and community" (105).

The new self moving towards empowerment can also *redefine* the relationship women have to the patriarchal family and their communities. Respondents in *all* of the associations in this study confirmed the liberating feeling that came out of connecting their own stories to the stories of other women.[7]

I'm definitely changed! Now I don't care about cleaning the house! I was always nervous about meeting new people; now, it don't bother me. I would have *never* done this (interview) three years ago! . . . I think my whole outlook has changed, my attitude about a lot of different things. . . . I think that now I am able to do things that I want to do, and that makes me a happier person. . . . Now I'm not letting (my son) manipulate me as much. It's getting easier now not to let him get through to me. Now he knows that I'm going to do what I want to do. . . . Three or four years ago I would let people walk all over me! . . . Now the rest of my family can depend on the rest of my family on the days that I am busy, and *they* can see that now. It's helped me a lot.

******

At one time, I felt like I was in a shell. I felt like I couldn't say nothing. I felt like if I'd say the wrong thing, I'd get belted for it. . . . Now, I'm a little outspoken! I don't mean to be, but instead of keeping it in, I let it out. It just comes out, and I feel free!

Nevertheless, the goal of the Gender Equity program in establishing the support groups was to assist women as individuals. Beyond the boundaries of the educational institution, the group has no reason to exist: it has no political agenda, and no mechanism for continuing beyond the time women are enrolled in the college. Women reported that their responsibilities as students, part-time workers, and as mothers meant that there were few opportunities to meet outside of required or structured situations. Although the director is involved in childcare issues for women at the state level, participants' interactions have been limited to peer counseling and mutual support, and no other issues have emerged for the group.

AN INCOME-GENERATING COOPERATIVE

And Then I Sew

Sometimes I get up a four o'clock in the morning (to sew). . . . I think that if I was making more money it would help, but I wouldn't want to take more time away from my family because my family comes first with me. I do everything else first, and then I sew.

The second association, an income-generating cooperative of approximately twenty homeworkers, was organized by a woman who returned with her author husband to her community of origin after an absence of many years. The couple were dedicated to "empowering women" by establishing a sewing business that would be collectively owned and programs associated with the sewing business, including a library and free clothing bank. In WID policy terms, organizing this group fits within the "Anti-Poverty Policy Approach" (Moser 1989) which addresses women's productive roles and assumes that increasing women's incomes will meet their practical gender needs and lead to their empowerment. The intentions of the organizers, however, are more complex, as they have been interested in fostering the kind of interactions among the women that could eventually lead them to address their strategic gender interests.

An important aspect of this almost entirely self-financed project is that the income generation is through homework: women sew specialty clothing at home and are paid by the piece. Homework allows women to compensate for inadequate family incomes while they continue to do reproductive and community work. From an analysis of the domestication of women's productive labor (Mies 1986), we can argue that a group organized around industrial homework has limited potential for addressing women's strategic gender needs. Women often must earn income because their husbands can no longer adequately support the family.[8] Homework does not appear to transgress the norms within conservative patriarchal families where the home is the site of women's labor, even though that labor is undervalued.

Additionally, because of the decline in social welfare and employee benefits, women are also needed at home to take on more extended caregiving work. At least three members are caring for sick husbands or parents in their homes. One woman commented about an original member who has since quit.

> (She) needed the money too. (She) had her husband sick at home and she done a lot of sewing just to get medicine for her husband.

Because a husband often won't admit that a wife's income is needed or that she is actually working by doing homework, there are additional strains on the family beyond the new demands on her time.

> I usually try to sew when (my husband) isn't there. . . . He don't appreciate it and he don't have much to say about it. I *was* sewing day and night—I like to do it! He got tired of hearing the sewing machine and got kind of cantankerous about it.

The husband forced her to stop sewing for a while, but she eventually decided that having the income and something of her own was "too important to me." She "refused to be controlled" and returned to the cooperative.

Observing that "most men treat their wife like they're just an old tennis shoe—just *there*," a respondent said of other members:

Her husband throws a fit sometimes if she has to be over here. He resented her taking the time and always wanted her to do something with him instead, like watch a ball game! I know we had one girl that had to quit because her husband was jealous. . . . I've seen a lot of men that if their wives made more money than they did or if they were a little bit smarter than them, they tried to compensate, I guess, by acting real macho.

Participation in the sewing cooperative includes weekly trips to the center to deliver, pack, pick up fabric and sewing assignments for the next week, and have a group meeting with the organizer. The overwhelming motivation for participation as reported by respondents is to earn an income, *not* as entrepreneurs but as wage earners. It is both the reason they answered a newspaper advertisement for home sewers and their goal for the future.

I'd like to see us have our own little shop here and have a regular income, pretty much what (the organizer) is saying. . . . Just be making more money, not have so many money worries. . . . As long as I'm making enough, I'll continue to do this, but if it comes to the point where I have to get a job, I will. Of course, if I can find one!

******

I believe she could have a good business, I really do. . . . I like to have my *own* money to spend.

Realizing that goal is complicated by the organizers' goal of a cooperative venture that goes beyond the boundaries of an income-generating project. However, the women were *not* initially organized into a cooperative but hired as sewers; this presents a contradiction that has led to some conflict. Despite good intentions, the project is a top-down intervention to expand the interests of the cooperative beyond sewing for money, and, in doing so, to address women's strategic gender needs. Organizers hope, for example, that the cooperative will give women the setting to challenge excessively controlling husbands and to improve the community.[9] They have started a free library and a clothing bank in the building rented for the sewing business,[10] and they encourage people from the community to come in and use the facilities.[11] They also have plans for educational programs.

Conflict within the group and between members of the group and the organizers is based on whether one sees participation in the group as a job or as an entrepreneurial venture with potential for expanding into other areas of development. The conflict centers around ownership, management, and liability issues in the sewing business: all issues that touch on a contested understanding of the meaning of "grassroots."

The group originally met in another woman's alteration shop and employed a cutter, who gave them pieces to take home and sew. One respondent said that she resents that the expenses of the cooperative, like paying for their own building, have meant that they can no longer afford a cutter; her labor has increased without an increase in pay. She also resents having to support programs within the cooperative building that *make more work* and *add to her costs*. This added burden is particularly difficult for home-workers, since they are *simultaneously* doing productive and repro-ductive work when they sew at home, and don't want additional domestic work at their place of employment.

(She) has a library in the front of the building. She said that this is something she had a dream about since she was a little girl so she is fulfilling her dream. It's a free library and it's OK, but somebody has got to pay the rent on the building. . . . I have yet to go up there that we haven't had to clean tables off, the counters off. It's loaded down with all kinds of clothes that people bring in and donate. I don't make the mess, and I don't see where I should have to come in and clean her building. . . . Now she wants us all to take turns and spend *a whole day* just to clean up, and we have to *pay* for someone to drive us there!

Because there is *not* a consensus on the cooperative, members of the group criticize the organizer for not being a better manager.

We need to get more formal. Sometimes it's real disorganized. It can be real havoc over here. But that's getting better.[12]

******

When we get there we have to check these things, bag them, and get the boxes ready to ship out. . . . Nobody has a station; everybody is supposed to know how to do it. . . . Well we're *not* equally sharing! But she says she is *not* the boss. She says: 'I want you to think of this as a cooperative thing.' But I can't personally understand how she can stand there and say (that). . . yet we cannot do one thing unless it's ok'd by her.

Weekly meetings have not become the forums for collective decisionmaking that the organizer had intended.

We have these meetings and she keeps saying she's going to make up a chart and show where all the money went to, and what we spent it on. . . . Well, it's almost a year now and she hasn't shown us not one! . . . I'm not concerned with how she spends it, I'm concerned about getting supplies. . . . I'd like to have my supplies that I can pick upon there on Fridays cause I have no other way of getting there. I have to depend on (another member) to get me there, so when I go, I expect her to have materials. I can take them home, sew them, and bring them back. . . . She could make money on that and be able to pick up a pay check.

Part of problem is geographic: mountainous terrain and the rural dispersion of the population.[13] Only a few of the women live in the community where the building is located. For the rest, it is a long and expensive drive, and they do not want to spend the whole day travelling to the location of the business without a guarantee of work to take home.

Without a regular income from the sewing cooperative, these women may be too financially vulnerable to stay with the business long enough to decide that a cooperative is what *they* want.

There's several girls—good sewers—that's quit. I mean these are originals that were with the company when it started. . . . I hated to see them quit. . . .

Q: Can you count on a certain amount of money every month?

No! I didn't work all winter. There was nothing. We turned in our last pieces in November and we didn't see (the organizer) again until she had a Christmas party. . . . She gave us a bonus, but we didn't get nothing else until work; so we just started back to work.[14]

One respondent told me of circumstances of another's departure.

The last time I saw her she said she had made two trips to the company and had only two pieces to sew, and for her to make the trip . . . for $20 wasn't worth it. . . . I haven't seen her for two weeks. . . . Another girl quit. Maybe her husband made her, but we weren't getting no work!

Even though the sewing business has helped some women as individuals to improve their material and psychological *condition* by getting out of the home, meeting with other women, and having an income, it has not led to the collective oppositional practice that would address their marginalized *position* (Young 1988).[15] Yet, as in the community college program, membership in the group has helped women to define themselves, if not their potential agency, within their communities.

When she first come up here she was real shy. But it has helped her. She laughs and talks more. She seems to have more confidence in herself.

******

Since I'm working, I feel—well, it's no skin off his back! I mean I'm the one sitting here hour after hour sewing and he shouldn't complain. There's all these things that I want to do, places to go. It's not just for me but for both of us. I help him with the bills!

Q: Can you save?

No, not really. There's too many things that go wrong and I've had to help.

Evaluations of WID projects in the third world have demonstrated how important concerns raised by the sewing cooperative are for a group to become the self-reliant and sustaining base for women's empowerment. The success of a dyed cloth cooperative in Mali, West Africa (Caughman and Thiam 1989), for example, was attributed to the project identifying and meeting *practical* gender needs with *strategic* implications, including the need for consistent and immediate financial returns even if small, the need for women to determine the structure of the group "even if the decisions appear illogical to outsiders" (45), and the need for training all women in the group to be responsible for bookkeeping and management. The most important need was for the women in the group to identify what they wanted to accomplish even if it appeared to be of limited value to the organizers.

A woman who has left the sewing business in Southwest Virginia told me how *she* would organize a cooperative. Her sense of collective responsibility is compatible with the lessons learned from development experience.

> To start out, I would get the whole group together and tell them that we have to look out for each other. Think about the other person, just don't think about how much money *I'm* going to make. You got to work together. You've got to set goals for what you're going to do and who is going to do what, let the group make the decisions as a group.

PUBLIC WORK

For homeworkers, the opportunities for empowerment through income generation are especially limited because the nature of the work further domesticates their labor (Mies 1986); not only is the dichotomy between productive and reproductive labor never resolved, social production is subsumed within reproduction; it is public work made private. Although the community college program served women who were being educated for participation in the laborforce, opportunities for them were still mostly limited to gender-segregated jobs in an increasingly polarized service sector. Only those enrolled in certificate programs for recently deprofessionalized services, like respiratory therapy technician, nurse's aide, or environmental technician, had a good chance of finding job at much more than minimum wage.

Organizing around issues of paid employment or "public work" is further complicated by the gendered changes in the global economy being played out in the mountains of Appalachia. Women in the mountains have had a tradition of paid employment, including

domestic and factory work, and understand the distinction between
public work and the undervalued work of the private sphere. When
they speak of "public work," they are talking about the work women
do *outside* the home that is "wage-earning labor performed outside
a household setting" (Hall 1986:361).[16]

Doing "public work" provides some opportunities for independence and greater control within the household. It also validates
women's reproductive labor in ways that domestic work and homework cannot.

> I used to feel like that, (like I wasn't worth very much com-
> pared to men). I started building up confidence in myself
> from the time I got my first job. I could do things that *I*
> wanted to do. . . . I didn't have any education . . . but I got a
> job as a cashier at a (supermarket). I thought: Oh my god!
> How am I ever going to do this: make change—a lot of people
> take that for granted. But I did fine! The more you do, the
> more you build yourself up. . . . I learned that to raise a fam-
> ily it takes a lot of ability—doing lots of things at
> once. . . . There's no such thing as being *just* a housewife be-
> cause it takes a lot of skill to be a mother and a housewife.

******

> I was working at (a company) . . . that made television and
> radio parts. It's out of business now. . . . I was making $1.25
> an hour, and boy, I was flying! But I had to quit the job
> when we got married.

Public work also presents situations where women confront
sexism and harassment in an environment where they may have
more authority (as workers) than in the home, and more freedom
to escape the consequences.

> There were a lot of men around that had this macho bull
> shit attitude, so I learned that I couldn't let them push me
> around if I was going to survive. I don't have to have any-
> one to take care of me or to boss me; I can make decisions
> on my own. I don't have to depend on someone else!

******

> (When a boss demanded sex from female teenage employ-
> ees as a condition of employment:) We said for him to wait

just a minute, and we went downstairs and took $17 more than he owed us (from the cash register) and we took off!

A problem with "public work" is that men still do *not* do private and community work. Public work is changing for women as industrial jobs become more scarce and the male living wage more unlikely. The woman in her 50s who had "never done public work" because her parents and husband wouldn't allow it may be joined by her granddaughters who may work outside the home but in narrower and more segregated labor markets. By the end of the 1980s, "nearly 80 percent of working women (were) secretaries, administrative support workers and sales clerks" (Greene 1992:168). Mies (1986) argues that the reorganization of capitalism under conditions of flexible accumulation will intensify women's work as *public housewives*, who as working women will fulfill the consumption needs of the men and a few women who are the beneficiaries of social production.

The next association, the Coal Employment Project, was organized in a time and under assumptions that have not yet accounted for these structural transformations that are changing both women's and men's work. As an association of women miners, CEP has attempted to promote equity for women in an old and male domain of public work, the mining industry. But as a group firmly grounded in the interests of the working-class of a single—some say dying— industry, it's challenge to women's subordination through their triple roles may not advance too far.

COAL EMPLOYMENT PROJECT

Just a Couple of Women

> I never thought that just a couple of women getting together and deciding that they had a problem and that they could do something about it, that it would last this long or work as well as it has.

Two respondents, including the woman who made the comment above, were among the small group of women miners who formed the Coal Employment Project (CEP), a national advocacy and support group for women miners.[17] Founded in 1977 "to help women claim their rightful place in the well-paid coal industry" (Hall 1990:53), the CEP has a mandate for change well beyond training and income-generation. While education and income groups help women develop self-esteem and some financial independence, they offer no opportunities for oppositional politics. Even though women joined CEP for similar reasons to women in other groups—they wanted to improve their working conditions and meet the needs of their families—they had already identified their *strategic* interest in pressuring the union and the industry for workplace equity, beginning with equal opportunity for employment.

Coal Employment Project was initially a legal project of the staffs of two public interest groups.[18] Activist and lawyer Betty Jean Hall found that they were "flooded with requests for help from women who were being turned down for mining jobs or who were suffering harassment on the job" (Hall 1990:56). The response to their publicity campaign to find out the extent of gender discrimination was so large that they realized that a few professionals could not help each woman. At a critical moment in planning, the professional organizers recognized that women could be given the opportunity to define their issues and to help each other. Hall says: "That was the beginning of our support group strategy" (56).

"She (Hall) came up here," one respondent said. "I think there were about ten of us then at one mine, and forty or fifty altogether in the company. And we talked! I was really bitching, and she said: 'What do you want to do about it?' So we talked and talked, and one thing led to another and we were going to have a conference."

Participation in CEP was the beginning of a gender consciousness even for women who were in nontraditional jobs and had to fight men to get them. One respondent initially resisted getting involved with CEP.

Someone in the local told me that they was having a women miners' conference and that I should go. And I said: 'I ain't got no problems!' I was in a job that was nontraditional, but I didn't think about it. I *had* to have a job to raise my kids and I needed a health card for them. I was in the mines to take care of my kids and I didn't think that I needed to get together with women miners from all over the country. I didn't think I needed anything.

On the suggestion of a male miner who thought she needed to "fight for her rights as a minority" and who talked to her children about CEP, the respondent not only went to the conference but became a leader in more than one grassroots association. She found potential for her leadership in CEP's local support groups.

By encouraging the formation of local support groups, CEP allowed women to identify their needs and how they would participate in the association. One CEP member felt strongly about the importance of "being there" for another women miner, of giving her a collective basis for her identity as a woman miner.

They have a support group that will meet in different areas. They're real important because a woman can realize that she's not the *only* one in the industry, that she's not the only woman that has had a discrimination problem, a problem getting childcare.

Hall (1990) described the "communications strategy" that came out of the support groups: "Women miners wanted to meet each other face to face and share their victories, problems, and stories" (56), and chose to do so through an annual conference and a newsletter. A respondent who is no longer a miner came back to the conference in 1990 and recalled the early years of the CEP.

You had different meetings at first. Getting together to find out what we thought about having a conference, what we wanted on the agenda, what issues needed to be addressed at the conference. One thing led to another and then we were going to have this conference, and she contacted women who worked in the coal industry all over the country. And we had our conference in West Virginia. I helped organize the first and the second conference.

Interests identified in the conferences led to week-long CEP workshops called "leadership and empowerment programs" (57). Although legal support services and litigation remained the "backbone" of CEP (ibid) to the director of that time, four women miners reported that the "backbone" was always the women themselves.

Of course, discrimination was one of the issues and we had a big workshop on discrimination. And we had a workshop on safety. Each year, that's the way it works. Now we've got districts and each district has a representative, and the representative finds out what that group thinks is important. They meet with other representatives throughout the year and they set up an agenda. . . . (CEP) keeps in contact with women in the mining industry—not just coal—and has programs if you get laid off, programs if you have a discriminations problem, especially if you have a discrimination problem! They help you with a lawyer, with which union representative you can get in contact with. They also try to keep current with civil rights issues and women's issues.

Women involved in CEP reported consciousness-raising about their collective problems based on gender ("Now I know I'm not the only one"), and their collective potential to address those problems ("I know now that I can help some other woman"). For women who have been socialized to both to mistrust and devalue their needs as women and as workers, a growing sense of self-esteem is part of the process of empowerment. It is important that this self-esteem came out of the conferences and support groups. There is evidence from development project experience, including those that specifically organize women as workers, that support groups and annual membership meetings that create policy by consensus are both a key to their success and a key benefit of participation. Two well-documented examples from India are the Self-Employed Women's Association (SEWA) (Moser 1989; Sen and Grown 1987; Sebsted 1982) and Working Woman's Forum (Chen 1989). Dissatisfaction with the primacy of legal advocacy over consensus policymaking led to the reorganization of CEP as a *membership* organization in 1988.

Respondents also recognized their success in pressuring organized labor to take into consideration women's gender needs.[19] One respondent observed.

Now the UMWA's backing the Coal Employment Project, the AFL-CIO is backing them and it's just incredible.

But there are also problems: both respondents were laid off from their jobs in the mines, and the social context for oppositional practice is limited to women *workers* in the coal industry.[20] Because there are so few women miners, CEP support groups are small and membership is dispersed, problems in fostering ongoing collective work. The former director has been criticized for her emphasis on legal services to the exclusion of expanding institutional support for other issues in the local groups. One respondent observed that when a group relies so heavily on professional expertise to fulfill its agenda, it loses the potential for everyone to participate equally.[21, 22]

CEP has been successful in bridging the production/reproduction divide in promoting worker benefits. In the early 1980s, one respondent was employed part-time by the CEP to work on a national Family Leave Campaign to giver workers "job-secure, insurance-secure time off from work to deal with the birth and adoption of children and the serious health condition of children and other family members" (Hall 1990:58). In 1983 the UMWA unanimously endorsed family-leave as a priority for its next round of collective bargaining. Betty Jean Hall described CEP's accomplishments.

> The original goal of women miners was to get a good family-leave clause in the UMWA contract. . . . Our work has now expanded to included other trade unions. The language developed by women miners has become the basis for proposed federal legislation and proposed state legislation in approximately thirty states. In addition, several major corporations . . . have implemented family-leave policies, based in large part on the same language (Hall 1990:58).

By transforming a *women's* issue into a *class* issue and a *UMWA* issue into a *national* issue, CEP members acted on their strategic gender interests for the benefit of a larger community. It is the kind of visionary work that represents feminist practice as proposed by Collins (1990) and third world feminists (Sen and Grown 1987): to work for the development of all, *begin* with the needs defined by marginalized women.

> We needed a way for women to come together and fight, and . . . it's been powerful! You know there's a lot of work that gets done, and it gets done by women. You know we've got men supporters, but it's women who are doing the work. 'Look,' we say, 'we need family support. We need to be able to take off when our children are desperately sick.' It's women that are pushing for things like that.

A similar process occurred with the issues of mine safety and worker protection. Two respondents noted that the entry of women in the mines improved safety conditions for all miners, because women miners were more conscientious and more likely to report safety violations.[23]

> It's women that are fighting for safety changes, that stay in there and will fight, you know, to the bitter end, and won't give in on one grievance. . . . A woman makes sure she knows what she's doing and researches it through and through. . . . One of the big things about women working in the mines was lifting heavy objects, right? There was a phrase put in the contract that said no miner has to lift any more than he or she is capable of lifting. That gave *them* (the men) a break! If I could say as a women I'm not putting my back out by lifting fifty pounds, he was now able to say that he wasn't going to put his back out by lifting hundreds of pounds. You know you've got these bosses that would say: 'I'm going to kill that woman,' or 'I'm going to kill that son of a bitch,' but *now* you don't have to lift what he says. You can say: 'My contract says I don't have to,' and there's no way in the world he can make you do it.

She continued by observing that men tend to "give up" on a grievance, that they are more bureaucratically compliant than women because they do not want to run the risk of failure, that they need to keep their "macho" or powerful image. "I love men," she said, "but their ego cannot take bruising."

CEP has also provided the context for a respondent to develop the global connections necessary for the mass political movement of working people she hopes will grow. "I don't think we will ever live in a democracy," she says, "until we have another party, and it would have to be made up by the working people." She does not want that movement to be dominated by the union: she sees a family and community-based organization that could grow out of the work that women did in the Auxiliary during the Pittston strike.

This woman has attended international conferences, travelled to China where she visited mining communities, and represented coal miners and their interests in various settings. This respondent also talked of meeting at a conference some Mexican women who were working in a garment factory that had moved from the Appalachian South to Mexico.[24] She said that after talking with the women, she realized how important it was to work for a dialogue between women in the North and South. Women in Mexico and the U.S. need to recognize that they *both* are exploited, she said, and that their struggle is against the corporations and not each other. She has continued to theorize, to expand her analysis, and to work in other grassroots associations for the alternative society she envisions.

Respondents were empowered by their participation in the Coal Employment Project, but they were not empowered by the CEP. Until 1988, CEP was an advocacy and not a membership organization, and the director and staff were not organizationally bound to respond to the needs identified in the support groups and conferences (Hall 1990). Consequently, it is important to make the distinction between the association as a *context* and women's *agency* for their own empowerment. Despite the emphasis of CEP's first director on litigation and the perception among some members that she did not want the association to respond to an expanding agenda emerging from the support groups, the limitations of CEP did not limit the agency of its participants.[25]

CHAPTER SEVEN

Class, Gender, and Resistance
in the Coalfields;
the Family Auxiliary

INTRODUCTION

Groups organized as planned interventions to promote development and change are limited in their potential for grassroots control and the expansion of their agenda; they are similarly constrained
when the group is confined to only one of women's triple roles. The
Family Auxiliary of District 28 of the United Mineworkers of America
(UMWA), a group closely associated with a labor union, has exhib-
ited these limitations to some degree, but the group has adapted
and expanded in response to the changes women experienced by
being part of it.

Women joined the Family Auxiliary to meet practical gender
needs and to protect *class* interests defined by the union and threatened by the coal company's attack on health benefits. Working-
class interests are oppositional: women knew that they were fighting
the company, the industry, the local police, the courts, and state
government, but as supporters rather than as workers. Women did
not organize on the basis of their strategic *gender* interests, which
reveal their position in relation to men, but those interests emerged
through their acts of resistance and newly-found solidarity.

WE COULD DO A WHOLE LOT DOWN HERE!

The Family Auxiliary is an association of wives, widows, mothers,
daughters, sisters, and other family members of coal miners. From
its beginning in the second half of 1988, the Auxiliary has been a
membership organization, but one with singular ties to the United
Mineworkers of America, a connection that has sometimes presented contradictions for the membership. The Auxiliary includes
retired and disabled male miners, but almost all of the membership is female; the work, particularly since the end of the coal

161

strike, is done by women.[1] Two women, an organizer for the Coal Employment Project and another laid-off woman miner, were hired part-time by the United Mineworkers International in June of 1988 to explore the possibility of organizing women in the different locals of District 28. The union contract with Pittston had expired in February 1988 and, to many union officials and miners, "the distant thunder" of a strike was "rolling across the . . . hills" promising a major confrontation with the industry (Yancey 1990:2).

"I would have done it voluntarily if I needed to," one woman commented; she felt the union chose her because she had volunteered with a miners' relief fund for several years and "knew that it had to be a whole group working together" to be successful. The other organizer noted that she had really begun organizing women for a possible strike well before the union contacted her:

> We knew that the way Pittston was acting, there would be a strike. I went to work for the union in '88, but I was involved before that, like for free. From November '87, I was organizing women.

She felt that working within the union structure was not the easiest or preferable way to organize women. She hoped to organize an auxiliary *independent* of the union by building on the support groups of the Coal Employment Project but was rebuffed by the then Director of CEP.

> When the strike was coming up, I wanted to organize under the CEP, but the Director of CEP said 'no.' She wanted to go into legal work and forget about the support groups, so she really didn't want this organized. So I just helped get it organized under the union banner.

With or without the sponsorship and ties to the United Mineworkers, the organizers knew that they had to go to men before women in the coalfields.

> We usually had to set it up with the local union men for them to bring their wives to meetings.

Assisted by a woman miner on the International staff,[2] the two organizers set out meeting with the leadership of all of the locals in the District. At first, some miners resisted their wives getting involved in the men's business of union politics. This attitude did not completely disappear as the strike unfolded and auxiliaries were never formed in some locals. But there were also "far-sighted men" that "started encouraging their wives to get involved."

> You have to remember that Southwest Virginia is sort of traditional: the men took care of the job, the work, and the women took care of the home. They just didn't get involved in whatever happened on the job or anything. They just went to church, stayed at home, took care of the kids, and that was it.

One respondent believed that the union's strategy to involve women was quite deliberate, an observation that foreshadowed later dissatisfaction with the union for both using the women and failing to recognize their accomplishments.

> This time around the International, everyone knew it was going to take a lot of work to get Pittston to give us a contract—well, they don't *give* you nothing; you've got to take it, know what I mean?

Nevertheless, the union told them "just get the women organized."

> Before the strike and during the time the guys were working without a contract,[3] our job was to get the women organized. They left it up to us to figure out how.

More and more women did come out to the auxiliary meetings being held all over District 28 in 1988 and into 1989. Rather than having one centralized organization, the women believed that it was better to have separate auxiliaries for each local or for a few locals.[4] That way, women would be working with their friends and neighbors and would not be expected to travel far to meetings.[5, 6]

> We figured out that if they had too far to drive, then they wanted to join the local in the vicinity where they lived. Yet, getting information from one local to another about what was going on and keeping the flow got to be impossible, so we started calling a monthly District meeting so

that *everybody* could come. . . . We held the meetings at District headquarters in Castlewood. That's how we got the
word back. That became our planning stage, where we decided what to do next.

Initially, the small number of women in the local auxiliaries
planned ways to educate themselves and their communities about
the issues in the union dispute with Pittston, and about how women
in other areas had become involved in strikes in the past.

We got talking to some women from Pennsylvania who had
been in the Canterbury strike and a few others up there.
One auxiliary had organized just around food banks, so we
got some of them to come down. The women began to figure
out that *we* could do a whole lot down here!

In the politics of gender, women defining the knowledge base for
the strike and participating in making the decision to strike was in
itself oppositional practice. In discovering the history of women in
their labor movement and validating women's right to knowledge
about labor issues, participants in the auxiliaries were changing
themselves and their relationships to their husbands. Their emerging class consciousness was also improving the relationship of the
miners and their union, and the union and the community.

First thing we worked on was educating the community
about the issues. And when we first started we had a lot of
men that resented it, that didn't want their wives involved,
and we still had some of that when we went into the strike.
When we started . . . we went down to Kentucky where
Pittston has a mine and we met the women that was in the
A.T. Massey strike. And we learned from those women!

******

A lot of women lived pretty close to one another, but they
hadn't been thinking about their husbands working for the
same company. You don't think about it! The men always
took care of their jobs and that was theirs, and we took care
of the families. Then a lot of men, when we first started
organizing, were totally against the women being involved,
but the auxiliary has the potential to make the union

strong. . . . It's like when one of the women, before she got involved, had told her husband to go ahead and sign the contract. She had never been involved in nothing and she thought that every individual went in there and signed a contract. Some of the women felt that their husbands should not go out on strike because they were going to miss a paycheck. When they got into the auxiliary, they started learning more about the union and a lot of them started educating their husbands.

IT REALLY PUT THE RADICAL IN US

The interests of the Auxiliary and union officials merged during the fourteen-month period before the strike when miners worked without a contract.[7] The women decided to keep a continuous presence picketing two days a week in front of Pittston headquarters, and about one hundred women walked the picket line regularly. They also decided to organize marches, to picket the homes of Pittston management and lawyers, and to pressure local businesses to take a stand on the union.

We'd have marches in every town to let the public know what was going on. . . . We did residential picketing before the strike. We went to Mike Odum's house,[8] and we went to those that was negotiating (for the company) on the contract. And these were well-to-do people who lived there! And we would ride around and flush all the security out. They had a red Blazer, a white Blazer, and a blue Blazer, so we'd call them 'red bird,' white bird,' and 'blue bird.' It was those things that really put the radical in us.

******

So we'd be on the picket line with out T-shirts on. And we'd talk to the merchants and get them to put our sign up: 'We support the UMWA.' And it really helped at Lebanon,[9] because when we started the union was getting cussed at every turn. And it took the women to talk to people, to let them know that without the union in that part of the country, who was going to spend money with them (the merchants)? Other jobs don't make enough! . . . They started realizing that it was going to hurt them too.

Local business persons quickly realized that displaying support for the union was in their self interest, even though none of the women would describe their actions as an attempt to boycott unsympathetic merchants.

Boycott? No! It's illegal to boycott! We was just taking our business to where we felt comfortable as individuals. That's where union people can help. If the store had a card in the window you went in and thanked them for supporting the unions. And if they didn't have a card, you didn't buy. . . . No boycott.

Boycott is when you write out pamphlets and stand on street corners and say: "Don't trade.' But if I walk into this place with four other women and ask them to put up a sign and they wouldn't, or if they say right out: 'We don't support the UMWA; all we want to do is to do business,' well, all they're really saying is that all they want to do is make *money*. Now if *I* make money, it's up to me to decide where I want to spend it. It's a free choice, and I could tell my friends: 'The best place to buy your groceries is Acme. They treat folks right.'

Boycott or not, it worked. Local restaurants donated food and drinks or paper goods to the miners' "Camp Solidarity," and women as consumers exercised their economic power by avoiding nonsupportive and nonunion stores. One respondent told me that even though there were thousands of people at rallies in St. Paul, and even though many of the people at the rallies smoked cigarettes, they wouldn't cross the street to buy from Food Lion.

Food Lion said they would shut their doors before they would support the UMWA, and we learned that Food Lion does not treat its employees right. . . . So, we'd get in our cars and drive back up to the Piggly-Wiggly to buy a pack of cigarettes or chewing gum, whatever we needed.

Support for the union may have been self-interested on the part of businesses that put up union signs, but the women succeeded in their campaign to develop a community basis for the strike.[10]

An important action, and reaction on the part of the coal company, for building the membership of the Auxiliary was a memorial service in June 1988. Auxiliary members were honoring the memory of miners, including Cat Counts, the woman miner killed five years earlier in an explosion at the McClure mine. The behavior of the coal company, its transgression of social and religious norms, and lack of responsibility to the miners killed, gravely offended the women. Revolutionary movements, as Scott (1985) reminds us, are built on profoundly reformist assumptions.

We did a caravan from Castlewood to Clintwood and stopped at McClure for the memorial service. And that was the one thing that really started cementing our work, because people saw that the Pittston company wouldn't even stop the trucks while we was having the memorial service for the people that got killed!

******

The Pittston company is a big business and they're insensitive; they don't care about people.

All parties concerned, both union leadership and the women in the Auxiliary, wanted this strike to be nonviolent. When the strike began in April 1989, the women would try to diffuse volatile emotions that usually ended in violent confrontation, to the benefit of the company.

A lot didn't think that there would be a strike, but personally I did. It was a very stressful time, those fourteen months that they worked without a contract. I mean the company was really pushing them to a quick temper!

******

If some of the men got really upset if something was happening on the picket line, the women would start singing 'Amazing Grace' and it would just sort of calm everything down. That was our goal—to keep the violence down.

One strategy of the women recalled by a respondent is similar to the manipulation of gender ideology in the tactics of Mexican women in the land invasions in the 1960s and 1970s and had the same effect of lessening the brutality of the police: the women surrounded the men to protect them from a menacing group of state police. If the police wanted to attack the miners, they would have to force their way through a line of women.

> Because the women placed themselves on the front lines, they eventually got arrested, but the police really didn't want to cross the women. They did arrest them finally, but the police weren't as rough on the women.[11] Then the men started seeing how the women being there could help, could keep our people from getting roughed up. How it could stop our people from getting an arm broke or even a bruise.

Union leadership also used assumptions about women's nature and gender roles to their advantage. Strike leader Marty Hudson told a reporter that "he used the women's audacity to prod the men—and keep them committed to civil disobedience, . . . throwing out reminders like 'the women did this'" (Yancey 1990:4).

Gender ideology influenced the response of Pittston management when thirty-nine women in the Auxiliary, identifying themselves to the media not by name but by calling themselves "The Daughters of Mother Jones" took over Pittston headquarters on April 18, 1989. This first attention-grabbing act of civil disobedience at the beginning of the strike provided the symbolic content its family-based and nonviolent characteristics.

Recognizing that the women would "play" their presence in Pittston headquarters "to the hilt" with the media, Pittston Coal President Mike Odum told his staff to treat the women graciously, offer them cokes, and to continue working.[12] But as the day progressed, "Mike Odum was becoming concerned," Yancey (1990) reported. "He worried about being responsible for the demonstrators camped out in his lobby, a concerned heightened by the fact that one women was seven months pregnant" (4).

The next morning, newspapers around the state headlined the women's takeover of Pittston headquarters. Union leadership claimed a victory and the press dutifully reported: "Wives, widows, and daughters of miners gathered in Lebanon for instructions from Marty Hudson, and then piled into vans and pickup trucks. . . . Just like that, the UMWA had seized Pittston headquarters—with women." (Yancey 1990:4). The women contradicted the reading that they were being herded into the frontlines of the strike by the union. From the standpoint of the women, this highly visible political action was not done *with* women but *by* women.

Well, we had been down there on the picket line for over a year and you know how people just get to talking. We were talking about how we would just *love* to go over there and just take it over, make them notice you, you know! We kept talking about it, and when the strike come, we started talking to Marty Hudson, and he kept saying: 'I don't know, well, maybe.' We wanted to do it before the strike but he didn't. Then we approached him one time and he said: 'Well, do whatever you want to.' I don't think he thought we would do it! But we did, and it was fun!

Picketing in the neighborhood of Pittston's president in Abingdon was also a grassroots idea that came from the Auxiliary. The women planned carefully to avoid arrest.

You know before the strike started the women got together and said: 'You know what we'd like to do? Picket Mike Odum's house! So we started thinking about it, figuring it out. We asked some people in the union and they really wouldn't give us no answer. We asked where he lived and nobody knew. We knew he lived in Abingdon, so we just looked it up in the phone book! It was one of those exclusive subdivisions, big fancy houses. So we just went in there and parked our cars and started walking up and down. He called the union and said he was going to have us put in jail but he never did. But he didn't like it! You know they could have got an injunction, but the ruling wasn't that clear. We would picket two or three hours a day for six months. We didn't do it every day or at the same time, because if we did, he would have had the cops out. We'd just pull up, start picketing, and before they could get it together, we'd be out of there.

Respondents recognized the psychological content of what they were doing. If the strike was a family issue for them,[13] it also must become an issue for Mike Odum's family.

From the time we started, they kept every shade in the house down. If his wife and children were there when we showed up, she put them in a vehicle and left. One time we saw (the lawyer's family) sneak in through a neighbor's yard. A bunch of picketers is not going to hurt anyone physically, you know, but mentally. Why does people in a little higher position feel that they have to hide? Because they know they're guilty! They know that they're not helping the working people get what they deserve. They know that they're taking it away from them.

Looking back, respondents recalled with humor how some men disapproved of their actions and how company officials underestimated them.

They (the men) still thought we was being too radical. Some of the guys did (think that), but we stayed there!
******

We maintained that picket line at Pittston, and the company didn't think too much about it at the time. I guess they laughed at us!
******

We walked the picket line in front of the Pittston office in Lebanon for over a year before the strike started. We put in two days a week. No matter what, we would be there. It would rain, the temperature would soar up over 100 (degrees), but *we would still be there* on them days. Pittston didn't think we would stay. They figured that when it got hot, we'd quit; that if it rained, we'd leave. But we didn't; we just set up a tent! When it came winter-time, we just boxed up the tent and set up a kerosene space heater and stayed right there. We even got so everyone would cook something and bring it to the picket line so anybody that came had something to eat.

For patriarchs within the home as well as the political economy, the women could be seen as 'disorderly' children. For the women, the longterm consequences of disrupting the company routine was often something to be enjoyed.

It was really an experience! They came in and said if we wanted to leave we could go out the front door at 5, but if we didn't, we'd have to go out the side door if we wanted to leave during the night. He (a company employee) went to lock the front door and broke the key off and had to put a chain and padlock on the front door. We told them that we came in the front door and that we were going to leave by the front door, and to this day, you just don't come in the front door and go to the personnel office! They put up a little partition in between and you have to talk on the phone when you come in the front door.

For all of the women, popular culture in a global setting provided a backdrop to strike actions. Films of earlier strikes influenced the women's decisions about strategy.

We thought we was going to get arrested and we didn't take no ID, and that's why we took the name 'Daughters of Mother Jones.' If we got arrested, we would get sent to jail. Because with Harlan County, USA—the movie about the strike—the women did the same thing and they were arrested. And we'd seen films on that. We had 'Harlan County' and 'Matewan' and we'd pass the word that the women should see them.

Filmmakers came to document events, including a college crew that later invited a member to a campus on the west coast for one week. At times, Camp Solidarity was a global village as visitors and supporters descended on Southwest Virginia. The Socialist Workers Party sponsored a caravan from New York City, and miners from Poland and the Soviet Union came to visit, as did labor leaders from El Salvador and Nicaragua. Women in the Auxiliary displayed pins and memorabilia on sashes over their camouflage strike shirts. One Auxiliary member told me she knew nothing about the world outside the mountains before the strike, but having people from other countries tell her that *her* struggles had global significance changed her more than anything else.

The women were quick to recognize the power of a media event, and included the press in the Pittston takeover in the first days of the strike.

The press was there—you *always* have your press! We wanted the people out there to know what was going on, so we had the press stay with us practically all the time, making them knowledgeable about what the company was doing to our health benefits.

*****

Each woman had a number—mine was '15'—so when they asked me my name, I would say 'Daughter of Mother Jones Number 15.'

They also reported that calling themselves "Daughter Number X" of the "Daughters of Mother Jones" added to their media appeal as well as their safety. Respondents felt that the press were more interested in some strike actions because it was exotic to have women involved in direct actions.

And the press came out because the women were sitting down in front of the coal trucks. It helped keep the state police in line! Then they arrested those two sisters in St. Charles. They didn't know then that they were sisters until they arrested them, and one man said that God would never forgive him for having to arrest two Catholic sisters.

IT KEEPS ON GROWING AND GROWING

The consistent and visible oppositional presence of the women in the Auxiliary took new forms when the strike began. The local auxiliaries now had steering committees that met together regularly, and all of the women met informally quite often as the pace of events quickened and there were more and more mass mobilizations. Women were now getting arrested, sent to jail, and engaging in diversionary tactics against the local and state police.[14] Some women, particularly those women who were less militant, took an equally important but less contradictory role as women: they cooked food for thousands at the union's "Camp Solidarity"[15] and sewed home fashion and clothing out the union-identified camouflage fabric.

Others travelled out of the area and out of the state. They kept a noisy and militant vigil at the jails in Roanoke when strike leaders were imprisoned. They also made several trips to Pittston's corporate headquarters in Greenwich, Connecticut[16] where they demonstrated at shareholder meetings and planted crosses on Pittston's lawn in memory of relatives who had died in the mines.

The auxiliaries helped identify women in the locals that had stock. Some of the women and some of the men had stock in the company. (An Auxiliary officer's) husband had it in there, and that's how we got into the meetings.

Not only were they keeping the pressure on Pittston, they were building self-esteem and solidarity among the women along class and gender lines.

I guess I would just have been settled down if it hadn't been for the strike. I didn't know that there were so many unions that goes up for contracts and has these problems. I mean it's not just the United Mineworkers, it's the paper workers, the steel workers. . . . If your numbers are united you can go far more than any corporation can go. I have learned that's number one. I go part as a number and part as a person that is united.

******

You got to realize that when I went out on the picket line at Pittston headquarters and I had just been a housewife before the strike. If I went by myself it would take a *lot* of courage, and it would be pretty dumb, too! But going out with *twenty other women that I know*, it don't take much courage!

******

I just feel like I'm a lot better person, and I have a greater understanding. I have a whole lot better understanding of how the union works! Because before, I didn't give it a thought. My husband would go out to work and bring home a paycheck and I didn't give a thought to what our union was about or what it did. If anything, being part of this has made me a stronger person. . . . This was a grassroots project right from the beginning, because women had never done anything before, never played any active part or done anything out of the ordinary or daring! But we have built ourselves up since then, and it keeps on growing and growing.

Yet the solidarity of women was increasingly at odds with the solidarity of men in the union. The consequences of occupying positions in class and gender hierarchies are interactive rather than additive; actively confronting those positions often created un- resolvable tensions for participants.

> If it hadn't been for the strike and the women getting in- volved together, I probably would have been the same as before: sitting at home, buying groceries, the typical house- wife routine. . . . I think that what the women did was unique because basically the union as a whole is male-oriented and dominated. There aren't many women in it or involved (in it) and they don't always encourage women. Let me put it this way: they don't want to be upstaged by women. They don't want women to do things that will put them where they're not on top. At all levels of the UMWA, it's male dominated. They're the ones with the leadership roles, and sometimes you get used by them. We know it. We were there when they wanted us to be there at a certain time and this and that because they knew we were successful and they took advantage of it.

******

> (This union official) made this remark that we couldn't go nowhere without the union. Then we later learned that two more (union leaders) made that we wasn't going nowhere without them. At that point in time, I felt like throwing in the towel. And then I said—you go out on these picket lines and you seen these people in *need*. . . . So I said they ain't telling us we aren't going nowhere! I don't care what they think!

The struggle to assert their authority as women with the men in the union is also a struggle to expand the agenda of the Auxil- iary beyond conventional boundaries of worker-based politics.

> If the union said no, we might go ahead and do it anyway! So far the union has liked our ideas, what we have done, and they might like the idea of us trying to keep the gar- bage out. They certainly liked the idea of us helping other unions. But I feel like we're more qualified now to make decisions, to do community work.

FOR ALL THE OTHER PEOPLE

The Auxiliary has participated regionally in the strike actions of other workers, and the Daughters faction[17] has frequently travelled out of state.

We work for our union and we're pleased to do it and proud to do it, and we enjoy it, But there are other things that we can work on, too. Like helping other unions, other auxiliaries.

******

Remember, we've gone out on the picket lines for *other* unions.

******

We go from place to place, because it's not just the United Mineworkers that needs our help, our support. There's hardly a week that goes by that we're not on the road. The struggles are so many! We go anywhere there's a picket line. The first time we went up to Greyhound, this guy who was up there on the picket line, this man had tears running from his eyes. We've travelled a lot. I mean we've seen the *same* security (forces)! They dress different, they go by different names, but it's the same ones. We've been to Greyhound, we've been up to Ravenswood, and we've been up to Volvo.

They are also considering expanding their work to include environmental activism to the extent that pollution affects people. There is a distinction, however, between environmentalists who work for the environment itself, to protect nature, and those who work to prevent negative outcomes of environmental degradation on people. There are class differences implied in the different emphases in these positions. It is people, not nature, that are at the center of these respondents' concerns. The burden is on environmentalists to enlarge their political work to be both responsive to and inclusive of the material needs of working-class people. Working-class persons in Appalachia, for example, may choose to strip-mine or be forced to strip-mine for economic survival until the human costs of environmental damage outweigh the exigencies of their economic reality.[18] There is also the issue of regional and cultural pride: women in the Auxiliary are furious that there is a move to dump the garbage of the *northeast* in old mine shafts.

> One issue that we ought to get involved in is the pollution. I wasn't aware so much before. but I heard that one of the power packs came up out of a strip mine and they called the toxic people to remove it and it had PCB in it. And I got to wondering. They done this the whole time around here! We have such a high cancer rate. I have a neighbor and her husband died of prostate cancer, and *her* neighbor dies of prostate cancer, and my daddy has bone cancer. They always talk about Oak Ridge and the high cancer rate. Well, just about everybody dies of it in this community. Around this area, it's mostly cancer. That is a project that we could really work on.

> ******

> We have been asked to take part in the landfill thing that is going on here in Wise County and Lee County. You know, they're trying to bring in this trash, this garbage from New York, and they're trying to bring it in here and dump it in our beautiful mountains! You know, at old, abandoned strip jobs. Well, we don't want their garbage!

Perhaps in coalition with other grassroots groups in fighting environmental pollution[19] and working for local community development, the Auxiliary can find an enduring and enlarging context to go beyond oppositional labor politics.

Some members of the Auxiliary have come to see the vision of the union as narrow and self-serving. They feel that the union "sold them out" in its need for a victory in Southwest Virginia: "All they really wanted was a contract that they could say was won with the strike," was a comment from a fiercely pro-labor member. Many men have *not* returned to work and more and more men are losing their jobs. Women fault the union for not seeing beyond the worker to his or her family, and further to the community.

> There's your own personal family and there's your union family. That's something that came out of the strike. There's a bond, a growing unity, a sense of family. We were united

towards the same goals, and we got to know each other and like each other.

One respondent contrasted a woman's analysis of working-class unity to that of men in the UMWA.

Men see their union brothers and sisters; women see their union brothers and sisters, but they also see their friends and their community. I love my husband, and I got involved in the strike for him and for our child. But I also got involved for me, and for all the other people.

The contradictions within gender relations take place in the home as well as the union: the women's growing authority within the strike sometimes strengthened relationships with husbands, and sometimes challenged boundaries and roles within marriages.

When the strike began and the men came out on the picket lines, some of them didn't like it that the women were still there. And some of them thought it was good! Sometimes they came together, and sometimes four or five wives would come together and four or five husbands.

******

You'd be surprised at the women that before the strike *never* went out of the home, except to buy groceries with their husband or mother-in-law or sister. During the strike their husbands started seeing how good, how much work the women were doing, and they encouraged them. A lot of marriages was really strengthened.

******

I've changed a lot being part of the strike. That's why I see these things about him today. I think I'm a lot stronger, but I'm afraid that he's threatened by the things I do. He's changed a lot, too, but not in the same way. I think now that he sometimes uses me as some kind of a crutch. before he didn't; everything was *his* way.

Conflict as well as solidarity was also brewing within the Auxiliary. "It's kind of sad," a respondent from a different association told me about the break in the Auxiliary. "You see women have been without power for so long, sometimes it's really difficult for them to deal with it when they get it."

WE WANT TO PASS IT ALONG

During the strike, women in the Auxiliary began to split over issues of leadership and accountability. Two factions emerged, associated with one or the other of the original organizers. The reasons for the split are complex and subject to highly contextualized interpretations. Both sides accuse the other of wanting to dominate the Auxiliary and both sides imply that funds were misappropriated by the other side.

The most hurtful event to the women in the larger group that remained the union-affiliated Family Auxiliary was a secret bid by a break-away faction of four women to successfully incorporate for themselves the name women used during the strike: "Daughters of Mother Jones." The break-away group was described by the others as more caught up under the direction of a charismatic leader and more interested in the public attention the "Daughters" got during the strike.[20]

It is a complex division, reflecting differences in personalities, the relationship to union leadership, and most clearly, use of power and leadership styles. The conflict was a subtext during my interviews with members of both sides.[21]

> There were two little cliques that worked against me. . . . got really mad. She had no permission (to sell shirts) and I have a really high temper. . . . They were just some glamour people, never a hair out of place.

> ******

> By that time we were going in different directions and I was with (one organizer) because I had seen (the other) for what she is. After that stunt she pulled in August,[22] I wouldn't have anything to do with her. . . . They let what they did, the publicity or any recognition they got, go to their heads. And they acted like they were above you, and would try to control you. They loved the limelight and the publicity and they would seek out after it. When we regrouped (after the strike), we still thought we had one organization, and they did that without telling us!

******

I've learned a lot; I've learned that you don't automatically trust everybody you meet. Most of the time that we were working together they were trying to figure out how to take over the Daughters of Mother Jones as theirs! I was real bitter for a while, but I'm not a bitter person.

Since the interviews were finished, a respondent has reported that the groups have worked together on a fundraiser for miners who haven't returned to work since the strike was settled. This rapprochement was possible, in part, because the membership of the Daughters has declined considerably since the end of the strike. According to the Auxiliary member, the Daughters have just about disbanded and their leader has returned to work underground as a miner.[23] In 1992, incorporation rights to the name "Daughter of Mother Jones" were still held by one woman, but as soon as she neglected to pay corporate taxes, the Auxiliary intended to claim the name. Since that time, the majority of Auxiliary members, according to one respondent, "no longer want anything to do with the name."

Speaking of the Daughters and the remaining member who still holds legal claim to the name, an Auxiliary respondent said: "She wants the name because they wanted control over other women. We don't want to own it, we want to pass it along. Once we get it, we're going to share it with *all* union women, not just women here. . . . Just look at their bylaws!" (A draft copy of the Bylaws of the Daughters of Mother Jones (Daughters, January 21,1990) states that "the executive board and officers will have final say on who will be allowed to join," while the bylaws of the Family Auxiliary open memberships to all persons in the District who support it goals and are associated with the U.M.W.A. "through family, community, or employment" (Family Auxiliary 1990).

Women in the Auxiliary report that several of the break-away group have met with them to try to work out their differences. The combined groups call themselves "The Freedom Fighters." These meetings have been facilitated by an African-American man who is president of a union local and has been described by an Auxiliary woman as the only man in the union who really gave the women credit for what they did in the strike. "He doesn't tell the groups what to do," a member reported. "He won't tell one this and the other that. He says that we should all sit down and talk, and he wouldn't discuss nothing outside of an open meeting." This man's leadership style, as reported by the woman in the Auxiliary, is more congruent with the consensus-building method observed in associations in this study and in numerous examples from women's groups in third world development experience (Yudelman 1987; Leonard 1989).

THE BIGGEST AND THE BEST PEOPLE'S ORGANIZATION

The years following the settlement have been unsettling for coalmining families. Respondents report that their victory over Pittston was illusory as so many union miners have lost their jobs since the resolution of the strike and many more never returned to work.

> Everybody thinks we got a big victory but there are still a lot of people still on strike and a lot of miners not working. And there's a lot of people out here who would like to see the leadership go.

Women also blame the union for being more interested in the symbolic content of their victory over Pittston than the actual terms of the settlement and how they affect people in the area.

Membership has also declined in the Auxiliary: approximately twenty women still participate, with "nine you can always count on." At the peak of the strike, you could get one hundred women out on the picket line and approximately three hundred women were regulars.[24] One respondent told me that although she thinks the Auxiliary should continue as an advocacy group for issues that affect working-class families, she can't attend too many meetings any more because she does not have the gas money.

The threat of a new strike looms over the depletion of coal-industry health funds to retired miners and widows, the same issue that galvanized women in the Pittston strike. The Bituminous Coal Operators Association (BCOA)[25] has joined the union in backing a congressional plan to tax all coal operators, union and nonunion, for every hour worked.[26]

Women in the coal counties report that conditions for coalmining families are worse in general than during the strike, with continuing recession and contraction in all job markets.

I wish I could be optimistic, but if you look at the unemployment, and how many women were really active in
the strike and all, and how many of their husbands is now
laid off, well—You know, no money coming in! Like
me. . . . There's quite a few women that does have the commitment and they have the knowledge to do it, but when
you start having to worry about day-to-day, about how we
are going to get food on the table, how are we going to keep
the organization together *and* keep the family together?

Becoming empowered—acting and reflecting of your class and
gender position—has revealed painful contradictions for some of
the women in the Auxiliary. The stress of the strike and its after-
math has been exacerbated by the changing relationships between
some women and men in the coalfields.

(My husband) has been very supportive because it's for the
union, but I don't know what he would do if it got too
radical for him. I've become very close to some of the women
and we talk about our private life. . . . It's a little scary because I have found myself . . . growing and developing and
maybe going in another direction. . . . The problems go on
more than you think. Its' just that you don't know about it,
but when you're talking you find out. . . . But the good thing
was that this was a family thing and it brought families
closer together and it educated families, the husbands, wives,
and kids that were old enough to understand.

Another woman expressed both sadness and outrage that so many
women *still* will not become involved outside the home, or will
return to the isolation of their homes if their husbands tell them to
do so.

No man has any right to tell me that I can't belong to the
Family Auxiliary. I love my husband, and I got involved in
the strike for him and for our child. But I also got involved
for myself, and for all the other people.

Neither the labor markets nor social service programs of an
economy under stress (Weiss 1990) offer any real opportunities for
a woman to resolve the contradictions of a marriage under stress.

Her options continue to be limited if she chooses to dissolve a marriage. Just as we must acknowledge that empowerment is more than economic freedom, we must also realize that a woman's lack of employment opportunities and training may make the implications of her increasing independence and self-esteem as a woman a frightening revelation.

The complexity of dealing with interacting structures of power in women's lives was recognized by one Auxiliary respondent who said that she was cautious about the Auxiliary taking on gender relations within the home, including violence against women, as a problem they should address.

> Before you can start working on problems within the home, you've got to have more than two or three people saying that they're having these problems. Like if you have a workshop and you start talking about it, you're going to have somebody say, 'she's talking about me,' and you're gong to lose them.

The women of the Family Auxiliary have strained against the lines drawn between the public and private spheres through their reproductive and community management roles. The have challenged the union's definition of class politics, and they have found strength in mutual support and consensus-building. Despite crisis when the group split, they are resolving their differences and planing for the future. Like the groups discussed earlier, the Auxiliary is restricted by the geographical dispersion of its members, and the Auxiliary has not yet directly addressed *women's* productive capacities. Also, the Family Auxiliary is still connected to the United Mineworkers, a tense union that may become more difficult in future. The one thing that women say they know for sure is: "The next time a strike comes, we're ready! The next time it's going to be even better."

Women saw themselves *in relation* to men and to workers when the strike began; the women in the Auxiliary now claim the right to issues beyond the self-interest of workers and wives. Their constituency is working-class people, and they think they can help them better than unions.

> I think that women's groups have done more for the UMWA and for the rank and file.[27] Even if it's not that well-known

a group, the women that belong jump right on it—pointing out things and getting things *done*.

Women in the Auxiliary have not yet found the best context for expanding their gender interests, although they have begun to identify and work towards them.

I see it as something that could go to anyone that's interested. And it's not just the union cause. Right now the union is working on national health care, and that's not only going to help coal miners. It's going to help all people all over, so why limit the Auxiliary? Here would be the ideal:—but with the structure of the unions and all of the stupidity that goes on in them, it would never work!—If every union in the country would try to work on a family auxiliary, then all the family auxiliaries could work together, now that would be ideal. It would be the biggest and the best people's organization. because the union's got the background of trying to help workers, and the women got the potential to make it strong. . . . The only way you're going to deal with the problems within the home is to point out that Mike Odum's job is in no way any more important than the coal miner's job, and that the coal miner's job is in no way any more important than what his wife is doing in the home.

Women's strategic gender needs, as articulated by the respondent above, cannot be met outside the intersection of gender and class: you cannot fight for justice in the home unless you simultaneously work for justice in the economy.

CHAPTER EIGHT

Community Development or Empowerment; Dungannon Development Commission and Ivanhoe Civic League

INTRODUCTION

Since the War on Poverty in the 1960s, grassroots community development groups have established a strong tradition in the Appalachian mountains. Often growing out of oppositional political movements,[1] groups have shifted to the work of grassroots development, focusing on infrastructure,[2] human services, local economic development, and protection of the environment. The issues are not isolated, and often groups are faced with a contradiction between economic development and other concerns. An example from Southwest Virginia is the dilemma of community groups who oppose attempts to import solid waste from the northeast as a strategy for economic development.[3]

The third arena for women's work, in addition to production and reproduction, is community management (Moser 1989), and it is primarily women in both the North and the South who do the volunteer work of sustaining and developing communities. This area of women's work has become especially important since the 1980s in developing countries and now in the United States, as debt crises, structural adjustments and the retreat of the welfare state transfer more of the responsibility for building and maintaining communities to women at the local level. This has also been true in Southwest Virginia, and two of the associations in this study, the Dungannon Development Commission and the Ivanhoe Civic League, are community development groups. Moser (1989) criticizes development planners for exploiting women's unwaged labor in community management especially in third world settings, arguing that there is ample evidence that women have been used as proxies for government and the market.

Although there are controversies about the use of women's labor and the responsibilities of the public sector, community development groups can provide a context for women's empowerment. The open agenda for community development has enabled the groups discussed in this chapter to avoid the confining characteristics of an income-generation or an industry-centered group. With historical, cultural, and geographic unity, they can come to common purpose and collective action more easily, and economically,[4] than other kinds of groups. Although maintaining grassroots control is a problem for all groups, we can find in these communities the creativity to negotiate and demand new forms of political, social, and economic power, for women as well as men.

DUNGANNON DEVELOPMENT COMMISSION

The Taste of Success

The Dungannon Development Commission (DDC) was formed in 1979 in response to the practical gender needs of one-hundred women working at a local sewing factory. Although the women were unionized, they were "afraid to make any waves," afraid of losing their jobs. They were, however, "complaining in the community" that the owner of the sewing business refused to make repairs on the building and that conditions were unsafe.

The roof was leaking and the rain would come in and hit the machines and the women would get shocks.

There were also stories that company owners had appropriated insurance premiums and women did not have the health care coverage they were promised.

Supposedly they were paying insurance but it wasn't getting sent to the insurance company.

******

When the women went to the hospital, they would find out they weren't covered. They didn't know they had recourse (with the union), so we just taught them that they did.[5]

DDC as a community organization began with reformist goals for improving working conditions in Dungannon: they wanted to buy the sewing factory building, make repairs, influence the owner to improve conditions, or bring in a better owner.

DDC got started over the working conditions in the sewing factory. It was owned by outside ownership and the conditions were bad. It was a sweatshop-type environment owned by a man in Pennsylvania. The women would freeze to death in the wintertime and just roast in the summer. They were lucky to have toilet paper. They wanted a better environment, a better place to work, and the women got together and said why not start our own organization and do something about it? So fifty of the townspeople got together because they wanted to buy that building and the business. They wanted a better working place from it.

As the group of women and their supporters began dealing with the frustrations of working towards those initial goals, their motivation for organizing began to move beyond the individual self-interest of workers in the factory. The women and men who began the DDC, a respondent observed, "wanted to see something *good* happen in Dungannon because they were born and raised here." The visible evidence of Dungannon's economic decline was noted by a respondent who returned home to Dungannon after a long absence.

Lord, you would have thought in twenty years there would have been growth of some kind! But the restaurant, hardware, dry goods store—they were not here. Everything was deteriorating, falling down.

The community involvement in issues usually the province of the union reflects the inadequacy of unions to address women's interests; this was one of the reasons the Coal Employment Project was formed. Forming outside pressure groups can influence unions to deal with gender issues, or give women a base outside union structures from which to validate their concerns. Whether to work inside or outside unions or political parties is a familiar debate in feminist analysis (Sargent 1981; Molyneux 1986). From a socialist feminist perspective, there is a need for outside pressure groups because of the limitations of an androcentric understanding of work, and because patriarchal power extends to all institutions (Sargent 1981). Men have power within the family, the union, and the workers' party as well as within capitalist firms. The formation the DDC, like the formation of the Coal Employment Project, did lead to union attention to the women's claims.[6]

The next thing you know, the union was having meetings down at the Depot. They started meeting with the same people and putting the heat on the owner. It was like they knew all along but they hadn't been calling attention to stuff.

The women may have been disenchanted with the union,[7] but the mood in the community was hopeful at the end of the 1970s. Volunteer efforts primarily of women were already well-established in the Depot community center.

They did have the Depot as a community center, and *again* it was women that did it. When they was moving the Depot over here next to the tracks, the men told the women: 'Well, you're all crazy. You'll never get that thing moved. Even when they was bringing it up the road here on this big tractor-trailer, they said: 'You'll never get it set up and going.' The men would just set back.

A women's club had raised several thousand dollars to move the Depot building, and then got a grant to renovate it and develop a center for older citizens. They were helped by a former Roman Catholic sister of the Glenmary order, a group of women who have worked in grassroots community development in Appalachia since the 1950s.

The Depot was also the setting for a community college economics class, and it was in this class that idea of forming a cooperative to buy the sewing factory began to emerge.

Folks in this area had never heard of the cooperative model. . . . I think the taste of success, the sense that 'we can do it,' gave them the courage, especially the women.

A COOPERATIVE SEWING INDUSTRY

The group began meeting in the newly renovated Depot building: "It just seemed natural," a respondent said, "to have their offices at the Depot." They made improvements on the building that housed the sewing factory, and the group began to coalesce as a community development association.

They went and fixed up the (sewing factory) building and got them some legal assistance about the insurance. And after they accomplished that, they said: 'Well, there are other things in town that need to be worked on, so why don't we form an organization to do that,' and the Dungannon Development Commission was formed.

However, their attempt to purchase the business failed: the owner's response to pressure for better conditions or to sell to a cooperative was "to file for Chapter 11."

During the time that the sewing factory was going through reorganization after the owner declared bankruptcy, the new Dungannon Development Commission worked with the women to establish a cooperative sewing business in another location. There was also another influential player: an "outsider," the Catholic priest who had taught the economics class, had started an organization called Human Economic Ministries. He could provide the technical assistance and an integrated project setting; this is the kind of professional input that is seen in the mainstream as a corrective to the problems associated with women's organizations (Buvinic 1986).

The DDC called a meeting and "eighty-seven women showed up who were interested in starting their own business." The priest met with them.

He seems to have all this knowledge. 'Yeah, we could do a sewing coop and we could all own the business and we could make money. Yes, it could work. Would I lie to you? And I've got all these connections, and I know people that's got all this money,' (he said.) So here go the women, and one of the first things they did was to become autonomous of the DDC.

The sewing coop had its own board, although DDC still provided "all kinds of technical assistance and support."

We would do anything around education with them. We set up a series of classes through (the community college) to get the women grants so they could study. We would help them with fundraisers,[8] all the time knowing that they were separate. But it was a community group that was trying to do something and DDC was about helping this community group; we weren't about claiming it was *ours*.

The original sewing factory re-emerged under the ownership of the brother-in-law of the original owner. The coop was in competition with the private industry but at that time there was enough work to go around, and because the hourly rate and piece rate at the coop was better, the brother-in-law had to pay his workers more.

IT WAS HOT!

Two respondents in this study joined the DDC about a year after these events and both became part-time staff almost from the beginning. One respondent was divorced and her children were grown; she could manage on a part-time stipend from the DDC. The other respondent was married, although her husband was not contributing any income at the time she joined. Both women had moved back to the area from urban industrial centers because of job loss and because their cost of living in Dungannon, especially for housing, would be so much lower.[9]

Like other community organizations, the DDC depends on volunteer labor and finds it easier to get funding for programs than for institutional support.[10] At the same time, development planners praise local control of grassroots initiatives (Chambers 1983; Leonard 1989) at all stages of planning and implementation. The problem this presents in poor communities is that the community associations that depend on volunteer labor and part-time pay have their reason for being in the economic conditions of the region: so few opportunities for paid work, and for women household heads, little chance of supporting a family. Women in all situations, even community work, must make do however marginally with what is available.

They had been around for about a year and they needed some new blood because a lot of them was tired; they really worked hard the first year. I came back to stay with mom and started doing volunteering, and they made me the president of the organization. They had hired a director of the organization, the only staff they had to begin with, but she had decided to quit after she had been with it for about a year; she resigned and went to work at the sewing factory. Since I was president, they said it was time I took care of the responsibilities of office. The money had run out and no other proposals had been written or grants had come in, so I was given $100 a month stipend to help defray some of my expenses, and for a long time, I lived on $100 a month.

The new director started right in, she says, on the education program. There were already community-based developmental and other classes offered through a nearby community college,[11] including the economic class that started discussion about the sewing coop. Using the economics class as a model, the DDC had something very different in mind when they started classes at the Depot.

There were these artsy-craftsy kind of classes: clogging, basket-weaving, stuff like that. When the DDC was formed we said: 'Wait! We want classes that will meet the needs of the community, and we have more needs than just making baskets. What about classes in community development?'

Like the Ivanhoe Civic League's community-based economics classes that would be formed a decade later, the DDC's classes represented an approach to development that linked economic development with "popular" education, in the control of the community and in response to its economic and social needs.

The DDC expanded the education program to meet personal and community needs. We created a curriculum and offered classes. First we looked at what Dungannon needed: everybody knew that Dungannon needed economic development, so the DDC created a community education curriculum that was actually on the books at Mountain Empire (Community College) until about three years ago.

******

It was hot! It was great; it was enthusiastic. A lot of the community, a lot of older persons participated a lot. A lot of students participated because the DECC (Depot Education Coordinating Committee) was really a hot committee.

MISBEHAVING

Buvinic's (1986) analysis of international development projects for third world women suggests that she would characterize the shift

in DDC from emphasis on the sewing factory to community education as evidence of the "misbehavior" of DDC as a development
project.[12] Buvinic claims that women's projects depart from planning objectives for income-generation and become welfare programs
during the implementation phase.[13] Women's projects "misbehave"
because gender biases lead to expectations that women's projects
have "social rather than production aims;" because these projects
are usually run by "women-based institutions" that do not have the
organizational capacity to implement economic objectives; and because "there are lower social and financial costs" in welfare projects
(Buvinic 1986:653).

DDC projects seem to support Buvinic's observation. The sewing cooperative was incorporated separately from the community
development organization, and the DDC turned its attention to
matters other than income-generation. Evidence of the welfare orientation of DDC from 1979 to 1989 is the listing of projects in their
brochure (DDC undated), including Depot classes, one-on-one literacy tutoring, parent effectiveness training, a Maternal Infant
Health Outreach Workers (MIHOW) Program, a crisis fund for emer-
gencies and for the elderly, and the SHARE food program.[14] In
addition, a respondent reported working on a housing program and
a community laundromat.

> We started this crisis center but it was a bandaid. But we
> were one of the first grassroots organization to get money
> from United Way. We talked them into $1500 so that we
> could provide emergency money for electricity and food. So
> we were thinking on a lot of levels at that time.

Despite the social welfare orientation of these programs, the
respondent above recognized the real benefit was in building the
organization: the programs were "bandaids" but the community
was getting healthy.

> It was like we realized that we *can* fight city hall, we *can*
> change things. We were getting Campaign for Human De-
> velopment funding and they really believed in systemic
> change, so it was like the whole world was opening up. You
> could do all this stuff, challenge the system, and we were
> getting paid for it!

DDC had open membership but centered around sixteen board members, the president and publicity director, and a book-keeper, all part-time paid staff.[15] As noted above, pay was low, and there were no lines drawn between part-paid and all-volunteer participants.

We were getting a small stipend from CHD (Campaign for Human Development) starting at ten and then going to twenty hours (a week), but we put in a whole lot more! There was mix of people. Most of them didn't have a lot of money. There was a few that had enough to be comfortable, but not a lot of money. They all wanted Dungannon to be better. . . . We followed Roberts Rules of order in the board meetings but it was real relaxed: we weren't too professional! We were eighteen (sixteen board and two staff) and we worked really hard together. If one person couldn't do something, then another person would jump in and help and not think anything about it! It wasn't because it was in the job description or whatever, it was that it needs to be done. If this person or that person was having trouble, we'd all help each other. We had a *lot* of volunteers that would help, a lot in the community that would come.

******

I started taking classes. I walked in one day and there was this newsletter on the table. I'm a writer and I said: 'Wow, this is really good!' And the next thing I knew, the DDC was meeting the next Wednesday and (they) asked me if I wanted to be hired to do the newsletter. I would be paid at $4 an hour for 40 hours a month, and that sounded like a lot of money at the time to me. So that's how I got involved in DDC; I was Publicity Director.

Not only was the community association generating social programs, it was sustaining its staff on grants and public assistance programs, using a welfare orientation to develop the organizational infrastructure for community-based economic objectives.

We were being paid part-time; we were all on food stamps, but we worked 40 to 60 hours a week. We were so enthused about what we were doing, that we were going to make a difference. Anyone in the community could join by paying $1 and the board was elected from an annual general membership meeting. It was an association of and for low-income people. . . . We had about fifty to seventy (people) involved, a big group in those days, and the majority were women.

Buvinic (1986) argues that such efforts are counterproductive to economic goals: "The standard design of a women's project," she says, "relies on a participatory style to identify felt needs and arrive at group decisions, while economic programs instead require centralized decisionmaking for successful implementation" (656). Even if Buvinic is correct, a negative interpretation of the DDC "style" may depend on defining success differently than the recipients of development assistance. Buvinic's objective is individual income-generation, an anti-poverty approach that falls within the theoretical limits of liberal feminism and liberal development theory or the modernization paradigm.

Buvinic privileges woman's productive work as the key to her private and individual liberation and criticizes welfare projects for furthering gender inequities by delivering services through women's organizations.[16] Implicit in Buvinic's (1986) claims and in the mainstream of women in development (WID) policy and planing is the assumption that the empowerment of women is an economic objective that can be delivered to women as individuals. Contrary to Buvinic, Mies (1986) argues that the new bond between capitalism and patriarchy in the new international division of labor creates dependent individuals rather than free workers. Through income-generation projects, women become "housewives" working for wages but even more dependent within the home and economy, and women who now labor in the sewing factories and service industries of Appalachia must compete with "housewives" in the South. Because patriarchy has not yet withered away, marginalization is a position within gender and other structural hierarchies: women cannot expect personal and political autonomy just because they have an income.

If Buvinic is critical of the emphases in women's groups as evidence of a welfare approach (Moser 1989), it is because she assumes that the market is a substitute for civil society. This offers little encouragement for those women in Appalachia who have been marginalized within their families and community institutions, and for whom real change must involve their relative position to men and dominant classes within civil society.

Dependence on welfare programs, like any form of dependence, is counterproductive. As Flora (1987) notes, "it is difficult to turn a welfare organization into a productive organization" (230). The key is whether the emphasis in on "welfare" or on "organization." The challenge to community organizations in a human service economy (Couto 1990) is to use welfare programs as a means rather than an end. The goal is to create collective alternatives to individual economic problems (Luttrell 1990) where resources are scarce and the market unsympathetic. Social welfare programs and services can be used to foster larger goals of community and organizational formation where people become *"shapers of"* rather than *"responders to"* the economy, but they must be *more* than mechanisms to receive resources. Luttrell (1990) states that the need for alternative and community-controlled economic development is "particularly true in Appalachia and the South, where economic development and control have rested in the hands of people outside the region and the culture of those who must live with the consequences" (227).

Community development approaches that demonstrate a concern for welfare rather than welfare programs can bring unanticipated longterm benefits to a community organization. For example, the concern for social welfare through a housing program in Dungannon contributes to economic development over time: after years of working for a housing program characterized as "the *only* way that very, very, very low-income people are going to have a decent, safe, and warm place to live," community efforts resulted in road, sewer, and water projects and, eventually, funding for housing.[17]

We were trying to get multi-family housing grants, applying to Farmer's Loan, but I didn't get anywhere. But (partially) because of that, we got a sewer system and a back-up well. And we got a paved road in town, so it's not been a total loss. Recently we got funded by the state to do housing. There's infrastructure now. We had to help the town with infrastructure, that's why it took so long!

The housing program will bring volunteers and materials into the community. A similar volunteer rehabilitation program though the

Ivanhoe Civic League, the final group dicussed in this chapter, has given the community both regional and national contacts that have been useful for developing other programs including economic development.

Moser (1989) recognizes that there may be a confusion between welfare and empowerment approaches in development planning because both emphasize women's organizations. In the welfare approach, the organization is a channel for the delivery of "information, education and sometimes free handouts" (Buvinic 1986:653). In the empowerment approach, information, education, and handouts can sometimes be channels for organizations "to raise consciousness to challenge (women's) subordination" (Moser 1986:1816). An example is the education program at Dungannon.

> We went around recruiting who *we* thought would be really good teachers for the Depot. We would also get the syllabus(es) from the college, look at them, and throw them in the garbage. Under the guise that we were doing the syllabus, we would switch it so that it would meet the needs we perceived. . . . When the college did have to send somebody to come down here, they lasted a quarter or less! There was this one English instructor who was a male chauvinist pig, and he walked into this classroom of twenty or more. The first thing he was doing was asking us what we liked to read. We has several women at the time who were really into fantasy novels, really intellectual stuff, and he said: 'I bet all you *girls* like to read is Harlequin romances.' We just tore him apart. We wrote a letter to the president of the college because he also made a racial slur and we called him on it: 'You can't do that here!' And then he started hitting on one of the students! But he only lasted one quarter. We got pretty good at screening teachers. . . . We started having psychology classes that centered around *women's* psychology, and we started working on what it meant to be female. We were pretty powerful back then.

DDC is not a *women's* organization, but it is an organization primarily of women. A respondent spoke of trying to involve more men in DDC activities but having problems because "their gender gets in the way." As in the other associations, there is consciousness-raising potential for women. The opportunity to hear other women's stories makes clear the gender and class contradictions poor women face in trying to provide for their families; this is a recognition of poor women's strategic gender interests. This respondent has changed her attitude towards her mother for making choices that hurt her as a child.

> The DDC furthered my education. It opened up a whole new—oh, how do I say this!—to try and make people's lives better, to help people help themselves. I've only got this wisdom since I've been back here! I guess my understanding about my mom and things. You have these groups of women and you hear some of the stories that women have! It's the other women, just getting together to talk, the sharing. DDC has enriched people's lives here. It has given them a voice. It's given them rights.

THE FAILURE OF SUCCESS

In September 1986, seven women from the DDC appeared in a Public Broadcasting Service film documentary on how communities are solving the problems of illiteracy and undereducation in the United States. The women had been filmed receiving associate degrees from the nearby community college and the Depot education program was presented as a hopeful model for other poor communities across the nation (Dungannon Times. Winter 1987:3): The following year in September 1987, the Office of Community Services of the Department of Health and Human Services awarded DDC $328,000 for economic development that centered around developing another sewing factory, the Phoenix Project (ibid:1).

Ironically, the success of the DDC's welfarist approach led to their ability to generate enough funding to undertake an income-generating project more congruent with Buvinic's (1986) perspective.[18] The grant, which included funding for twenty low-income housing units and a revolving community loan fund to assist further economic development, offered the possibility of an ideally well-funded and productive program.

The opportunity to expand the employment base in the community came when the privately-owned sewing factory burned down. Some members of the community allege that it happened "in a mysterious fire that allowed (the owner) to collect the insurance." There were more women who wanted to work in the sewing industry, and more possibilities for contracts, than the sewing coop, still in operation, could handle.

> At the time the factory burned down, the women came to DDC and said: 'You all do something about this. We're desperate.' So (another respondent) went around with these hand-made posters: 'Sewing Factory—Can We? Should We?.'

Rather than rising from the ashes of the old, exploitative sewing industry in the mountains, the Phoenix Project destroyed itself and burned a hole in the community base of the DDC in the process. The accounts from respondents and others about the causes vary in detail but the spirit of the stories is the same: some members of the community were interested in dominating the project to the exclusion of educating the women about good business management; there were bitterly divisive conflicts in the community and in the Phoenix Project over the separation of the project, project control, and management decisions. Additionally, in the four years it took to get the factory into production, the sewing industry had contracted significantly; the Phoenix Project lasted only one more year.

> We had to build it from the ground up. We had the land, that was all. When we found that the land wouldn't perk, we worked with the town and got a sewer grant. That's why it took four years for it to get going.

An analysis by DDC members can be interpreted as a critique of income-generation projects in general: the Phoenix Project was attempting to meet women's practical gender needs (for material well-being) but neglecting their strategic gender needs (for class and gender equity), and, in doing so, the women were subordinated on the basis of their lack of expertise and economic vulnerability as *women*.

> It closed in just a little over a year. By that time the market was really bad, and they didn't have contacts with key folks—it's a cut-throat industry—key folks like the contractors. And there was a problem with the management. We advertised all over, but we couldn't get anyone with good management experience.

The sewing coop endured longer than the Phoenix Project, four or five years according to one respondent. Yet, the coop also did not develop the consensus style of decisionmaking and flexibility that evidence from other associations have shown to be a more important organizational capacity for women's groups than specialized knowledge and administrative structures. According to some women, this was especially true because of the class and gender hierarchies embedded in the relationship of the priest and the women.

It was one person, it was one star. He hooked two or three women in the community who were real go-getters but they were also totally infatuated with this man—not in the sexual way, but like: 'Oh gosh! Here's somebody with so much knowledge!'—a savior kind of thing. He was real paternalistic.

Respondents from the DDC feel that the sewing coop failed, in part, not for lack of "centralized decisionmaking" (Buvinic 1986:66) but because of it.

They ran into some money difficulties but that's not what killed the coop. What killed it is that there are all these women and they did not continue in the education process; *they* never owned the process in the first place. Education would take place only when (the priest) had time for it; it was not a continuum, and the women needed it. In a coop you've got to challenge each other all the time and there's got to be a safe place to do that. There was a lot of bickering, but it was only a symptom. Like the manager brought in her daughter and started paying her more than anybody else. And they had a board, but the board just bickered. He (the priest) knew it was going down the tubes, so he just backed out! And the *worst* thing he did before he left was to mess with one of the women in the community. You don't do that! So the coop eventually dies, but it shouldn't have. It was a good idea.

Flora (1987) has observed for some third world women's income-generating projects that "the organizational structure and the centralized control of resources of intermediary groups often means they have difficulty transferring responsibility to the members of the groups that they have formed. Group responsibility is thus never formed. Paternalism is difficult to break" (230). Although the intermediary group, Human Economic Ministries, consisted of only two men, the same pattern appears to have emerged in the sewing coop. Even if the sewing coop had succeeded and met the economic objectives that mainstream WID policy suggests is "empowerment," the women in Dungannon would still be caught in patriarchal structures within the nexus of work and community; it is difficult to imagine how they would then work against patriarchy at home.

THAT WAY IS NOT WHAT WE'RE ALL ABOUT!

The damage done to the DDC as a community organization by the failure of the Phoenix factory, and by association the failure of the sewing coop, was even more disturbing. Respondents felt that as the DDC had achieved national attention and a large grant, more affluent and more powerful interests in the community wanted to "get on board." In an evaluation of income-generation projects for rural women in Latin America, Flora (1987) has observed that "the infusion of outside funds led to further disintegration of the women-based community organization" (228). Because the community development model in Dungannon provided for an open membership and a consensus style, it was vulnerable to attempts by "important" persons to be elected to the board, and when elected, to influence "less important" people in a direction that was less "grounded" in the needs of poor people in the community.

> People came on the board that didn't want to have anything to do with low income people.
>
> ✳✳✳✳✳✳
>
> As the board changed, we had to fight for any kind of vision at all around the education program or anything. Things got really bad. And they were holding these secret meetings away from the DDC building. They had this evaluation and they put me through the ringer. The personnel committee was meeting and evaluating people and I got a very bad evaluation. They said I dressed too loud and I used too colorful language. And you know what I said after I came out of that interview? I said: 'Jesus fucking Christ! What are they trying to do to me!' They all heard, and the minister (on the executive committee of the board) wanted to fire me immediately.

Confusion, anger, and mistrust abounded. One respondent commented that it was very difficult for poor women to resist the expertise of outsiders (in the sewing coop) and the demands of elites (on the DDC board). Although she left the DDC for a time following the crash of the Phoenix Project, she has "empathy" for the women who opposed her during that chaotic period.

> Right now you've got staff and board people, and a couple of trouble makers because they've been done dirty. So what? So they may have stabbed me in the back! It was *because they wanted to survive*. Those women (who were involved in the Phoenix debacle) were *used*. I feel kind of sorry for them. They've got kids and their spouses don't work and they're really having a rough time. I forget what they've done before. They're good workers and they've made this organization home before. They was fighting for their own survival, for where their next paycheck was coming from. I can see that.

She also recognized that particularly in the context of Appalachian communities, you destroy the base of a community group if you exclude some women.

> But they are community! You know what I'm saying? They've got big followings, big families! The majority of the community is made up of those two families. If you hurt one, you're going to hurt all of their kin people and all of their friends. That's community.

Another respondent left because she "had this vision that the DDC used to have and didn't have any more." She has formed an educational and training program for poor women in the mountains and continues to work with her colleagues at DDC.

> For me to survive, there had to be something better. I couldn't go back to being a nursing assistant. I *couldn't* go back to that! The alternative was to create another organization and to be doing the kind of stuff that I wanted to do. There was another woman that had the same vision and was going through some bad stuff with her organization, so we got together and said: 'Either we're going to be belly-

aching all our lives or we're going to do this.' So we started
(another organization) . . . and got $20,000 funding our first
year!

The woman who returned to the DDC struggles against disillu-
sionment. At the time of the research, her office was in the DDC-
operated laundromat, symbolically separated from the organization
but accessible to the people in the community.

Those people were finally voted off, but now the town is
divided. You've got your lower income people that's kind of
lingering back right now, and we don't have a lot of participation like before. It was worse before I came back. Right
now I'm kind of in the hot seat, trying to be a liaison and
smooth the ruffles over here. It's a hard struggle, especially
since I'm standing alone right now. Because the new group
of people on board don't know what grassroots community
is all about.

The DDC continues to function: it has four persons on staff
including this respondent, and continues with its education program, a MIHOW program, and literacy classes. It was funded in
1991 to do a housing project that took over ten years to be realized.
By 1994, they were exploring "eco-tourism" as an alternative development strategy, using a hunting lodge built for railroad executives
as the site for a conference and tourism center. Yet the organization
has moved into more bureaucratic than participatory community
development. Many less people in the community are involved, and
this respondent continues to struggle with the contradictions created by its former success.

People elect board members because, I guess, they think
they'll do a good job. 'This person is in business,' or 'that
person has a lot of contacts.' One time there was an officer
who wanted to get rid of every low-income person on the
board that we had! 'Oh, we don't need them. They're just so-
and-so down the street.' And I keep saying that it's not
always the person that knows, or the business person. This
is *supposed* to be low-income! I say to be that way is *not*
what we're all about. We're about teaching people to take
control of their own lives.

IVANHOE CIVIC LEAGUE

I've Never Seen Anything Like This

(C)ase studies (from Latin America) demonstrate that women derive power when they form multipurpose organizations. Indeed, the most successful cooperatives tended to expand the community development model. (Flora 1987:234)

******

What you do determines your future, not what outsiders do for you. There is no scientific equation to assure economic development. We see it happening in places you wouldn't even dream possible. (Charles Yates of the Department of Economic Development in Rice 1986).

A successful multipurpose organization in Southwest Virginia that has expanded the community development model is the Ivanhoe Civic League, discussed in earlier chapters. The Civic League organized in reaction to news that the county was going to sell an abandoned industrial park rather than bring industry to the moribund and "mean little town"[19] of Ivanhoe.

All of a sudden, there was this article in "The Southwest Times" that they were going to put it up for auction! When some of us read it in the paper, we got together a meeting. We just started having meetings and one thing led to another and we formed the Civic League. We had maybe seventy-five to one-hundred come to meetings, and the community really stayed together.

******

The Ivanhoe Civic League was born in '86 and came out of a need and a want in the community to have some kind of control over our lives.

Since that time in 1986, the Ivanhoe Civic League has abandoned an industrial strategy in favor of a diverse and community-based strategy for human economic development. A visiting state official told the community less than a year after they organized: "I've been in economic development for over 20 years and I've never seen anything like this" (Rice 1986).[20]

The Ivanhoe Civic League began with the notion that it could accomplish something local economic development authorities could not: bring in new industry and restore the town to its past prosperity. But conflict with local bureaucracies and the reality of a declining U.S. industrial base created the conditions for a change in direction. The first industry the Civic League attracted early in 1987, a manufacturer of parts for wood chippers, couldn't raise enough capital to begin production. When the group tried to get county development authorities to accept their proposal for a tourist business, a move that would require officials to expand the conventional definition of businesses suitable for the industrial park, they met opposition. By January 1992, the Civic League had still not attracted an outside industry; instead, they were developing industries that "come from the people."

The people, in this case, were a small group of women and men galvanized into action by a woman from the community who emerged as a powerful and visionary local leader. Maxine Waller was in her second term as Civic League president while I was interviewing women in Ivanhoe. Maxine drew no salary for her work; she received a stipend for travel and other expenses including her home phone bill, but she had no income. A housewife and mother who had never finished high school, Maxine came to Ivanhoe when she married her husband, M.H. almost two decades ago; she became active in school and church groups, what she now calls "conformist-type stuff." Maxine's nonconformist ideas about community development have influenced the direction and the spirit of the Civic League. Among her most creative efforts, which she says were inspirations based on faith, were the "Hands Across Ivanhoe" fundraiser and the "Jubilee Week" festival.

A small community on the New River in Southwest Virginia, Ivanhoe was "built by the iron furnaces" (Lewis 1990) and thrived on mining and mining-related industry.[21] Rural decline followed the closing of the carbide plant and the zinc mines: the town lost its school, local businesses, a theater, the railroad, and three-quarters of its population. Those workers who did not leave must travel long distances to find jobs (Waller et al. 1990). The husband of the president of the Civic League, for example, was a zinc miner until the company closed in 1981; at the time of the study, he was travelling forty-five minutes to work in an army ammunition plant. Although neither he nor his wife liked the idea of weapons-related work, they realized it was a good job considering what is available: furniture and sewing factories and the cotton mill in the region have also closed, and there's not much else. The couple was concerned that he would lose his job due to defense cuts and his lack of seniority in the ammunition plant; because her position in the Civic League is voluntary, they will face financial crisis if this happens.

The development challenge to the Ivanhoe Civic League is a substantive one in light of the position of small, rural communities in regions where the industrial base is declining and people have neither the education nor the opportunities to enter higher-paying jobs in the service sector. The Ivanhoe Civic League and the women who are the majority of its leadership and participants have chosen to answer this challenge on ideological, political, and social, as well as economic, grounds.

"They have waged a remarkable campaign to educate themselves about the economy, to develop their own community-centered development, to start a literacy and training center, [and] to make officials become accountable to them for the development of their community" (Gaventa and Lewis 1988:2). It required a redefinition of development from conventional models of economic development to a multifaceted and innovative community development model.

Their efforts have been assisted by community development professionals, social and political activists, and former adversaries or skeptics in local government and other institutions who have experienced a conversion commensurate with Ivanhoe's growing fame. Evidence of their success is in the newspaper, journal, and magazine articles, the Ivanhoe newsletter, and print memorabilia of Ivanhoe events that spill out of three large file folders, (personal collection) and attest to Ivanhoe's rapid ascension in the constellation of grassroots community development groups.

A list of the Civic League's accomplishments is impressive: 1) a community survey to create a data base and assess community needs; 2) a volunteer program that brings university students into Ivanhoe for an "alternative spring break" and introduces them to many of the elderly residents whose homes are in need of repair; 3) a graduate equivalency degree (GED) program whose graduates include Civic League president, Maxine Waller; 4) a community education center, "Ivanhoe Tech," which houses the GED program, youth programs, community college classes and other multigenerational educational programs; 5) community-building fund-raising events, including "Hands Across Ivanhoe" (See discussion); 6) the publication of two-volume local history; 7) a planning grant to begin a youth radio station and other programs specifically for young people in the community; 8) a MIHOW (Maternal-Infant Health Outreach Program); and 9) an annual "Jubilee" celebration in July, which is tied to all of the other programs and to Ivanhoe's creative economic development plans.

BUILDING BRIDGES

Expanding the community development model has led the members Ivanhoe Civic League on a path towards empowerment, not just for women but for the entire community. Part of the process has been to resolve interpersonal contradictions rooted in the political economy and to include as many persons as possible. Although not entirely successful, the Civic League has built bridges across divisions within and outside the community based on class, race, age, gender, region, and probably other dimensions.

It began with the "Hands Across Ivanhoe" fundraiser planned out of Maxine Waller's dining room. The financially successful event also brought family members home who had left the area, bridging the gap in Ivanhoe's collective memory and community history, and eventually contributing to the community history project. It also involved building bridges to local business persons who were solicited for corporate contributions and to local officials who couldn't ignore the much publicized event.

> When we had 'Hands' we got a lot of terrific publicity. I mean it was all over the United States! Even Ken Reed from Voice of America came down here and broadcast in forty-something countries overseas. A lot of reporters came.

The Civic League formed as a membership organization almost from the beginning, and bridged differences in the town that had emerged over race.[22]

> It's a grassroots nonprofit organization, for the poor people, and by the poor people. Our dues are one dollar. Some people think they should be higher, but if they are, the poor people can't belong.

Lewis (1990 A) says that "since the emergence of the Civic League, there has been an increasing cooperation among black and white residents working together to rebuild the community" (243).

Our first meeting was interracial. Black and white people came, so from the very beginning, black and white people were on the board. We make sure that we are inclusive of black and white, not because it's in the bylaws—it ain't— but because we're a *people's* organization.

"Men and women were equally involved," in forming the Civic League, says Maxine Waller, although there is only one man on staff. Even though the leadership of the Civic League is female, its strength as an organization of women is, paradoxically, to include men, but on the women's terms.

Some men couldn't handle it, and they're not with us today. Some women couldn't handle it.

The work that appears to remain to be done is in building bridges to those women and men who are threatened by women's equality.
     Another bridge was created with the "Alternative Spring Break" program in Ivanhoe begun early on with Marquette University students.[23] Today, students from nearby Virginia Tech and other colleges and universities go to Ivanhoe go to help repair homes, usually of elderly citizens. They discover that they take more than they give in this community; rather than being the teachers, they are the learners.[24]

The students have learned. What I have heard from a lot them is that they really have never stopped to think that *a lot of people* live like the people here. They didn't realize that not everybody had a bathroom in the house; they didn't realize that people could live and survive on the income that a lot of people around here do.

By 1993, the Civic League had taken on the characteristically ambitious project of developing a program for placing student and other volunteers—even international volunteers from various countries, including Russia—in different communities in the region as well as Ivanhoe. This is not only "popular" education, it is a way for the community to support other programs through administrative charges included in this one.[25]
     The Ivanhoe community is enriched by their interactions with the volunteers; the presence of outsiders who are college students

draws considerable interest among Ivanhoe's teenagers, and creates connections between old and young in the community.

> The best way it's affected the community is that people here see these kids from everywhere. They come here and I'm sure their parents have quite a bit of money. They work hard—*they* really don't have to!—but they come and give up their vacation to help other people. They've done a lot of work for the senior citizens and I think it's bridged the gap between young people and older people.

******

> One time last year we had forty kids here at one time. And then our kids will come and volunteer because they like visiting with the college kids, too. Therefore, a lot of our young people have met senior citizens they probably didn't know before.

The Civic League is multigenerational in its development strategies, recognizing that you build bridges to get somewhere. Young people are central to longterm development, and they are both nurtured and encouraged to be leaders.

> So now we've got clogging classes, and we've got as many older people as younger people. You've got quite a few over there that's over forty, and that little girl over yonder, she's six. And they dance side by side.

******

> The kids are taking more of a role (with the community drama). That's what we were hoping. We want the young people to learn to do some of this stuff because it would be education for them. If they know how to do it, they could go to other communities and learn other people how.

REVERSALS IN LEARNING

> No pedagogy which is truly liberating can remain distant from the oppressed. . . . The oppressed must be their own example in the struggle for their redemption. (Freire 1972:39)

The Civic League has also bridged the ideological divide between traditional Appalachia culture and middle-class institutional culture by establishing community college classes that reflect *their* interests and expertise. This has validated Appalachian ethnicity within the institutions of the mainstream and created an environment where education is "all around you."[26]

> Once I got involved in the Civic League, it (education) kind of went together. It was easier to get involved in education when you see it all around you.

On a hot summer night, I watched a clogging class taught by a young man from the community take place in the Ivanhoe Tech store-front office and educational center.[27] Maxine Waller pointed to the group, which included her teenage daughter, Tiffany, and a wide range of young and old and enthusiastic participants, and said:

> Here tonight we've got a dancing class. I mean there's (name of person) and she's clogging and having the biggest time there ever was. Who would ever have thought (she) would be taking a *dancing* class? Because dancing is supposed to be ballet, or modern, or jazz stuff. Be we developed a class that people was interested in. And (name of person) was one who said: 'I want to take clogging. I've always wanted to clog.' So we've got a class and it's a *dancing* class.

Chambers (1983) acknowledges a "theme of reversals" in his book to practitioners about "putting the last first" in the rural development of the third world. A theme of reversals also runs through the programs of the Ivanhoe Civic League and creates opportunities for new leaders, new planners, and new experts. If education can be a means to "conscientizacao,"[28] awakening the poor towards political action and empowerment, there is evidence that it is happening at Ivanhoe. The educational philosophy in Ivanhoe is what Freire calls "co-intentional education," where "teachers and students (leadership and people), co-intent on reality, are both Subjects, not only in the task of unveiling that reality, and thereby coming to know it, but in the task of recreating that knowledge" (Freire 1972:56).

I think the greatest thing about the Civic League is that everybody gets involved in it, and it seems like they get more involved in education. A big part of it *is* education. It's kind of like everything else: after you get in there, you find out that it's something to be enjoyed, not something that you have to do as a job. Then you just want to grab it and run with it! . . . If I had has this when I was fifteen years old, I'd probably be a doctor or a lawyer now. I started late in life, but it's not too late.

A year after its formation, the Ivanhoe Civic League found that it had met official resistance and failed to bring in outside industry. The community invited Helen Lewis, a sociologist with the Highlander Center, to organize an economics discussion group for six weeks to help them decide what to do next. In the discussion group, they learned about why the industries in their region were continuing to move south, this time to Mexico and beyond. They learned about the shift from an industrial to a service economy and what this meant for them as undereducated workers. At the end of the six-week course, they decided to do a community needs survey to help them develop new strategies for development.

We did a survey and a lot of people on the survey said that they would like to get their high school diploma and maybe a little college. So we learned from the survey that a lot of people wanted education.

Education was at the center: it was not an alternative to economic development, but central to the community taking charge of economic development. They began a GED program and community college classes. Maxine Waller and other members of the group attended a Highlander Center leadership training workshop;[29] Helen Lewis of the Highlander Center began working with the community on a history project that would result in the publication of two books about Ivanhoe (Lewis and O'Donnell 1990 A,B). All programs, in one way or another, involved people educating themselves and others.

The Maternal-Infant Health Outreach Worker program is a good example of the empowering potential of an alternative educational program that is integrated into other development strategies.

And we did another survey from the MIHOW outreach and a lot of women that we talked to wanted to finish high school but they didn't have a babysitter. So that's how the MIHOW program started last fall: GED with child care!

One respondent had stopped working in the community for a few years because she had to take care of her grandchildren when her daughter and daughter-in-law went to work. She came back to her community work because she had an opportunity to be educated, work with young people, *and* get a small temporary salary while she was learning.[30]

We took health (as part of our MIHOW training) and we got credit for that as a college class. I've got nine credits so far! I want to take computer. MIHOW is a wonderful program. It's working with pregnant women. You go in and you talk to young girls and mothers. You tell them what drugs, what whiskey, what cigarettes, even aspirin can do to an unborn child. And even though . . . I've raised two children and helped raise my grandchildren, I learned things I didn't know: how important it is to eat the right foods, how to feed your children to get good nutrition, that you need to play with them, do things with them. It's a wonderful program.

PLANNING OUR DESTINY

We've always been on the tail end of two counties, the forgotten end. Other places get support, but we never get support from county officials. . . . We started going to some IDA (Industrial Development Authority) meetings and we got them to rescind the sale of the land. We did it by having a few fusses! We stayed on *their* tail, attending the meetings and all. They seen, I guess, that we really meant what we were saying.

The process of doing the survey gave the women who participated more self-confidence, and brought more people into the community group.[31] They decided to take their case to public officials outside of the local area.

We chartered a bus and took a busload of people to Richmond. We went to talk to officials down there. We talked to
the governor and to Danny Bird from Wytheville—I think
he was our representative down there—and he set us up in
these meetings. Everyone was waiting on *us*! They said we
were the first busload of people that came to the capitol to
talk to anyone. We got a lot of publicity.

The group began to shift their emphasis from "chasing smoke-
stacks" to a different kind of development. Income-generation was
not enough; they had learned *that* in the mines, the carbide plant,
and in the sewing factories. What they wanted was *human* economic development, a development of the whole community, of their
social, cultural, and political power, as Appalachians, as women,
and as a rural place.

Essential to taking control of the development agenda was
asserting their political power. This was difficult at the local (county
government) level; the Ivanhoe community may have had more
success in making their case at the state level that in the local
planning environment where the county government has political
control over the community. Ivanhoe has never been incorporated
as a town, although a group unsuccessfully petitioned the court for
incorporation in 1948 (Lewis and O'Donnell 1990:193). Consequently,
it does not have the power to tax or to control land use; there *is* no
local government, only county government.

Currently, Ivanhoe only has the power to solicit money, not to
raise funds locally, which reinforces dependency on outside sources
of revenue. As a community distinct from the more metropolitan
areas of the county that have traditionally taken money *out* of
Ivanhoe, the residents of Ivanhoe find themselves without basic
civic rights and responsibilities.

This does not mean that the dialectic of political struggle has
not opened up the political process in some ways. Using what they
learned in the community economics discussion groups, the community found themselves educating the local development authorities about what was realistically possible for a rural community in
Appalachia at the end of the twentieth century. Although community members consciously reject dependence, reliance on outside
funds may be encouraging it in different ways.

We have learned so much. We've learned that we don't have
to let them—the county officials—run everything. We can

sort of plan our own destiny. We take charge. It's opened up so many different things, like education, like housing. It's so much! It's not like when we were sitting at home and letting the county run everything and take everything away from us. We are bringing some of it back into the town, some of what was taken away.

The process of political empowerment is not without costs and disappointments. It took several years for the county planning authorities to sanction Ivanhoe's plans for a community tourist business, and Maxine has written and spoken about the hostility of local government bureaucrats.

The first thing that happened is that we were treated as radicals, as bad children. Our governments in Wythe and Carroll counties kept throwing out all these big educated words that mean nothing and these theories that mean nothing to nobody. That's not living and eating and sleeping and walking and thinking. That's not reality. They do that to throw poor people off. They have this other language and they think that you don't understand it (Waller et al. 1990:22).

CREATIVE MISBEHAVIOR: USING OUTSIDERS FOR MUTUAL BENEFIT

As in the case of the Dungannon Development Commission (DDC), the Ivanhoe Civic League used a concern for social welfare and funding from outside agencies to accomplish its purposes. At the time of the research, at least three staff members are were receiving a stipend from VISTA (Volunteers in Training for America), a "war on poverty" program originating in the 1960s. The Ivanhoe model of the VISTA program, unlike its predecessors, does not bring in outsiders to "help" but provides an income to members of the community to continue their volunteer development work. This creates an institutional capacity for development that Buvinic (1986) recognizes as important to successful projects. Although the staff depends on this funding, it is not an end in itself (welfare), but a means to creating local opportunities for income-generation (community development).

We have these VISTA positions (in housing, youth, and education), and most everything we do comes under one of those things. All of what the college kids do comes under housing and the rest of it is under education in one form or another.

The VISTA program and other funding sources have come to the Ivanhoe Civic League through alliances the group has made with supportive institutions, like the Highlander Center, and individuals in the region who support community-based alternative development work. Their allies have included ministers,[32] community development workers, scholars, artists, and administrative staff at nearby service and educational institutions. Maxine Waller has been the central contact for these relationships, and she has made it clear that it is an exchange relationship. For example, in exchange for letting Helen Lewis write a case study of Ivanhoe, Helen Lewis agreed to help with the Ivanhoe oral history project.

I cut a deal with Helen Lewis. I cut a deal with Carol Wesinger, a Lutheran minister that's worked in Appalachia for twenty-five years. I cut a deal with Sister Claire McBrien, and they came and led the economics discussion group.

Forming multiple outside relationships in order to solicit funds is part of the community development strategy in Ivanhoe. It works well because these relationships are mutually beneficial and because the community does not depend on a single broker. The contradiction, as noted before, is that it does create dependency on funding that should be available to the town through revenues it has generated and legally collected, if, and when, Ivanhoe is incorporated and a local business succeeds. A further contradiction is that it is precisely the support of these outside brokers that is allowing for the breaking of exploitative relationships of dependency to the county, to outside capital, and to outsiders in general.

JUBILEE

Maxine said she was lying in bed one night reading the bible. She was reading about the year of Jubilee, and then she knew. So we decided that we would try it.

In July, 1987, the Ivanhoe Civic League hosted a week-long festival in the river-front area of the industrial development land. The community had cleaned brush, installed outdoor lighting, and built a stage and concession stands (Gaventa and Lewis 1988): this was now "Jubilee Park," named to commemorate the biblical Year of the Jubilee,[33] "when land and other property . . . was redistributed to its original owners to maintain equality and community systems of mutual support" (Flora 1990:28).[34]

In learning about changes in the economy, the women decided that they could be part of the development of the tourist industry in the region. The state was building a hiking and biking trail along an abandoned railroad track by the river, and the industrial site included river frontage. After the Jubilee festival of 1987, the Civic League petitioned the development authorities for twenty acres of riverfront to develop a community-owned recreation area that would include bike rentals, camping, and concessions. This was only the beginning of a campaign of persuasion that would last for years; they would face many obstacles, including intransigent and skeptical officials, a lack of resources, and disappointment and a "slackening of energy" (Lewis and O'Donnell 1990A:210) among the members.

Nevertheless, the work to make "Jubilee Park" more than the home of Ivanhoe's annual home-coming festival continued. The oral history project had led to the production of a community drama that is performed yearly during "Jubilee;" the first one was titled "It Came from the People." Ivanhoe teenagers now make the giant puppets for the drama and look to the time when the week-long summer festival not only brings back people who have left, but attracts other tourists because of Jubilee's proximity to the state park.

Plans for the community-owned business are under continuous revision and discussion; there is a committee responsible for development of the site. In the years since 1986, the climate for development in Ivanhoe has changed: the "experts" are now within the community, and look forward to developing the kind of civic autonomy and income sources that will decrease their dependency on outsiders. In a book chapter co-authored by Maxine Waller, she says:

I don't know the answer to the economic crisis, but I know it has to come from the people. It has to come out of the hands of the so-called system and the so-called powerful people, and come back to the people—the dinner buckets of

America and the dinner buckets of Korea and the dinner
buckets of the Philippines. (Maxine Waller, Ivanhoe Civic
League. In Gaventa et al. 1990:25)

FROM THE PRACTICAL TO THE STRATEGIC

The Ivanhoe Civic League broadened its community development
agenda almost from the beginning to move from practical (concrete) to strategic (power) needs. Molyneux (1986) and Moser(1989)
use the terms to refer to those needs women have either rooted in
traditional gender roles (practical) or presenting a challenge to
them (strategic). Strategic *gender* needs are those that address
women's relative power to *men* as well as to dominant classes.

The Civic League has from the beginning addressed strategic
class needs, but only indirectly addressed gender needs. Moser (1989)
has observed that the movement in third world grassroots women's
associations towards empowerment most often does not begin with
strategic gender needs; they *emerge* from women meeting their
concrete needs.

At the core of the process in Ivanhoe and elsewhere is a growing recognition among women that, as a group, they have some
power within their communities, and from that power they define
themselves as autonomous persons. As persons, women become more
than someone *in relation* to others at home; they discover that they
can also have power within their homes.

They kind of got empowered by the Civic League. They'd go
home and talk this and that and the other, and their husbands would come down on them real bad.

For some women, like women in the Family Auxiliary, a conscious understanding of their strategic needs has placed them in
the middle of a contradiction that will be difficult to resolve. At
times the conflicts over commitments to the community association
are subtle: a husband might resent not coming home at lunch to
prepare dinner, or staying out late too many nights.

He doesn't care a lot about my position because I put in a
lot of hours. Like when we had the college kids come in. I
would stay down here with them until bed-time. Like I say,
I love it! The more I got into it, the more I *want* to be in it.

And I have a hard time, sometimes, drawing the line and saying that I had to separate this part of my life.

According to Maxine Waller, some women have had to drop out of the Civic League because their husbands did not appreciate their autonomy, their new-found self-esteem that made them less dependent. In finding their "power to" effect change in the community, they have challenged husbands' "power over" wives (French 1985).

The process of empowerment needs to be part of the group or collective agenda if individual change is to be sustained. For the Ivanhoe Civic League to reach out to those women who have not been able to make a bridge from community work to home, it must continue to offer the support services that allow women to push at the boundaries of gender roles. Programs like GED and MIHOW are important not because of their welfare components but because they give women safe spaces in which to grow personally and politically. It is yet unclear if the Civic League has a commitment to *gender* struggle, even one that takes it down a practical path.

The transition for women from articulating and acting on practical gender needs to acknowledging and acting on strategic gender needs is *part* of the process of empowerment. Although the process may be difficult, it is almost inevitable when women become more self-confident, have more self-esteem, and have a sense of themselves as persons in addition to their relationships and roles within families.

CHAPTER NINE

Alternative Visions

But we must have before us a vision of the kind of world we want. We want a world where inequality based on class, gender, and race is absent from every country, and from the relationships among countries. We want a world where basic needs become basic rights and where poverty and all forms of violence are eliminated. Each person will have the opportunity to develop her or his full potential and creativity, and women's values of nurturance and solidarity will characterize human relationships. . . . It must be fostered by mass movements that give central focus to the 'basic rights' of the poor, and demand a reorientation of policies, programmes, and projects toward that end. . . . The transformation of the structures of subordination that have been so inimical to women is the other part of our vision of a new era.[1] (Sen and Grown:1987:80–81)

INTRODUCTION

This has been a story about survival and oppositional politics by women who confront structural positions of class, gender, and ethnicity. It has aimed to create knowledge that fosters resistance, and resists the prevailing assumptions about women and development. Respondents in this study have revealed the complexities and interactions of class and gender oppression: these are not additive positions, and planning interventions cannot disassociate "development for the poor" from "development for women."

For example, women have theorized about their position in relationship to men and to dominant classes in ways that have shown the importance of questions of sexuality and personal life, a terrain usually ignored in theory and practice (Hartsock 1983).

I think that my sense of classism came out of my sense of sexism as it existed in the mountains. I knew that there

219

were some people who had 'power over.' I could recognize it in different situations, and I knew who I was in society. And then it clicked with me that there were other coal miners' children who were feeling the same thing. That we were all *this* little group, and there was *that* group up there. So I guess I had a sense of knowing who had 'power over' and who was 'under.'

The significance of this understanding of patriarchal capitalism is to confirm the failure of Marxist theory to recognize the theoretical importance of conflict outside of class conflict, delimiting the revolutionary and redemptive potential of women's groups.

In her study of Black feminist thought, Collins (1989) has said that "the material conditions of race, class, and gender oppression can vary dramatically and yet generate some uniformity in the epistemologies of subordinate groups." In this spirit, I have framed this research, basing an understanding of empowerment on knowledge generated by working-class Appalachian women. They give us an alternative vision of a just society; this vision, as articulated by Sen and Grown (1987,) can emerge even from the first world, "from the vantage point" (23) of working-class women in Southwest Virginia.

The women who have told their stories for this study participate in grassroots associations, identified in some progressive analyses of social change as central to strategies for the empowerment and development of all persons (March and Taqqu 1982; Sen and Grown 1987; Moser 1989). Whether the women in Southwest Virginia can contribute to building the mass movement that Sen and Grown[2] envision is a question for the future.[3] For the time being, we can begin by acknowledging how women have change themselves and their everyday reality through that participation.

TRICKLE-UP REVOLUTIONS

Only power that springs from the weakness of the oppressed will be sufficiently strong to free both. (Freire 1972:28)

Empowerment is trickle-up revolution.[4] It is trickle-up because its direction is from the grassroots to the centers of power, and it is revolutionary because it implies fundamentally challenging old power relationships based on the oppositional dichotomies of patri-

archal capitalism. The process of empowerment also implies reject-
ing coercive power in favor of a creative and dialogical understanding of power that allows for self-development within collective
development. Empowerment is defined in this study as a process
through which marginalized persons can realize their potential for
human agency through collective social action. It is the social rather
than individual practice of becoming "fully human" by acting and
reflecting upon the world in order to transform it (Freire 1972:42).

Power is a gendered concept; unless the power relations of
gender are challenged, no person can be empowered. Essential to
that challenge is an understanding that the division of labor is
fundamentally gendered, and that working-class women are subordinated to men as well as to men and women of dominant classes.
This skeletal definition is given substance through the interactive
process of research: the definition of empowerment is both defined
and derived from the experiences of women in this study.

DIVERGENT UNDERSTANDINGS

(I)t is less the penetration of elite beliefs among the poor
than the capacity of the poor to pierce, in almost every
particular, the self-serving picture presented by the
wealthy. . . . The penetration of official platitudes by any subordinate class is to be expected both because those platitudes are unlikely to be as cohesive or uniform as is often
imagined *and* because they are subject to different interpretations depending on the social position of the actors.
Such divergent understandings are, in turn, rooted in daily
experience. (Scott 1985:319)

******

Authentic thinking, thinking that is concerned about *reality*, does not take place in ivory tower isolation, but only in
communication. (Freire 1972:64)

Critical consciousness is learned rather than taught (Freire
1972). The elite beliefs and official stories of "big white men"[5] (Mies
1986) are continuously scrutinized within women's "sphere of greatest freedom" (Anderson et al. 1990). A woman's consciousness[6] of
the everyday reality of being female, of being working-class, pokes
holes in the narratives of the powerful.[7] The women who took the

blows from husbands, for example, knew that they were hit because they were *women* in relation to the men who hit them. They
also knew that they were deflecting blows from children, and that
there were few, if any, possibilities to keep their families together if
they left. The women who are workers in the sewing factories or
homeworkers who sew do not bother with the platitudes of management or organizers; as women, they have neither the time nor
the social right to define themselves solely as workers. Women who
closed the doors on a person suspected of being a social worker also
knew that when they opened them, they might become objects of
assistance rather than subjects of change.

Those who dominate within and without the home rule "not so
much by sanctions and coercion as by the consent and passive
compliance" (Scott 1985:316) of subordinates. This does not mean,
however, that subordinates *accept* their domination. Scott (1985)
criticized Gramsci and other Marxists whose theories of hegemony
"and its related concepts of false consciousness, mystification, and
ideological state apparatuses . . . mislead us seriously in understanding class conflict" (317).

Scott's first observation, that "the concept of hegemony ignores
the extent to which most subordinate classes are able, on the basis
of their daily material experience, to penetrate and demystify the
prevailing ideology" (317), has been supported throughout the analysis of women's life stories in this study. His second observation is
that "theories of hegemony frequently confound what is inevitable
with what is just, an error subordinate classes rarely, if ever, make"
(317). Knowing the difference was apparent, for example, in a
respondent's acquiescence to a second marriage to a man she feared
would abuse her. Because she and her children were dependent on
a mother who was also poor, she could not afford to reject an offer
to marry.

Scott further observed that "the rank and file of nearly any
manifestly revolutionary mass movement will show that the objectives sought are usually limited and even reformist in tone" (318).
This observation is important if we understand empowerment as a
process of moving from reformist strategies to meet "practical gender needs" to revolutionary strategies to meet "strategic gender
needs" (Moser 1989). If reformist strategies are not "obstacles" but
"the only plausible basis" (Scott 1985:318) for revolution, we can
better understand the reformist goals of the women in this study
and how a liberatory process can emerge from a reformist agenda.

Both community development associations in this study were formed to bring traditional industrial development to their communities, and the traditional division of labor by gender was not challenged. Women in the union auxiliary initially defined themselves as supporters of working-class men whose interests were represented by the union, rather than as working-class women who also had a right to determine the agenda outside of the control of the union. A reformist definition of empowerment would stop with individual achievement, like earning an income or getting an education. Women in the Gender Equity and income-generation groups, and even Coal Employment Project, wanted a secure and adequate income above all else. Half of the respondents were either enrolled in a community college program or had recently finished their high-school education through their association. Yet in recognizing the contradictions that getting a community college education presents for her community work, one women noted: "When I start to go to school I won't have that much time to work on this, and that part just about kills me!"

Education itself need not be a reformist end but a path to alternative development, as the women in the Dungannon Development Commission and Ivanhoe Civic League have demonstrated. Women in other groups have also recognized the need for claiming their own knowledge and sharing it. Like the Ivanhoe Civic League, the women in the Family Auxiliary and Coal Employment Project have initiated history projects[8] where the potential for "authentic thinking" is in the collecting and the telling of *their* stories:

The Pittston women should be able to share what they learned first-hand, I mean experience. There's no books now that can tell you.

Finally, Scott notes that the "breaking of the norms and values of a dominant ideology" is usually the prerogative of dominant rather than subordinate classes (318). If working-class women are unreceptive to a top-down strategy for development or empowerment, it is because they do not have the luxury or safety to publicly pursue ideological critique. If they are unreceptive to liberal and radical feminist agendas that ignore class, they recognize that their empowerment is connected to the empowerment of working-class men.

WOMEN'S COMMUNITIES

What Scott (1985) calls "everyday forms of resistance" are mobilized within a collective context in the process of empowerment. Because women and men experience social life differently, women create communities and a culture of their own out of their "divergent understandings" of social life. Like other groups that are relatively less powerful, women create a "world of community and collectivity where resources are shared" (Hooks 1989:76). Working-class women's communities in Southwest Virginia reflects alternative values and knowledge, networks of communication, and systems of reciprocity and support; they also reflect a sense of place.

Jo Carson, an Appalachian poet, playwright, and performer says of herself: "I am a woman of place."[9] To be Appalachian is to be ethnically "other", and women in this study have challenged ethnic stereotypes of Appalachian people as symbolic forms of oppression. They have also asserted Appalachian culture and kinship as a base for new forms of political community. Appalachian women's culture is shared in conversation across the kitchen table.[10] It is what women talk about right after the PTA meeting, cleaning-up after the church supper, smoking cigarettes during break at the shirt factory, deciding who gets what "homework"[11] for the coming week, passing time while standing in the damp cold on the picket line.

In the context of this study, women's culture subverts controlling ideologies about women and working-class Appalachian people. Significant voices in feminist theory have attempted to equate women's culture,[12] particularly that which is rooted in the experience of mothering (Ruddick 1980; Elshtain 1982 A,B), and oppositional politics. Smith (1979) has claimed that "all women's culture represents a functional grab for power"(xx). But women's culture is not necessarily oppositional: to be oppositional, it must be politicized beyond the boundaries of women's experience and present some challenge to the powerful.

The communities in this study may be fertile ground for the growth of women's culture as a way for women to articulate their interests in a world dominated by "big white men." To some extent, they have also been transformational environments, with evidence in the ways women in the Coal Employment Project and Family Auxiliary challenged the controlling images of women in the industry, the union, and their own homes, and similar challenges to public authorities and institutions that came from the community development groups in Dungannon and Ivanhoe.

Hooks (1989) draws a distinction between survival and opposition in her discussion of the African-American's "counter-hegemonic value system." Marginality provides "the space for the formation of an oppositional world view" and an alternative culture, but it must be accompanied by "conscious efforts to oppose" if "it is to provide a sustained blueprint for change" (76) and to sustain the integrity of those cultural values.[13]

Just as opposition is more than alternative cultures, it is also more than individual consciousness-raising.[14] When respondents left exploitative work and family relationships, their own consciousness may have been raised: they may have *questioned* the right of a man to batter, of an employer to take advantage of them, and of a social worker to demean them as working-class Appalachian people. But they did not necessarily actively *challenge* the right of men to batter, of capitalists to exploit, or of the market to define culture. They did not have the critical consciousness (Freire 1972) that is grounded in the political or collective *practice* of opposition.[15] In this sense, challenge or opposition is a political act; personal experience is politicized, but politics is more than individual action.

There is evidence in this study that women become involved in grassroots associations because they articulate "practical gender needs" (Moser 1989)[16] which are not being met within the normative institutions of contemporary market capitalism including the family. If respondents define families as both a source of domination and resistance, their political work is more than an enlargement of their social roles within this institution. To meet their needs as mothers, women must do more than enlarge their mothering: the social context for oppositional practice then is not a group of workers, not a group of mothers, but a group of women.[17]

GENDER PLANNING FOR EMPOWERMENT

If there was a compelling message to development planners from the research conducted during the United Nations Decade for Women (1976–1985), it was that projects fail because of "a lack of baseline information about the socioeconomic situation of project beneficiaries" (Sen and Grown 1987:45). This study has explored how women in the coalfields and surrounding areas of Southwest Virginia are marginalized as women and as working-class Appalachians. Through their life stories, respondents have deeply detailed the oppressive reality of women's lives, their "habits of surviving," (Scott 1991), and their commitment to social change.

If development practice aims to eradicate structures of oppression and conditions of poverty and marginalization, there is a need in development policy to center on a vision from the vantage point of poor women (Sen and Grown 1987). In development practice, there is also a need for women-centered programs and projects because women are subordinated to men of all classes and find within associations of women the personally political space to develop the collective consciousness for social change. Women understand that their gender needs disappear in male-dominated groups, and when you miss the women, you miss the family.

At the same time, the planning emphasis on "women in development" must shift to a broad commitment to "gender in development" or gender planning (Moser 1989).[18] This does not imply leaving women out, but bringing the consideration of gender as a *relationship* to all development planning.

In the mainstream or liberal development discourse, it has become almost axiomatic that women are constructed and treated as a group—*women* in development—in order for them to become self-interested individuals. Increasing income and achieving gender equity—with different understandings about which comes first—are the measures of progress, of development, and of empowerment. It is a colonizing discourse (Mohanty 1991).

Development planners must reject the assumptions that have informed the shift towards the "efficiency approach" in women in development planning in favor of an empowerment approach to gender planning. If implicit in the women in development policies of the 1980s has been the assumption that empowerment is individual economic improvement, which will, in turn, lead to greater equity between women and men, this study has offered an alternative analysis. Empowerment is social, political, economic, and ideological autonomy; it is both collective and personal rather than individual. It occurs within the intersection of family, work, and community as women simultaneously confront structures of gender, class, ethnicity, and position in the local and global economy. It relies on "co-intentional" education but education, in itself, is not enough. It relies of income-generation, but income alone is not enough. To become "shapers" of their economy, grassroots associations must pursue the development of social capital and see this social investment as a basis for economic growth.

The contradictions are many: it is difficult for groups to resist both the welfare and efficiency policy models. As people in Southwest Virginia "come together within their communities in response to economic decline," (Luttrell 1990:227), what is emerging is a new model for a human service economy, a model that "meets human needs as a form of economic activity in itself, not merely as a consequence of other economic activity" (Cuoto 1990:253). Development practice must follow the leadership of the women who are building this model.

> We are giving birth to a new way of life for the Appalachian people. I feel like I'm nurturing a baby and we are going to have to be stronger than most people. I think we are progressive. We are dealing with something entirely different from what has been done before. We have been so creative. . . . We have gone out of the system and started thinking in terms of reality.

BUILDING FOR CHANGE

Development begins with the development of associations that become its collective context. Building women's and community organizations, as Moser (1989) notes, is central to the empowerment approach in planning. The goal of "empowering ourselves through organization" articulated by DAWN (Sen and Grown 1987)[19] is being met by grassroots women's associations in Southwest Virginia. From this study, several organizational characteristics have emerged; they have to do with structure, external linkages, leadership, and a commitment to social investment.

Women's groups share a rejection of bureaucratic structures in favor of nonhierarchical and consensus-building forms of organization. Instead of promoting centralization and professionalization for women's groups (Buvinic 1986), it is more helpful to understand that structure must emerge from the context of women's lives and their collective experience. The women in the Auxiliary, for example, found that being part of the union revealed the union's gender bias; in privileging both class struggle and corporate accommodation, the union could not offer them the family-centered vision of social change that emerged from their participation with the union.

There is a need for women's community associations to form multiple external linkages for funding and technical assistance. The Ivanhoe Civic League has creatively used connections to outside funding sources and to outsiders, and they have also demonstrated the importance of resisting dependency on them. Although community development and women's projects may "suffer from inadequate funding and managerial support," they can also suffer from an infusion of money and outside expertise; this was evident in the case of the Dungannon Development Commission, where the problem of "too much funding (was) as serious as too little" (Sen and Grown 1987:44–45).

Strong leadership is important because women must struggle at the level of consciousness to overcome their vulnerability to dominant classes and to men. But the authority for that leadership must come from consensus rather than control. Leadership must emerge from the group: no matter how well-intentioned, outsiders cannot make the experiential connection that is conducive to the trust needed for leadership to be shared. There must be space for cooperative and collective decisionmaking, and strong leaders are those who are committed to passing their leadership on to others.

You got to be a good listener. And I don't mean just sitting there and letting the words roll through your head. You got to listen! You got to *hear* what people are saying: if the leader don't listen, you're not going to be in tune to what *they* want to do. If you got a group of people here—I don't care how strong they are, how committed they've been—if you take over as a leader and you start telling people what to do, they're not getting a chance to be heard. They're not getting a chance to bring *their* ideas. There is no leader in the world that can continue leading people that way. You got to listen to what they want to do and help work out a plan. That's number one as a good leader. Number two is that you got to help all the potential leaders in your group to *become* leaders. If something happens to the leaders, you got to have people who can carry on. And you got to have a heck a lot of patience! Cause there's going to be a heck of a lot of starts and wrong turns, and it's going to have to get started again in the right direction. And I'm not saying that it's the people that's going the wrong way: a lot of times even the best laid plans, when you get out here, you see it's better to turn left instead of right. Then you've got to be ready to regroup and bring all your people up to speed, ask them what they think. Any organization that I'm in, if I can't have at least a say in it, I'm not staying long!

When a strong leader emerges, particularly is she is a woman, there are pressures from outsiders to define her as an "exceptional woman." People within communities then feel distanced from the power she has come to represent as an individual. Maxine Waller is such an "exceptional" woman, and she understands the pressures on her: "I'm good copy," she says. Maxine recognizes the danger in this aspect of success and resists the diminution of community power through her individual fame, yet it is difficult to imagine the Civic League without her. However, this may be an outsider's problem; the women in the community feel that they would carry on.

I think that it would go on, the Civic League. It would suffer a great deal. Maxine studies a lot, she reads a lot, and she knows what's going on everywhere, not just here. In reading about other places, it helps her to see what we needs here. Maxine is a very bright women. To me, nobody would fill her shoes, but to me, the Civic league would go on.

******

(If Maxine were gone) somebody else would take over tomorrow. They may not be as forward and all as Maxine is, but I think someone would take over; it wouldn't fold. It would be hard, because we all look up to Mac. She gets these great ideas. But I really don't believe that it would fall apart.[20]

CONCLUSIONS

Development, like empowerment, is a struggle concept that is finally defined by those who struggle. Development and empowerment convey the same meaning when they emerge from the oppositional struggles of subordinate groups of women; without women's empowerment, development is incomplete. For women, the process of empowerment must include both women's strategic and practical gender needs, but not necessarily at the same time.

As women empower themselves, development practitioners can be there to facilitate the process by supporting the formation of women's organizations and organizations of women. They can also help poor women to meet their practical needs in ways that allow for the emergence of feminist issues. They can provide resources and mitigate threats to successful but vulnerable women's organizations.

Women's organizations and community development groups are often vulnerable to takeover by men or by more powerful interests in the community; women may encounter resistance from men, and support services are need to help them in a transition to economic independence from their husbands.

Development relies on the "bottom-up" struggles of women. It is important to support their personal and collective agency as historical actors rather than to further oppress them by seeing them as victims; what can bring us together are the coalitions we can build. Development practitioners can assist women's community organizations to articulate strategies to meet their strategic gender needs; they cannot impose them. In the end, together we can seek to realize the just world that we want.

NOTES

NOTE TO CHAPTER ONE

1. I use the term "third world" as a political and ideological concept that reveals the power relationship between peoples of the historic and geographic periphery and peoples in core countries. I also use the term to refer to groups in the core countries that have been systematically exploited on the basis of structural positions within the economy and justified on the basis of some collective socially-defined characteristics, such as women, Blacks, and Appalachian people.

NOTES TO CHAPTER TWO

1. This discussion of the interpretive, critical, and standpoint perspectives in feminist methodology follows Nielsen (1990A).
2. Collins (1990) warns that the implications of standpoint approaches located within the "dichotomous thinking" of Marxist theory, could "invoke criteria for methodological adequacy characteristic of positivism" (207).
3. Although I used an interview guide, the interview was still open-ended, and in many cases stories went far beyond the guide. The guide was continuously revised in subsequent interviews to explore each woman's story and to allow for a reflexivity among the twelve respondents.
4. The research process included the following stages:
   1) Identification of key informants in the area of interest.
   2) Identification of grassroots associations with the help of informants.
   3) The observer-as-participant: attending meetings of the associations for purposes of observation and selection of respondents.
   4) Selection of women to be interviewed.
   5) Establishing the relationship of the researcher and respondents.
   6) Data collection: intensive interviews.
   7) Data analysis and revisions of interview guide.
   8) Evaluation of reliability and validity.
5. The analysis will show that two of the associations, the Gender Equity Program and the income-generating cooperative, did not actually satisfy criteria three and four, although they have been represented as doing so.

6. One of the community development associations is in a town not located in a coal county. This town is more like the coal counties, however, than the counties that surround it. It is an historic mining community and its only industries have been mining or mining-related.

NOTES TO CHAPTER THREE

1. Women who participate in an insecure as well as low-paid labor force in the sewing factories of Appalachia, for example, are also "housewives" engaged industrial production.
2. "The new strategy of obscuring women's productive work for capital is propagated under the slogan of 'flexibilization of labour'. Not only are women pushed out of the formal sector . . . they are reintegrated into capitalist development in a whole range of informal, non-organized, non-protected production relations, ranging from part-time work, through contract work, to homeworking, to unpaid neighborhood work. Increasingly, the dual model according to which Third World labour has been segmented is re-introduced into industrialized countries. Thus we, can say that the way in which Third World women are at present integrated into capitalist development is the model also for the reorganization of labour in the centres of capitalism" (Mies 1986:126–127).
3. With the entry of women into the coal industry as workers in the mid-1970s, demands within the union for safety regulations and worker benefits increased (as reported by respondents; and Hall 1990).
4. Collins (1990) observed a similar conservatism in Black women's struggle for group survival through community work (141–154).
5. Union man Jack Bartee "rented" his abandoned campground to the UMWA in June of 1989. "I let 'em have it for $1 for as long as they needed it. I even put the dollar back in the relief fund, so I came out zero in the deal" (Yancey 1990:9). According to Yancey, Camp Solidarity became the "heart of the strike" (ibid).
6. "Educated Black women traditionally were brought up to see their education as something gained not just for their own development but for the purpose of race uplift. This feeling was so strong that the women founding the National Association of Women's Clubs chose as their motto 'Lifting As We Climb'" (Collins 1990:149).
7. Parenting, according to Chodorow, is preferable to mothering for both parents and children.
8. Despite prohibiting legislation, young boys worked underground with their fathers, first as helpers, and as apprentices by their late teen years. They did the supportive and less skilled jobs, and often returned to those jobs when they were too old for the strenuous job of cutting coal (Shifflett 1991:94–101).

9. Despite reconstructive surgery, this miner has difficulty swallowing, speaking, and cannot taste anything. Under Virginia law, he was not compensated for the use of the inside of his mouth because it does not directly relate to his work. His wife used the example of a college professor who earns her living by lecturing, and who probably would be compensated for those kinds of injuries.

10. "In each generation there has been a major structural reduction in coal employment . . . During the 1930s, the world depression, combined with the early stages of mechanization, led to layoffs and short weeks. . . . Then during the 1950s and 1960s, while the rest of the economy was booming, two-thirds of the coalmining labor force was displaced by the next wave of mechanization. They migrated for the most part to the industrial cities of the Midwest" (Yarrow 1990:39).

11. I intentionally go back and forth among various dimensions of physical and sexual abuse because they are related in women's lives. For example, the woman who is beaten by a father who "brought the blood" is beaten because she is a girl, even if he also was abusing his male children.

12. "Accurate estimates of the extent of incest and sexual abuse are very difficult to establish. Man–girl incest is said to involve at least 1 percent of all girls, although one in five girls . . . say that they have had sexual experience as a child with a much older person (Finkelhor 1979)" (Andersen 1988).

13. Although the interview guide included an indirect question about incest, both women who volunteered that information did so before the question was asked. One women was just beginning a process of healing through disclosure, and the other has recently discussed the experience openly with siblings.

14. The number of children born to mothers of respondents in this study reflect the high birth rates of earlier generations of Appalachian women: most women reported at least nine siblings.

15. The line between pressure to become sexually active and acquaintance rape may be difficult to draw. "Rape is either seen as a man's prerogative or a crime against the honor of a woman's family or husband, not as a violation against the woman. In fact, the Latin root of rape means 'theft,' and most cultural responses to such violence emphasize reclaiming woman's lost value, not prosecuting the offender. In many countries . . . the cultural 'solution' to rape is to have the young woman marry her rapist, thus legitimizing the union and preserving the family honor" (Heise 1991:4–5). Heise cites reports on this "solution" from Fiji, the Philippines, Thailand, Mexico, and Peru. Instance of teenage marriage in the United States may be disguised forms of the same practice.

16. "Population-based surveys suggest that between 21 and 30 percent of U.S. women will be beaten by a partner at least once in their lives

(National Committee 1989). Battering also tends to escalate and become more severe over time. Almost half of all batterers beat their partners at least three times a year (Strauss et. al. 1980)." (Heise 1993:172)

17. Studies (Stark 1984; Stark and Flitcraft 1989), conclude that abuse may be the most important precipitating factor in female suicide attempts (Heise 1993:173–4).

18. All of the respondents now have children, but one was abused in her first and childless marriage.

19. "In the United States, battery is the greatest single cause of injury to women, accounting for more injury than auto accidents, muggings, and rape combined (Stark and Flitcraft 1991)" (Heise 1993:172).

20. "Preliminary results from a large, prospective study of battery during pregnancy in the United States indicate that one out of *every six* pregnant women are battered during their present pregnancy (McFarlane 1991)" (Heise 1993:183).

21. "Other studies indicate that women battered during pregnancy run twice the risk of miscarriage and four times the risk of having a low birth weight baby compared with women who are not beaten (Stark et. al. 1981; Bullock and McFarlane 1989)" (Heise 1993:183).

22. In the period 1969–1983, the divorce rate in the coal counties was lower than the divorce rate for the state as a whole, although both divorce rates were increasing and the gap was narrowing. In the period 1981–1983, the divorce rate per 1,000 population was 4.7 for the state and 3.9 for the coal counties (Kraybill et. al. 1987). The national divorce rate in 1985 was 5.0 per 1,000 persons in the population (U.S. Bureau of census 1986).

23. One respondent's children were abused by both their father and stepfather.

NOTES TO CHAPTER FOUR

1. The terms "South"and "North" refer to the political geography of the divisions between periphery and core in the global economy.

2. Collins (1990) observes that Black female domestic workers do not perceive their domestic work *within their own homes* as oppressive. In this instance, having a home of one's own is in itself a site of resistance and a source of empowerment.

3. Yarrow (1990) sees the decline of U.S. production and aggressive efforts to de-unionize what is left of coal jobs in Appalachia as evidence of multinational firms "coercing mining families and communities to subsidize their profits in the name of making the industry competitive" (39).

4. "Back then they used to get their house coal in the mines," a coal-mining woman told me of her mother's generation. Women also

worked in the mines during periods of labor shortages like WWI, but their presence was "invisible" to the men, a common phenomenon noted in the Women in Development literature (See World Bank 1979; and commentary by Rogers 1979).

5. Like contemporary stories told to me, Hall's subject spoke of her father's death in a mining accident when she was a child. "The family kept body and soul together grinding corn for their neighbors and tending the farm. . . . While her brothers followed their father's lead to the coal mines, she pursued the two most common occupations of the poorest mountain girls: agricultural labor and domestic service" (Hall 1986:361).

6. Subsistence production—growing much of the household food in large gardens—is not practiced by this generation of women. Even those women whose husbands are unemployed or threatened with lay-offs don't consider growing their own food a reasonable option for supplementing family income. One woman spoke of how blackberries and rutabagas, poor people's food, were "disgusting" to her because they reminded her of the hardships of her past.

7. "The textile industry has always been a stronghold of women's labor" (Hall 1986:355).

8. Not all marriages were oppressive in the same ways. For this respondent, as for others, marriage gave her the social sanction and financial security to enroll in a traditionally female vocational school. Other women gained limited freedom in working outside the home even though their conditions of employment were exploitative and they still did all of the household labor.

9. This practice was confirmed by an employee of another sewing factory in the area. After two years, it was unusual to have a two-week pay period when she made the production quota *and* worked forty hours a week. I visited this factory and found hazardous working conditions. The work areas were crowded and there were no clearly marked or easily accessible exits. The floor vibrated, lint filled the air, there was no ventilation or air conditioning, and the noise was deafening. This woman reported a noticeable hearing loss in two years, and her fingertips were numb.

10. I met with three of the respondents shortly after the Clarence Thomas-Anita Hill Senate Judiciary Committee hearings. I joined them at the end of a gathering of grassroots women organizers from the mountain states of the South. Several women from their respective associations were also there. The women were very clear in communicating that they believed Anita Hill had been "set up"; they said that there was "no woman alive who has ever worked" who didn't know what Hill meant, and that Anita Hill was telling the truth. The women reported that in their meetings they had decided to write "I believe Anita Hill" on all of the money that passed through their hands, because "that's what those guys in power understand—money".

11. Complicating industrial decline and the weakening of the union is the fact that Virginia is a "right-to-work state" where unions cannot legally halt production even during a strike. This not only limits labor's potential but increases the length of strikes. In a film (Johnson 1986) about the 1984 strike against A.T. Massey, a subsidiary of Royal Dutch Shell and Flour corporations (Yarrow 1991:46), a corporate official said that damage done by miners and loss of production was negligible. With international sources of raw materials and labor, the strike in right-to-work states seems to have lost its meaning.

12. "In the United States, women did not enter underground mining until 1973, according to government records, although a few apparently worked underground during WW II" (Shifflett 1991:81). A slightly different picture is presented by Betty Jean Hall, a founder of the Coal Employment Project (CEP) in 1977, the organization that opened up the industry to women through litigation. Hall (1990) notes that CEP filed "a major lawsuit against 153 coal companies and mines the year after we got started . . . with great fanfare in the national press. . . . The percentage of women hired as miners increased from 2.0 percent in 1976, the year before we started our work, to 11.4 percent in 1979. Since 1979, women have averaged a little better than 8 percent of the total hired in any given year. The number of women hired as underground coalminers soared from 0 in 1972 to 830 in 1978" (56–57).

13. Another woman employee of a sewing factory reported an annual *net income* of $7,000. She could not afford to buy health insurance from the company; it would cost approximately *half* her net income.

14. She reported that she had completed a training program at a public vocational school. Classes were held in the evenings after work; completing the program qualified you for an apprenticeship in the mining industry.

15. Several women mentioned the television shows "Ozzie and Harriet", "Donna Reed Show", "Leave it to Beaver".

16. One woman's husband died before their child was born.

17. For a woman trapped inside the home by her caregiving responsibilities and the ideology of a patriarchal household, this "freedom" is a contradiction.

18. The "outside organizer" in both insider and outsider. She was born and raised in the community, but moved West as a teenager. She has been, among other things, a professional folk singer, and returned several years ago to the community with her husband, a science-fiction writer. They are committed to development work through the sewing cooperative, and have opened the community's only library.

19. The use of "motherwork" and "homework" as one word, rather than two, supports the theoretical assertion that "home" and "mother" cannot be disassociated from "work": that the exploitation of

women's reproductive labor within this marginalized setting over-proletarianizes these women.

NOTES TO CHAPTER 5

1. With thanks to Elizabeth Spelman.
2. For a critique of "culture of poverty" based on class, race, and gender, see bell hooks, "The Myth of the Black Matriarchy," in *Ain't I a Woman: Black Women and Feminism*, Boston: South End Press, 1981.
3. "All of these problems of conflicting values . . . have a familiar ring, and one recognizes that they are the same problems that have attended the transition from agrarian to industrial society in other parts of the nation, and indeed, throughout the world" (Ford 1991:101).
4. The "invisibility" to development planners of women's everyday reality and contributions to social, economic, and political development has become an axiomatic observation in the "women in development" literature.
5. The UMWA union is an institution of community because it has historically been the location for the expression of collective working-class interest in the region. It is also a provider of collective goods to working-class families, such as strike funds and collective food supplies.
6. See Shifflett (1991:101–106) for a discussion of occupationally related disease and injury among miners.
7. The incidence of mining-related injury and disease among family members of these respondents is difficult to represent numerically because not all women necessarily reported all incidents to me. They would not, for example, have any reason to report incidents that had happened to brothers or uncles or cousins if they did not directly relate to other areas of inquiry. One woman's father had lost his leg in a mining accident but continued to mine coal on his belly; she did not consider him disabled. Since I did not directly question women about their family history concerning these health issues, the picture is incomplete.
8. "Feminist clinicians who have studied incest have challenged traditional Freudian assumptions about incest that children lie or fantasize about incestuous sexual encounters. Incest victims do try to stop the incest by seeking help or striking back, though often they are not believed. . . . Mothers may be aware of incestuous abuse, but they are typically powerless to stop it. A mother may be a silent bystander because her emotional and/or economic dependence on her husband prevents her from confronting the situation (Armstrong and Begus 1982). Particularly in families where mothers are usually powerless because of battering, disability, mental illness, or repeated

childbearing, there is an especially high risk of sexual abuse, especially among daughters who have taken on the household responsibilities . . . (Herman and Hirschman 1977)" (Andersen 1988:172–173). The mother of the above respondent matches this profile.

9. I heard similar complaints about this center from other women in the area. This presented problems for me as a researcher because I was also from the university.

10. With the ratification of the UMWA contract in February, 1990, "the union granted Pittston the flexible work schedules the company said it needed to be more productive in an international market" (Yancey 1990:16).

11. Vance Security, owned by former Secret Service Agent Chuck Vance, "are the high tech heirs of the Baldwin-Felts detectives that companies imported during the organizing campaigns of the '20s and '30s. . . . From its first job in the Massey strike, Vance Security had grown into a 410 million-a-year company with a roster of Fortune 500 clients; at the National Archives, Vance men guarded the U.S. Constitution" (Yancey 1990:4).

12. Judge McGlothlin increased fines against the UMWA throughout the strike; at the end of the strike in February 1990, they exceeded $64 million. At one point in 1989, "he threatened to bankrupt the UMWA if miners continued to ignore his order" (Yancey 1990:8:16).

13. Two pro-labor coalfield lawyers, Frank Kilgore and Scott Mullins from St. Paul, Va., represented more than 2,500 people in strike-related cases. These "individual misdemeanor cases were clogging the courts." Women were full participants in acts of civil disobedience, and since most of them were not miners, they did not risk losing their jobs if convicted. Kilgore and Mullins, who worked all of the summer of 1989, said that "their goal was to keep the court record of the strikers clean so that they could go back to work" (Yancey 1990:8).

14. "There . . . has been a history of subordination of local politics to manipulation by outside (and inside-owned) business interests. The advent of federally-subsidized, but locally distributed, welfare programs in the 1930s made local politics in much of Appalachia an instrument of political control for business interests, a situation that largely persists today" (Clavel 1983:117).

15. "I picked up the *Roanoke Times*," said Maxine Waller, "and right beside the obituary column it said, 'Property to be sold: money to be taken to Wytheville and Hillsville to build factories and employ people, to put in their industrial parks' " (Lewis and O'Donnell 1990 A:197).

16. The effects of educational-funding inequities on poor women's lives in Virginia was made clear by a sewing-factory employee in Dickenson County who was not a respondent in this study. She reported that

"paying for school" for four daughters was extremely difficult on her $8,000 per year income, and that the cost of keeping children in public school was often a determining factor in decisions to drop-out of school before graduation. In Dickenson County, unlike the more affluent county where I live, parents must purchase books for their children; I rent books provided by the county at a much lower cost to me. If public funds are available to subsidize book purchases, the woman above either did not know about them or would not use them, confirming the observation that poor women are estranged for the social welfare system.

17. The consistency of standardized test score gaps may support her analysis.

18. I observed elaborate plastic flower arrangements in one community. This may explain the origin of this form of conspicuous consumption.

19. This may contradict the liberal position on busing children to achieve integration and therefore assimilation.

20. "Self-depreciation is another characteristic of the oppressed, which derives from their internalization of the opinion the oppressors hold of them" (Freire 1972:49).

21. These include on-site community college classes and vocational gender equity programs.

22. The distinction between Christendom and christianity is made in the theology of liberation. Schooled in the work of revolutionary and theologically-based popular movements in Latin America, religious workers are very much involved in "the church of the people" in Southwest Virginia. This connection is rooted not in institutions but in faith. National denominations often fund counter-hegemonic movements in Appalachia that local churches resist. It may be the result more of their geographic and social distance rather than their commitment to revolutionary praxis.

23. The potential within the African-American institution of the prophetic church for a Black woman's culture of resistance is explored by Gilkes (1985).

24. Although the position of the priest within the Roman Catholic Church is clearly more privileged, other respondents who were not raised as Catholics recognized the distance between their position as women and that of decisionmakers within the churches.

25. A similar phenomenon was observed by Warren (1991) in recent interactions with indigenous Guatemalan anthropologists. Her own work was moving towards the post-modern stance of questioning the possibility of cultural universals. As she critiqued North American assumptions about static Mayan ethnicity and assimilation as *ladinoization*, or "becoming the ethnic other" (10), the Guatemalans were moving towards a Mayan essentialism. In a forthcoming essay, she writes: "The most difficult dilemma now is the successful inven-

tion of a pan-community Mayan identity. . . Wider identifications are crucial, they argue, if Mayans are to avoid modern forms of the divide and conquer strategy historically used by dominant groups" (ibid:18).

26. In the mountains, divisions on the basis of class may be interpreted as equally important as divisions based on race. African-Americans in Appalachia came to work in the coal fields or migrated west after slavery to the Piedmont and beyond. In the oral histories of Black women in southwest Virginia (Lewis and O'Donnell 1990B; Johnson 1985 film), women speak of their identity as mountain people having as much significance as race. For example, the blues, defined by them as the music of the Black urban South, seemed strange to them.

27. The "militant antiscientific fundamentalism" observed by Ford (1991:94) may also be interpreted as a way to subvert the collusion of Christianity and capitalism (Weber 1958).

28. "The mountain women who people nineteenth-century travel accounts, novels, and social surveys tend to be drudges who married young and aged early, burdened by frequent pregnancies and good-for-nothing men. Alongside that predominant image is another: the promiscuous mountain girl, responsible for the supposed high rate of illegitimacy in the region" (Hall 1986:376).

29. This observation has been made about the articulation of capitalism and vestiges of pre-capitalist modes of production in the geographic third world. Particularly in the case of southern Africa, kinship ties through non-market and subsistence production served both as a retreat from *and* as a basis for capitalist exploitation (Wolpe 1980). Following Engels (1978), Meillassoux (1981) introduced gender to the discussion of the exploitation of a domestic mode of production. His work has been criticized by feminists who argue that once again, the economism of Marxism "offer(s) no satisfactory theory . . . of the oppression of women, . . . of why women's valuable fertility should lead to their alienation from all rights in themselves" (Redclift 1987:135).

30. In a 1929 strike among women workers in a Tennessee rayon factory, "one woman remarked, 'I haven't forgotten to use a hoe,' while another said, 'We'll go back to the farm.' Such threats were not just bravado" (Hall 1986:370).

31. "The southern lady . . . does not fit into the mountain landscape; she is too ethereal. Instead, Appalachian authors have championed strong women, who can manage the household and the children as well as milk the cows and cultivate the fields. They have been tall women, either physically or spiritually or both, because—as an old mountain saying explained—'a tall woman casts a long shadow' " (Matthews 1987:39).

32. Although all of the respondents recognized the economic and gendered constraints on their mothers' lives, those respondents who were sexually abused as children could not fully forgive their mothers for allowing the abuse to happen.

33. In addition to the newspaper reporter's claim, the same analysis was offered in overheard and direct conversation with current and former union officials, both male and female.

34. The name "Daughters of Mother Jones" is a contested term between two factions that emerged in the association at the end of the strike. The struggle over this symbol will be discussed in Chapter 6 in the context of the contradictions women experience when they both resist and gain power.

35. Ella May Wiggins, a leader in a 1920 textile strike, "joined the long line of working-class heroines who served with devotion" but Hall (1986) is also more interested in heroines "cast from a more human mold" (355).

36. This is a common critique of the "add women and stir" approach.

37. See the autobiography (Jones 1972).

38. A sensitive treatment of the position of the outsider from a planning perspective is in Robert Chambers, *Rural Development: Putting the Last First*, 1983.

39. Hall (1986) researched women strikers in the 1920s in Tennessee: "Trixie Perry took the stand in a dress sewn from red, white, and blue bunting, and a cap made from a small American flag. The prosecuting attorney began his cross-examination: 'You have a United States flag cap on your head?' 'Yes.' 'Wear it all the time?' 'Whenever I take a notion.' You are dressed in a United States flag, and the colors?' 'I guess so. I was born under it, so I guess I have a right to.' (373) . . . (W)ith the language of dress—a cap made of an American flag, an elegant wide-brimmed hat—they claimed their rights as citizens and their place in female community" (375).

40. On "Labor Sunday" 1989 I attended a UMWA rally in St. Paul, Virginia. The crowds pressed into the ball field to cheer on union leadership, including President Richard Trumka, Vice President Cecil Roberts, and local President Jackie Stump, and to wait for the helicopter arrival of Jesse Jackson who was making his second speech supporting the strikers. Under the tents, women from the auxiliary cooked and served enormous amounts of food—beans, cornbread, meat—which they distributed to the long lines without charge: a few cans sat at the ends of the table for donations. They were dressed in their camouflage outfits with badges and buttons from unions and supporters all over the world: several women proudly displayed union buttons from "communist" countries like the Soviet Union and Nicaragua. On the periphery of the crowd, tables were set up and in addition to the leaflets and solicitations from grassroots political and environmental groups from all over the country, women and men sold a variety of camouflage-decorated goods and jackrock jewelry, including earrings and a necklace for a child made of re-worked "jacks" in many colors interspersed with bows and beads.

41. I follow Collins (1990) use of capitalization of "Black" as a socially constructed category to differentiate African-American persons.
42. Similar mechanisms have been observed in Appalachia (Beaver 1991; Lewis and O'Donnell 1990A).

NOTES TO CHAPTER SIX

1. The Coal Employment Project, for example, was organized in part because the United Mineworkers did not represent women's interests.
2. In WID planning, women's projects and women's associations are usually confined to practical gender needs, and gender is usually a coda in discussions of social movements. Castells (1984) and Fainstein and Fainstein (1979, 1982), for example, acknowledge that class consciousness is shaped by participation in community organizations, but they are not interested in gender unless it is subsumed in class. For Castells, "the relationship of gender itself was determined, in its content and evolution by production relationships (class position of males) and by power relationships (state enforced family relationships). . . . (F)eminist consciousness . . . is part of a broader historical tendency: the calling into question of the hierarchy over the relationships of production, power, and experience" (308–309).
3. Two of the women were respondents in this study. One of the respondents has also been involved in an association of women miners.
4. Since the completion of the study, the director has left the program. Since she was active at the state level in promoting the program and raising funds, it is unclear what shape the program will take in future.
5. This group, like the income-generating group, did not emerge from the collective identity of the participants but relies on professionals and outsiders to encourage the creation of collective identity.
6. Based on discussion with directors and participants in two Gender Equity Programs in Southwest Virginia. In a public presentation and discussion with participants from both programs, women spoke of how they had found the strength to leave abusive husbands or boyfriends, to plan for the future, and to deal with substance abuse.
7. The comments below were from women in several associations and should not be attributed only to women in the Gender Equity program.
8. Several women are wives of miners who have been laid off. Other husbands are also unemployed, including at least one man who is too ill to work.
9. Based on conversations with organizers. Increasing women's community management work, a characteristic of the "Efficiency Approach" to WID, can also be exploitative.
10. At the time research was conducted, they were in the process of forming a legal cooperative and purchasing the building.

11. The library of donated books is in a large room that used to be a clothing store on the main street of town. It is comfortable, colorful, and inviting, with displays of books and other items that directly relate to the interests of the organizer and her author-husband. There are sofas to sit on and toys for children in this large space. The smaller and windowless room in the back are where the sewing business sorts, packs, and distributes material.

12. There was considerable difference in the extent the participants were willing to criticize the organizer. The woman who was reserved in her critique was interviewed twice in a back room of the cooperative's building, where there was a chance the organizer or other women could overhear our conversation. All of the other respondents in this study were interviewed at least once in their homes. There are contradictions in this woman's appraisal of the situation with the sewing cooperative. On the one hand, she says she agrees with the organizer that "it's a cooperative" and the other women are at fault for not taking more initiative. Yet, she also says that "it's good to follow (the organizer) because she started it." I have since heard from another member that she has left the group.

13. This is a problem for all of the women who belong to associations that draw members from outside their immediate communities.

14. Interviewed 6/91.

15. Another problem may be time. At the time of the study, the sewing group had been in existence for a little over a year.

16. I heard the term "public work" used by several women to refer to paid employment in sewing factories or service jobs.

17. One respondent was paid for a time as a part-time organizer for two groups in this study, but most of her work is voluntary.

18. CEP began with a $5,000 grant from the Ms. Foundation (Hall 1990:56).

19. "The development of a positive working relationship with the UMWA did not happen automatically," Hall (1990) observed. "Early on, we sought for many months to obtain some sort of official endorsement from the union, not for CEP as an organization but for the concept of women miners. We got nowhere fast" (59). Women are only 1 percent of UMWA membership (57).

20. There will be fewer women underground in the mines one respondent observed. Women are "new" miners and their numbers dwindle with recession as they are the first laid off. Even so, Hall (1990) claims that attendance at CEP conferences has increased in the last several years.

21. Beyond this observation, a respondent would only talk about this problem off the record.

22. At the time of the study, another respondent was hopeful that a woman miner was the new director: "For the first time now the director is a miner, a black lady named Carol." Since the completion of

the research, the CEP has changed directors again, selecting a long-time activist and miner with experience in more than one of the associations in this study.

23. This observation was also made in the film *Coalmining Women* by Elizabeth Barret (1982).
24. She is not sure but thinks the company was Maidenform.
25. There are few direct quotes from one respondent concerning CEP because she asked that the tape recorder be turned off while we were discussing this association.

NOTES TO CHAPTER 7

1. Women organized the group and carry it on; it was, for a time, a "ladies auxiliary." Some men were involved during the strike.
2. Marat Moore has since left her position in the UMWA and is working on a history of the women's participation. She is credited for her commitment to the union cause *and* her deep respect and appreciation for the work of the women in the strike. Another International staff person, Nmonde Ngubu, a labor organizer and cultural worker/singer from South Africa, also advised the women during the strike and contributed to the formation of their international analysis.
3. Pittston dropped out of the BCOA in February and the strike began in April 1989.
4. A respondent estimated that there were thirteen or fourteen locals that had auxiliaries. Estimates of women who participated in the strike range from 150 to 500, but two respondents thought that there were probably fifty highly active members, women who regularly participated in the meetings and decisionmaking process.
5. If your husband worked at a mine a long distance from home and there was a closer local, you could join the auxiliary near your home rather than the auxiliary affiliated with your husband's union membership.
6. An important constraint on an organization that spanned several counties was the cost of telephone calls. Long distance charges, especially to women who would be facing the enforced frugality of a strike, were to be avoided. Setting up local auxiliaries that would meet together once a month cut down on telephone costs, especially later in the strike when phone chains were in use almost daily.
7. February 1988 to April 1989.
8. Odum became President of Pittston Coal in January 1989.
9. Location of Pittston headquarters.
10. Community support was so strong that "when state police brought the first busload of arrested strikers to the Dickenson County Jail on April 24 (1989), residents mobbed the streets, businesses shut their doors

and some miners escaped from the courthouse on a rope. On April 26, the crowds were so thick that troopers were afraid to unload arrested strikers. Instead, they took them on an eight-hour ride to Honaker" (Yancey 1990:2).

11. They were not always less rough: a respondent recalled an incident where a woman miner was "slammed up against a door."

12. "We don't want your scab pop," was the reply of one of the respondents.

13. In April 1989, the first month of the strike, high school students in all of Dickenson County's three schools walked out in protest against the coal company, and the protests spread to other schools in the region. All summer, children joined their parents on the picket lines (Yancey 1990:5).

14. Including changing road signs to trick the police.

15. In a field near Carterton, over 70,000 supporters from all over the U,S. and other countries "passed through this 'Hillbilly Woodstock' " (Yancey 1990:2).

16. One respondent said she went two or three times, and that they were demonstrating at stockholder meetings before the strike.

17. Part of the Auxiliary has exclusive rights to the name women used in their first action in April 1989 to occupy the Pittston building, the "Daughters of Mother Jones."

18. The environmental movements of third world women come closer to a mediating position. For poor women protecting their livelihood, as in the Chipko Movement in India, spirituality and the natural world have not been completely severed from their class-based and material needs.

19. Since the research period, I have not heard environmental action articulated as a goal for the group. There have been more pressing needs for women in just supporting each other in the face of further economic decline.

20. I heard reports which remained unsubstantiated by respondents that rumors of "Hollywood" interest in the Daughters of Mother Jones led the break-away group to claim control of the name. I also heard reports that were supported by respondents that the break-away group was less interested in being part of the union, and that their leader was angered that union officials were not giving her the accolades she felt she had earned.

21. I did not refuse when the President of the Auxiliary requested that I carry a message to the leader of the "Daughters." She wanted me to let the other woman know that she hoped they would be able to talk and bridge their differences. It was a gracious gesture that I saw repeated many times by women in this association. I was rebuffed, but learned several months later that the break-away group had joined in at least one event with the Auxiliary.

22. Publicly accusing a member of stealing money earned from the sale of T-shirts.
23. An auxiliary member reported the following incident: When the leader of the break-away faction was called back to work as a coal miner on a panel in a nonunion mine, she was told by the coal company that she couldn't work because she did not pass the physical. When she informed the company that she had not had a physical and that she intended to file a lawsuit if they blocked her employment, the company said it was all a mistake.
24. I have also heard that 500 women came out on the picket line during the first week of the strike in April 1989.
25. BCOA negotiates with the union as an industry. When Pittston pulled out in 1988, the union knew there would be a strike.
26. They want nonunion operators, an increasing proportion of the industry, to share in the burden of contributing to the fund. They argue that 60 percent of the retirees and widows are collecting on the basis of employment with companies now out of business, and 15 percent worked for nonunion or no-longer unionized companies (Karr 1992).
27. This respondent was referring to both the CEP and the Auxiliary.

NOTES TO CHAPTER EIGHT

1. An example is Mud Creek Clinic of Floyd County, Kentucky, a community project that grew out of a rural welfare rights movement (Johnson 1986).
2. The success of citizens of the coal camp of Trammel, Virginia in buying their homes is an example of a group that organized around inadequate rural housing.
3. This concern was stated by members of the UMWA Family Auxiliary and other women in the region.
4. The costs of telephone calls and transportation were cited as important obstacles by women in four groups in this study.
5. After the creation of DDC, two respondents got together with legal aid and had a "Know Your Rights Workshop."
6. A respondent showed her understanding that gender consciousness is not biologically determined: Observing that all of the sewers were women, she also noted that the manager was a woman: "She was local, but she was strictly company."
7. I wasn't involved in all of that," a respondent commented, "but I know that it's left a bad taste in some of the women's mouth because of it. You can mention unionizing a shop and they go bananas: 'I don't want nothing to do with the union!' "

8. In 1983, I attended a fundraiser and dance at the Depot with a group of women from Africa, Asia, the Middle East, and Latin America, participants in a U.S.A.I.D. management training course who were visiting development projects in Southwest Virginia.

9. As discussed in Chapter 5, a contradictory strength of Appalachian communities is the acceptance of grown children returning home when they are having financial or marriage problems. Also, although housing is inadequate and often substandard, those who do own their own homes on family land often own them outright; those who rent can find housing that is much less expensive than in urban areas.

10. This observation was made by Maxine Waller of the Ivanhoe Civic League. You need the institutional support to write the proposals and reports for project funding, but few funding agencies want to pay you for something that has no measurable "product."

11. Developmental classes are remedial in content to prepare students for secondary education.

12. The DDC did not abandon its interest in the sewing factory or in economic development, but from the perspective of these respondents, other areas were more significant.

13. Because these educational classes were not directly related to employment—they were not vocational classes—they can be characterized as welfare programs. The educational component of income-generation projects is described by Buvinic (1986) as "teaching a new skill or upgrading income-generating skills women already have" (1).

14. A regional food cooperative with national affiliation.

15. A man was the part-time book-keeper, but neither respondent considered him a participant in the decision-making process.

16. An example in Dungannon (and in Ivanhoe) is the MIHOW (Maternal-Infant Health Outreach Workers) program.

17. These efforts were begun before DDC was organized, and it was not until 1990 or 1991 that the housing program was funded. The housing program involves rehabilitation and construction, and will offer low-interest loans to participants. The other area of the program is an all-volunteer rehabilitation program because "the people who need it don't have any income." The respondent is raising money and donated materials and working with a housing agency that gives her technical assistance.

18. The DDC staff person hired to administer the grant commented that "the overall goal of creating 100 jobs is still the driving force" (Dungannon Times. Winter 1987:1).

19. An Ivanhoe respondent's words to describe how outsiders view Ivanhoe.

20. The anticipated economic miracle in Ivanhoe centered around community control of an industrial park left to the town when the last

manufacturer, National Carbide Company, shut down in 1966. Rice (1987) reported that "many residents of Ivanhoe recall that the town began to die even before the carbide plant closed. The real money in Ivanhoe was in the hands of absentee parent companies, which successfully blocked a move by a large contingent of residents in 1957 to incorporate the town. The area was honeycombed with mine shafts and houses crumpled into sinkholes. Many of the unfortunate residents received no compensation"(34).

21. Ivanhoe had been mined for over 100 years (Waller et al. 1990). "Wealth from lead, iron and zinc deposits (had been) produced for the great benefit of Wytheville, Richmond, and the rest of the state and the nation as it industrialized" (Lewis 1990:241).

22. Lewis (1990 A) says that "(f)rom its early days, Ivanhoe was in many ways a racially integrated town," but that with population decline and growing unemployment, Ivanhoe had begun to become "hostile territory" for the Black population (243).

23. An activist campus minister, Jan Tobias, who moved to Marquette from Virginia Tech, brought Maxine Waller to his campus for one month as a visiting lecturer and helped begin what became the student volunteer program.

24. Based on personal conversations over the years with many student volunteers who go to Ivanhoe.

25. They received financial support from the Kellogg Foundation.

26. The DDC had attempted the same kind of validation but not necessarily on cultural grounds.

27. The name Ivanhoe Tech calls attention to the large state university nearby, both in the differences in these settings for education and because students from Virginia Tech go to Ivanhoe to work and learn, especially during the "Alternative Spring Break." Ivanhoe Tech is located in a building that used to be the company store.

28. This is Freire's (1972) term that "refers to learning to perceive social, political, and economic contradictions, and to take action against the oppressive elements of reality.—Translator's note"(19).

29. The Highlander Center in New Market, Tennessee, founded my Miles Horton, has been an extremely important institutional catalyst for social change in the region, and has facilitated many of the efforts of the DDC, the Family Auxiliary, the CEP, and the Civic League.

30. This was particularly important to her because she needed the income to pay for medication for her and her husband.

31. Since the completion of the research, the Ivanhoe Civic League has done another survey to consider the need for a sewer system in the community.

32. During the Civic League's first two years (1986–1988), I worked with two campus ministers who were supporters.

33. Leviticus 25: 9–13.
34. Flora (1990:28) discusses the Year of Jubilee as a "mechanism of land access" in traditional agricultural communities.

NOTES TO CHAPTER NINE

1. From the title of a book (Sen and Grown 1987) presenting the analysis and program of DAWN (Development Alternatives with Women for a New Era), a group of third-world activists, scholars, and practitioners.
2. Sen and Grown (1987) articulate the position of DAWN, Development Alternatives for Women in a New Era.
3. An international mass movement of working families that is organized by women is a vision of one of the respondents in this study.
4. Empowerment as it is used here stands in opposition to Marxist assumptions about vanguard politics. It rejects the notion that revolutions require the mass mobilization of workers through the agency of a few enlightened leaders who have a clearer understanding of the struggle.
5. Mies (1986) uses the term "big white men" because "men play a decisive role as 'agents of capital' (Mies 1982). This role, however, has to be differentiated according to class, as well as race, and the location in the international division of labour" (142). The term can be extended to the agents of capital in Southwest Virginia who have power over small white women and small white men. As patriarchy is neither first cause nor ahistorical, it is equally important to acknowledge the power that some (big) women have over other (small) women.
6. Women's consciousness can be interpreted as female consciousness, what Lutrell (1988) describes as the impetus to women's collective activism, but not the character of the activism itself. I prefer to use the term "women's" rather than "female" as the latter is associated with biology not society.
7. This statement follows Scott (1985), who addresses the issue of ideological hegemony in Marxist theory based on his research with poor peasants in Malaysia. I generalize from his argument to working-class persons as a group and to women in particular because women confront gender ideology not independent from class ideology but as a specific set of ideological practices that relate to them as women and not to working-class men. As a member of an association told me: "If cleanliness is next to godliness, why is it that women have to do the cleaning?"
8. An advantage of the Ivanhoe Civic League, centralized in one community, is that oral histories could be more easily researched and discussion groups could be more easily facilitated.
9. Personal conversation 4/94.

10. All conversations, like all kitchen tables, are not alike. "Big white women" cannot claim the culture of "small white women" or women of color. Their are many things that divide us within our experiences of gender, class, race, sexuality, and position in the international division of labor. See Moraga and Anzaldua (1983) published by Kitchen Table: Women of Color Press as antidote to the feminism of big white women.

11. Sewing. Deciding how to divide the garments to be sewn among the women who are part of an income-generating group.

12. This is also a universalist claim to women's culture. The differences in women's cultures are as important as the similarities.

13. Hooks (1989) observes that without an *oppositional* stance, it is possible that some African-Americans have effectively changed their own culture by assimilating the values of the privileged (78).

14. Radical and cultural feminists suggest that consciousness-raising as feminist practice is in itself oppositional. Elshtain (1981, 1982 A and B) goes further and see women's culture, specifically white middle-class mothering, as not only oppositional but politically redemptive.

15. You may realize that *you* have been oppressed, and you may question the right of those that oppress you, but you may not challenge those who have power over you because you define yourself as powerless.

16. Moser (1989) uses Molyneux's (1986) discussion of practical and strategic gender interests as gender needs. Needs are practical representations of interests: a woman's practical need, such as family leave policy within an industry, may satisfy her practical gender interest of caring for a sick child.

17. A selection criteria for the women in this study was that they be involved in an association where women constitute the majority of membership and leadership positions, not that the associations be limited to women or women's needs.

18. Caroline O.N. Moser is currently completing a book on "gender planning" (personal conversation 3/92).

19. Development Alternatives for Women in a New Era.

20. Nevertheless, in 1994, I was told by people associated with the Civic League that Maxine would like to step down as president, but is having a difficult time finding someone who is willing to replace her in that position.

BIBLIOGRAPHY

Acker, Joan, Kate Barry and Joke Esseveld. 1983. "Objectivity and Truth: Problems in Doing Feminist Research." *Women's Studies International Forum*. Vol.6. No.4. 423–435.

Afonja, Simi. 1990. "Changing Patterns of Gender Stratification in West Africa." In Irene Tinker, ed. *Persistent Inequalities: Women and World Development*. New York, NY: Oxford University Press. 198–209.

Andersen, Margaret L. 1988. *Thinking About Women: Sociological Perspectives on Sex and Gender* (second edition). New York, NY: Macmillan.

Anderson, Kathryn, Susan Armitage, Dana Jack and Judith Wittner. 1990. "Beginning Where We Are: Feminist Methodology in Oral History." In Joyce McCarl Nielsen, ed. *Feminist Research Methods: Exemplary Readings in the Social Sciences*. Boulder, CO: Westview Press. 94–112.

Austin, Ernest H., Jr. 1966. "One View of Yesterday's People." *The Appalachian South*. 1 (Spring/Summer).

Bachrarch, Peter, and Morton S. Baratz. 1970. *Power and Poverty: Theory and Practice*. New York, NY: Oxford University Press.

Barret, Elizabeth. 1982 (film). "Coalmining Women. Whitesburg, KY: Appalshop.

Barrett, Michele. 1980. *Women's Oppression Today: Problems in Marxist Feminist Analysis*. London, England: Verso.

Barrios de Chungara, Domitila. 1978. *Let Me Speak: Testimony of Domitila, a Woman of the Bolivian Mines*. New York, NY: Monthly Review Press.

Barry, Kathleen. 1979. *Female Sexual Slavery*. Englewood Cliffs, NJ: Prentice-Hall.

Beaver, Patricia Duane. 1991. "Family, Land, and Community." In Bruce Ergood and Bruce E. Kuhre, eds. *Appalachia: Social Context Past and present* (third edition). Dubuque, IA: Kendall Hunt. 299–307.

Behar, Ruth. 1990. "Rage and Redemption: Reading the Life Story of a Mexican Market Woman." *Feminist Studies*. Vol.16. No.8. 223–258.

Belenkey, Mary Field, Blythe McVicker Clinchy, Nancy Rule Goldberger, and Jill Mattuck Tarule. 1986. *Women's Ways of Knowing: The Development of Self, Voice, and Mind*. New York, NY: Basic Books.

Beneria, Lourdes, and Shelly Feldman, eds. 1992. *Unequal Burden: Economic Crises, Persistent Poverty, and Women's Work*. Boulder, CO: Westview Press.

Beneria, Lourdes, and Gita Sen. 1986. "Accumulation, Reproduction, and Women's Role in Economic Development: Boserup Revisited." In Eleanor Leacock and Helen I. Safa, eds. *Women's Work: Development and the Division of Labor by Gender*. South Hadley, MA: Bergin and Garvey.

Bernard, Jessie. 1981. *The Female World*. New York, NY: Free Press.

Best, Bill. 1973. "From Existence to Essence: A Conceptual Model for An Appalachian Studies Curriculum. (Ed.D. Dissertation, University of Massachusetts.)

Billings, Dwight. 1974. "Culture and Poverty in Appalachia: A Theoretical Discussion and Empirical Analysis." *Social Forces*. 53. 315–323.

Billings, Dwight. 1976. In Bruce Ergood and Bruce E. Kuhre, eds. *Appalachia: Social Context Past and Present* (second edition). Dubuque, IA: Kendall Hunt.

Bookman, Ann, and Sandra Morgen, eds. 1988. *Women and the Politics of Empowerment*. Phildelphia, PA: Temple University Press.

Boserup, Ester. 1970. *Woman's Role in Economic Development*, New York, NY: St. Martin's Press.

Burkett, M. Sexton. 1990. "Directory of Economic Development Leadership in Southwest Virginia." Blacksburg, VA: Virginia Cooperative Extension Service at Virginia Tech.

Butler, Janice R., and Linda M. Burton. 1990. "Rethinking Tenage Childbearing: Is Sexual Abuse a Missing Link." *Family Relations*. 39. 73–80.

Buvinic, Mayra. 1986. "Projects for Women in the Third World: Explaining their Misbehavior." *World Development*. Vol.14. No.5. 653–664.

Carbonell, Dina, Lois Glass, Suzanne Gosselin, Carol Mamber, Jill Stanzler, Alice Friedman, Margaret Lazarus, Lynn Rubinett, Lena Sorensen, Denise Wells, Nancy Wilbur, Terrie Antico, and Wendy Sanford. 1984. "Violence Against Women." In *The New Our Bodies, Ourselves*. Boston Womens's Health Book Colective. New York, NY: Simon and Schuster. 99–117.

Cardenal, Ernesto. 1982. *The Gospel in Solentiname*. Vols. 1,2, and 3. Maryknoll, NY: Orbis Books.

Castells, Manuel. 1983. *The City and the Grassroots: A Cross-Cultural Theory of Urban Social Movements*. Berkeley, CA: University of California Press.

Caudill, Harry M. 1962. *Night Comes to the Cumberlands*. Boston, MA: Little Brown.

Caughman, Susan, and Mariam N'diaye Thiam. 1989. "The Markala, Mali Cooperative: A New Approach to Traditional Economic Roles." In Ann Leonard, ed. *Seeds: Supporting Women's Work in the Third World*. New York, NY: Feminist Press (CUNY). 31–48.

Chambers, Robert. 1983. *Rural Development: Putting the Last First*. New York, NY: Longman Scientific and Technical.

Chen, Marty. 1989. "Developing Non-Craft Employment for Women in Bangladesh." In Ann Leonard, ed. *Seeds: Supporting Women's Work in the Third World*. New York, NY: The Feminist Press (CUNY). 73–98.

Chinchilla, Norman Stoltz. 1990. "Revolutionary Popular Feminism in Nicaragua: Articulating Class, Gender, and National Sovereignty." *Gender & Society* Vol.4. No.3. 370–397.

Chinchilla, Norma Stoltz. 1991. "Marxism, Feminism, and the Struggle for Democracy in Latin America." *Gender & Society* Vol.5. No.3. 291–310.

Chinchilla, Norma Stoltz and Martha E. Gimenez. 1991. "Guest Editor's Introduction." *Gender & Society* Vol.5. No.3. 286–290.

Chodorow, Nancy. 1974. "Family Structure and Feminine Personality." In Michelle Zimbalist Rosaldo and Louise Lamphere, eds. *Woman, Culture, and Society*. Stanford, CA: Stanford University Press. 43–66.

Chodorow, Nancy. 1978. *The Reproduction of Mothering: Psychoanalysis and the Sociology of Gender*. Berkeley, CA: University of California Press.

Clavel, Pierre. 1983. *Opposition Planning in Wales and Appalachia*. Philadelphia, PA: Temple University Press.

Coles, Robert. 1971. *Migrants, Sharecroppers, Mountaineers*. Boston, MA: Little Brown.

Collins, Patricia Hill. 1989. "The Social Construction of Black Feminist Thought." *Signs: Jounral of Women in Culture and Society*. Vol.14. No.4. 745–773.

Collins, Patricia Hill. 1990. *Black Feminist Thought: Knowledge, Consciousness, and the Politics of Empowerment*. Boston, MA: Unwin Hyman.

Cone, James H. 1972. *The Spirituals and the Blues: An Interpretation*. New York, NY: Seabury Press.

Cook, Judith, and Mary Margaret Fonow. 1990. "Knowledge and Women's Interests: Issues of Epistemlogy and Methodology in Feminist Research." In Joyce McCarl Nielsen, ed. *Feminist Research Methods: Exemplary Readings in the Social Sciences*. Boulder, CO: Westview Press. 69–93.

Couto, Richard A. 1990. "Toward a Human Service Economy." In John Gaventa, Barbara Ellen Smith, and Alex Willingham, eds. *Communities in Economic Crisis*. Philadelphia, PA: Temple University Press. 251–262.

Dalla Costa, Mariarosa, and Selma James. 1972. *The Power of Women and the Subversion of the Community*. Bristol, England: Falling Wall Press.

Daughters of Mother Jones. January 21, 1990. "Draft Copy of Bylaws." (Author's collection.)

Davis, Angela. 1981. *Women, Race, and Class*. New York, NY: Random House.

Davis, Angela. 1990. *Women, Culture, and Politics*. New York, NY: Vintage Books.

Denzin, Norman K. 1978. *The Research Act: A Theoretical Introduction to Sociological Methods*. New York, NY: McGraw-Hill.

Denzin, Norman K. 1984. *Interpretive Interactionism*. Newbury Park, CA: Sage Publications.

Dietz, Mary G. 1987. "Context is All: Feminism and Theories of Citizenship." In Jill K. Conway, Susan C. Bourque, and Joan W. Scott, eds. *Learning About Women: Gender, Politics, and Power*. Ann Arbor, MI: The University of Michigan Press. 1–24.

Dobash, Rebecca, and Russell Dobash. 1979. *Violence Against Wives: A Case Against the Patriarchy*. New York, NY: Free Press.

DuBois, Barbara. 1983. "Passionate Scholarship: Notes on Values, Knowing and Method in Feminist Social Science." In Gloria Bowles and Renate D. Klein, eds. *Theories of Women's Studies*. London, England: Routledge and Kegan Paul. 105–116.

Dungannon Development Commission. Dungannon, VA. (Undated brochure. Author's collection.)

Eisenstein, Zillah R., ed. 1979. *Capitalist Patriarchy and the Case for Socialist Feminism*. New York, NY: Monthly Review Press.

Elshtain, Jean Bethke. 1981. *Public Man, Private Woman: Women in Social and Political Thought*. Princeton, NJ: Princeton University Press.

Elshtain, Jean Bethke. 1982A. "Feminist Discourse and Its Discontents: Language, Power, and Meaning." *Signs* Vol.3. No.7. 603–621.

Elshtain, Jean Bethke. 1982B. "Antigone's Daughters." *Democracy* Vol.2. No.2. 46–59.

Engels, Friedrich. 1978. "The Origin of the Family, Private Property, and the State." In Robert C. Tucker, ed. *The Marx-Engels Reader* (second edition). New York, NY: W.W. Norton. 734–759.

Erickson, Thomas H., Philip Newell, Owen Owens, and Wayne C. Stumme. September 22,1989. "The United Mineworkers of America Strike Against the Pittson Coal Company: A Report to the Religious Community." New York, NY: Office of Economic Justice, UCBHM.

Fainstein, Norman, and Susan Fainstein. 1982. *Urban Policy Under Capitalism*. Beverly Hills, CA: Sage.

Fanon, Frantz. 1966. *The Wretched of the Earth*. New York, NY: Grove Press.

Fay, Brian. 1986. *Social Theory and Political Practice*. Boston, MA: George Allen & Unwin.

Fay, Brian. 1987. *Critical Social Science: Liberation and its Limits.* Ithaca, NY: Cornell University Press.

Ferguson, Kathy E. 1984. *The Feminist Case Against Bureaucracy.* Philadelphia, PA: Temple University Press.

Fisher, Steve. 1990. "National Economic Renewal Programs and Their Inplications for Appalachia and the South." In John Gaventa, Barbara Ellen Smith, and Alex Willingham, eds. *Communities in Economic Crisis.* Philadelphia, PA: Temple University Press. 263–278.

Fisher, Stephen L. 1991. "Victim-Blaming in Appalachia: Cultural Theories and the Southern Mountaineer." In Bruce Ergood and Bruce E. Kuhre, eds. *Appalachia: Social Context Past and Present* (third edition). Dubuque, IA: Kendall Hunt. 185–194.

Fitchen, Janet M. 1991. *Endangered Spaces, Enduring Places: Change, Identity, and Survival in Rural America.* Boulder, CO: Westview Press.

Flora, Cornelia Butler. 1987. "Income Generation Projects for Rural Women." In Carmen Diana Deere and Magdelena Leal, eds. *Rural Women and State Policy: Feminist Perspectives on Latin American Agricultural Development.* Boulder, CO: Westview Press. 212–238.

Flora, Cornelia Butler. 1990. "The Social and Cultural Dynamics of Traditional Agricultural Communities." In Miguel A. Altieri and Susanna B. Hecht. *Agroecology and Small Farm Development.* Boca Raton, FL: CRC Press, Uniscience Books. 27–34.

Fonow, Mary Margaret, and Judith Cook, eds. 1991. *Beyond Methodology: Feminist Scholarship as Lived Research.* Bloomington, IN: Indiana University Press.

Ford, Thomas R. 1991. "The Passing of Provincialism." In Bruce Ergood and Bruce E. Kuhre, eds. *Appalachia: Social Context Past and Present* (third edition). Dubuque, IA: Kendall Hunt. 80–103.

Forester, John. 1989. *Planning in the Face of Power*. Berkeley, CA: University of California Press.

Foster, G.M. 1973. *Traditional Societies and Technological Change* (second edition). New York, NY: Harper and Row.

Foucault, Michel. 1972. *The Archaeology of Knowledge*. London, England: Tavistock Publications.

Foucault, Michel. 1978. *History of Sexuality: Volume One*. New York, NY: Random House.

Foucault, Michel. 1979. *Discipline and Punish: The Birth of the Prison*. New York, NY: Vitage Books.

Foucault, Michel. 1980. *Power/Knowledge*. New York, NY: Pantheon Books.

Freire, Paulo. 1972. *Pedagogy of the Oppressed*. New York, NY: Herder and Herder.

French, Marilyn. 1985. *Beyond Power: On Women, Men, and Morals*. New York, NY: Summit Books.

Friedl, E. 1975. *Women and Men*. New York, NY: Holt, Rinehart and Winston.

Friedmann, John. 1987. *Planning in the Public Domain: From Knowledge to Action*. Princeton, NJ: Princeton University Press.

Funiciello, Theresa. 1990. "The Poverty Industry: Do Government and Charities Create the Poor?" *Ms.* November/December.

Gaventa, John. 1980. *Power and Powerlessness: Quiescence and Rebellion in an Appalachian Valley*. Urbana, IL: University of Ilinois Press.

Gaventa, John, and Helen Lewis. 1988. "Case Study: The Ivanhoe Project" (draft). New Market, TN: Highlander Center.

Gaventa, John, Barbara Ellen Smith, and Alex Willingham, eds. 1990. *Communities in Economic Crisis*. Philadelphia, PA: Temple University Press.

Gender & Society. 1990. Vo.4. No.3.

Gilkes, Cheryl Townsend. 1985. "'Together and in Harness': Women's Traditions in the Sanctified Church." *Signs*. 10. 4. 678–699.

Gilligan, Carol. 1982. *In A Different Voice: Psychological Theory and Women's Development*. Cambridge, MA: Harvard University Press.

Glaser, Barney G., and Anselm Strauss. 1967. *The Discovery of Grounded Theory*. Chicago, IL: Aldine.

Gramsci, Antonio. 1971. *Selections from the Prison Notebooks*. London, England: Lawrence and Wishart.

Greene, Gayle. 1992. "The Empire Strikes Back." *The Nation*. February 10. 166–170.

Habermas, Jurgen. 1976. *Legitimation Crisis*. London, England: Heinemann.

Hall, Betty Jean. 1990. "Women Miners Can Dig It, Too!" In John Gaventa, Barbara Ellen Smith, and Alex Willingham, eds. *Communities in Economic Crisis*. Philadelphia, PA: Temple University Press. 53–60.

Hall, Jacquelyn Dowd. 1986. "Disorderly Women: Gender and Labor Militancy in the Appalachian South." *Journal of American History*. 73. 354–382.

Harding, Sandra, ed. 1987. *Feminism and Methodology: Social Science Issues*. Bloomington, NY: Indiana University Press.

Hartmann, Heidi. 1979. "Capitalism, Patriarchy and Job Segregation by Sex." In Zillah R. Eisenstein, ed. *Capitalist Patriarchy and the Case for Socialist Feminism*. New York, NY: Monthly Review Press.

Hartmann, Heidi. 1981. "The Unhappy Marriage of Marxism and Feminism: Towards a More Progressive Union." In Lydia Sargent, ed. *Women and Revolution: A Discussion of the Unhappy Marriage of Marxism and Feminism*. Boston, MA: South End Press. 1–41.

Hartmann, Heidi. 1986. *The Science Question in Feminism*. Ithaca, NY: Cornell University Press.

Hartmann, Heidi. 1987. "The Family as the Locus of Gender, Class,and Political Struggle: The Example of Housework." In Sandra Harding, ed. *Feminism and Methodology: Social Science Issues*. Bloomington, IN: Indiana University Press. 109–134.

Hartsock, Nancy C.M. 1983. *Money, Sex, and Power: Toward a Feminist Historical Materialism*. New York, NY: Longman.

Heise, Lori. 1993. "Violence Against Women: The Missing Agenda." In Marge Koblinsky, Judith Timyan, and Jill Gay. *Women's Health: A Global Perspective*. Boulder, CO: Westview Press. 171–195.

Hochschild, Arlie. 1975. "The Sociology of Feeling and Emotion: Selected Possibilities." In Marcia Millman and Rosabeth Moss Kanter, eds. 1975. *Another Voice*. New York, NY: Anchor Books. 280–307.

hooks, bell. 1981. *Ain't I a Woman: Black Women and Feminism*. Boston, MA: South End Press.

hooks, bell. 1989. *Talking Back*. Boston: South End Press.

Horkheimer, Max. 1972. "Authority and the Family." In *Critical Theory*. New York, NY: Herder and Herder.

Illich, Ivan. 1978. *Toward a History of Needs*. New York, NY: Pantheon Books.

Inkeles, Alex. 1969. "Making Men Modern: On the Causes and Consequences of Individual Change in Six Developing Countries." *American Journal of Sociology.* 75. 208–225.

Jaggar, Alison. 1988. *Feminist Politics and Human Nature.* Totowa, NJ: Rowman and Allanheld.

Jaggar, Alison, and Paula S. Rothenberg. 1984. *Feminist Frameworks: Alternative Theoretical Accounts of the Relations Between Women and Men* (second edition). New York, NY: McGraw-Hill.

Jaquette, Jane. 1982. "Women and Moderization Theory." *World Politics.* 334. No.2. 267–284.

Jarrico, Paul, Michael Wilson, and Herbert Bieberman. 1954 (film). "Salt of the Earth." Chicago, IL: Films, Inc.

Jay, Martin. 1973. *The Dialectical Imagination: A History of the Frankfurt School and the Institute of Social Research, 1923–1950.* Boston, MA: Little Brown.

Joekes, Susan. 1987. *Women in the World Economy.* New York, NY: Oxford University Press.

Johnson, Ann. 1985 (film). "Mabel Parker Hardison Smith." Whitesburg, KY: Appalshop.

Johnson, Ann. 1986 (film). "Mud Creek Clinic." Whitesburg, KY: Appalshop.

Jones, Mary Harris. 1972. *Autobiography of Mother Jones.* Edited by Mary Field Parton. (1925. Chicago: Charles Kerr.) Reprint. Chicago, IL: Illinois Labor Historical Society.

Kahn, Kathy. 1973. *Hillbilly Women.* Garden City, NJ: Doubleday.

Karr, Albert R. 1992. "Union, Nonunion Coal Companies Head for Showdown on Retirement Benefits." *The Wall Street Journal.* March 3. A4.

Kelly, Liz. 1988. *Surviving Sexual Violence*. Minneapolis, MN: University of Minnesota Press.

Kelly-Gadol, Joan. 1987. "The Social Relation of the Sexes: Methodological Implications of Women's History." In Sandra Harding, ed. *Feminism and Methodology: Social Science Issues*. Bloomington, IN: Indiana University Press. 15–28.

Kessler-Harris, Alice. 1982. *Out to Work: A History of Wage-Earning Women in the United States*. New York, NY: Oxford University Press.

Kingslover, Barbara. 1989. *Holding the Line: Women in the Great Arizona Mine Strike of 1983*. Ithaca, NY: ILR Press.

Klein, Renate. 1983. "How to Do What We Want to Do: Thoughts about Feminist Methodology." In Gloria Bowles and Renate Duelli Klein, eds. *Theories of Women's Studies*. Boston, MA: Routledge and Kegan Paul.

Koop, C. Everett. 1989. "Violence Against Women: A Global Problem." Address by the Surgeon General of the U.S. Public Health Service at a Conference of the Pan American Heath Organization. Washington, DC. May 22. Cited in Lori Heise. 1993.

"Violence Against Women: The Missing Agenda." In Marge Koblinsky, Judith Timyan, and Jill Gay. *Women's Health: A Global Perspective*. Boulder, CO: Westview Press. 171–195.

Kopple, Barbara. 1976 (film). "Harlan County, USA." New York, NY: Cinema Five.

Kraybill, David S., Thomas G. Johnson, and Brady J. Deaton. 1987. "Income Uncertainty and the Quality of Life: A Socio-Economic Study of Virginia's Coal Counties." *Virginia Agricultural Experiment Station Bulletin 87-4*. Blacksburg, VA: Virginia Polytechnic Institute and State University.

Lacy, Donald P., Pamela D. Gibson, and Mark D. Miller. 1990. "Southwest Virginia: A Regional Profile." Blacksburg, VA: Virginia Cooperative Extension Service at Virginia Tech.

Leiss, William. 1976. *The Limits of Satisfaction: An Essay on the Problem of Needs and Commodities*. Toronto, Canada: University of Toronto Press.

Leonard, Ann, ed. 1989. *Seeds: Supporting Women's Work in the Third World*. New York, NY: The Feminist Press (CUNY).

Lewis, Helen Matthews. 1970. "Occupational Roles and Family Roles: A Study of Coal Mining Families in the Southern Appalachians" (dissertation). Lexington, KY: University of Kentucky.

Lewis, Helen M., Sue E. Kobak, and Linda Johnson. 1978. "Family, Religion, and Colonialism in Central Appalachia or Bury my Rifle at Big Stone Gap." In Helen Lewis, Linda Johnson, and Donald Askins. *Colonialism in Modern America: the Appalachian Case*. Boone, NC: The Appalachian Consortium Press. 113–141.

Lewis, Helen, Linda Johnson, and Donald Askins. 1978. *Colonialism in Modern America: the Appalachian Case*. Boone, NC: The Appalachian Consortium Press.

Lewis, Helen, and Susanna O'Donnell. 1990A. *Remembering Our Past, Building Our Future*. Ivanhoe, VA: Ivanhoe Civic League.

Lewis, Helen, and Susanna O'Donnell. 1990B. *Telling Our Stories, Sharing our Lives*. Ivanhoe, VA: Ivanhoe Civic League.

Lewis, Helen. 1991. "Fatalism or the Coal Industry?" In Bruce Ergood and Bruce E. Kuhre, eds. *Appalachia: Social Context Past and Present* (third edition). Dubuque, IL: Kendall Hunt. 221–229.

Lewis, Oscar. 1961. *The Children of Sanchez*. New York, NY: Random House.

Lewis, Oscar. 1966. "The Culture of Poverty." *Scientific American* 215. 19–25.

Lofland, John, and Lyn H. Lofland. 1984. *Analyzing Social Settings: A Guide to Qualitative Observation and Analysis* (second edition). Belmont, CA: Wadsworth Publishing Company.

Loof, David H. 1971. *Appalachia's Children: The Challenge of Mental Health*. Lexington, KY: University of Kentucky Press.

Lorde, Audre. 1983. "The Master's Tools Will Never Dismantle the Master's House." In Cherrie Moraga and Gloria Anzaldua, eds. *This Bridge Called My Back: Writings By Radical Women of Color*. New York, NY: Kitchen Table, Women of Color Press. 98–101.

Luck, Maura. 1991. "Gender and Library Work: The Limitations of Dual Labor Market Theory." In Redclift and Sinclair, eds. *Working Women: International Perspectives on Labour and Gender Ideology*. London, England: Routledge. 25–41.

Lukes, Steven. 1974. *Power: A Radical View*. London, England: Macmillan.

Luttrell, Wendy. 1988. "The Edison School Struggle: The Reshaping of Working-Class Education and Women's Consciousness." In Bookman and Morgen, eds. *Women and the Politics of Empowerment*. Philadelphia, PA: Temple University Press. 136–156.

Luttrell, Wendy. 1990. "Community-Based Economics Education: A Personal, Cultural, and Political Project." In John Gaventa, Ellen Smith, and Alex Willingham, eds. *Communities in Economic Crisis*. Philadelphia, PA: Temple University Press. 227–241.

MacKinnon, Catharine. 1982. "Feminism, Marxism, Method, and the State: An Agenda for Theory." In Nannerl O. Keohane, Michelle Z. Rosaldo, and Barbara C. Gelpi, eds. *Feminist Theory: A Critique of Ideology*. Chicago, IL: The University of Chicago Press. 1–30.

MacKinnon, Catherine. 1987. "Feminism, Marxism, Method, and the State: Toward a Feminist Jurisprudence." In Sandra

Harding, ed. *Feminism and Methodology: Social Science Issues*. Bloomington, IN: Indiana University Press. 135–156.

Maggard, Sally Ward. 1986. "Class and Gender: New Theoretical Priorities in Appalachian Studies." In Jim Lloyd and Ann G. Campbell. *The Impact of Institutions in Appalachia*. Boone, NC: Appalachian Consortium Press. 100–113.

Maguire, Patricia. 1984. *Women in Development: An Alternative Analysis*. Amherst, MA: Center for International Education, University of Massachusetts.

March, Kathryn S., and Rachelle Taqqu. 1982. "Women's Informal Associations and the Organizational Capacity for Development." Ithaca, NY: Rural Development Committee, Center for International Studies, Cornell University.

Margolis, Diane Rothbard. 1989. "Considering Women's Experience: A Reformulation of Power Theory" *Theory and Society*. Vol.18. 387–416.

Martin, D. 1976. *Battered Wives*. San Francisco, CA: Glide.

Matthews, Alice E. 1987. "Tall Women and Mountain Belles: Fact and Fiction in Appalachia." In James C. Cobb and Charles R. Wilson, eds. *Perspectives on the American South*. Vol.4. New York, NY: Gordon and Breach Science Publishers. 39–53.

McClleland, David C. 1966. "The Impulse to Modernization." In Myron Weiner, ed. *Modernization: The Dynamics of Growth*. New York, NY: Basic Books. 29–39.

Meillassoux, Claude. 1981. *Maidens, Meal, and Money: Capitalism and the Domestic Community*. Cambridge, England: Cambridge University Press.

Mies, Maria. 1986. *Patriarchy and Accumulation on a World Scale: Women in the New International Division of Labour*. London, England: Zed Books.

Mies, Maria, Veronika Bennholdt-Thompson, and Claudia von Werlhof. 1988. *Women: The Last Colony.* London, England: Zed Books.

Mies, Maria. 1991. "Women's Research or Feminist Research? The Debate Surrounding Feminist Science and Methodology." In Mary Margaret Fonow and Judith Cook, eds. *Beyond Methodology: Feminist Scholarship as Lived Research.* Bloomington, IN: Indiana University Press. 60–84.

Millman, Marcia, and Rosabeth Moss Kanter, eds. 1975. *Another Voice.* New York, NY: Anchor Books.

Mitchell, Juliet. 1971. *Woman's Estate.* New York, NY: Pantheon Books.

Mohanty, Chandra Talpade. 1991A. "Introduction: Cartographies of Struggle: Third World Women and the Politics of Feminism." In Chandra Talpade Mohanty, Ann Russo, and Lourdes Torres, eds. *Third World Women and the Politics of Feminism.* Bloomington, IN: Indiana University Press. 1–47.

Mohanty, Chandra Talpade. 1991B. "Under Western Eyes: Feminist Scholarship and Colonial Discourses." In Chandra Talpade Mohanty, Ann Russo, and Lourdes Torres, eds. *Third World Women and the Politics of Feminism.* Bloomington, IN: Indiana University Press. 51–80.

Molyneux, Maxine. 1986. "Mobilization Without Emancipation? Women's Interests, State and Revolution in Nicaragua." In Richard R. Fagen, Carmen Diana Deere and Jose Luis Coraggio, eds. *Transition and Development: Problems of Third World Socialism.* New York, NY: Monthly Review Press and Center for the Study of the Americas. 280–302.

Moore, Henrietta. 1988. "Women and the State." In *Feminism and Anthropology.* Minneapolis, MN: University of Minnesota Press. 128–185.

Moraga, Cherrie. 1986. "From a Long Line of Vendidas: Chicanas and Feminism." In Teresa deLauretis, ed. *Feminist Studies:*

Critical Studies Bloomington, IN: Indiana University Press. 173–190.

Moraga, Cherrie, and Gloria Anzaldua, eds. 1983. *This Bridge Called My Back: Writings By Radical Women of Color*. New York, NY: Kitchen Table, Women of Color Press.

Morgen, Sandra, and Ann Bookman, 1988. "Rethinking Women and Politics: An Introductory Essay." In Ann Bookman and Sandra Morgen, eds. 1988. *Women and the Politics of Empowerment*. Phildelphia, PA: Temple University Press. 3–29.

Moser, Caroline O.N. 1989. "Gender Planning in the Third World: Meeting Practical and Strategic Gender Needs." *World Development*. Vol.8. No.11. 1799–1825.

Moynihan, Daniel Patrick. 1965. *The Negro Family: The Case for National Action*. Washington, DC: Government Printing Office.

Nash, June. 1990. "Latin American Women in the World Capitalist Crisis." *Gender & Society*. Vol.4. No.3. 338–353.

Nash, June. 1979. *We Eat the Mines, the Mines Eat Us*. New York, NY: Columbia University Press.

Nielsen, Joyce McCarl, ed. 1990. *Feminist Research Methods: Exemplary Readings in the Social Sciences*. Boulder, CO: Westview Press.

Nielsen, Joyce McCarl. 1990A. "Introduction." In Joyce McCarl Nielsen, ed. *Feminist Research Methods: Exemplary Readings in the Social Sciences*. Boulder, CO: Westview Press. 1–37.

Oakley, Ann. 1981. "Interviewing Women: A Contradiction in Terms." in Helen Roberts, ed. *Doing Feminist Research*. London, England: Routledge and Kegan Paul. 30–61.

Petchesky, Rosalind. 1979. "Dissolving the Hyphen: A Report on Marxist Feminist Groups." In Zillah R. Eisenstein, ed. *Capitalist Patriarchy and the Case for Socialist Feminism*. New York, NY: Monthly Review Press.

Photiadis, John D., and Harry K. Schwarzweller. 1970. "Change in Rural Appalachia." In Max E. Glenn, ed. *Appalachia in Transition*. St. Louis, MO: The Bethany Press. 69–81.

Porter, Iana, and Kathryn Ramey. 1990 (film). "We Won't Go Back: Women in the Pittston Strike." Olympia, WA: Evergreen State College.

Redclift, Nanneke. 1987. "Rights in Women: Kinship, Culture, and Materialism." In Janet Sayers, Mary Evans, and Nanneke Redclift, eds. *Engels Revisited*. London, England: Tavistock Publications. 113–144.

Reinharz, Shulamit. 1992. *Feminist Methods in Social Research*. New York, NY: Oxford University Press.

Rice, Russ. 1986. "Yates Says Ivanhoe On Verge of New Industry." *Southwest Virginia Enterprise*. October 11.

Rice, Russ. 1987. "Hands Across Ivanhoe." In *Journal of the Appalachian Regional Commission*. Vol.20. No.1 (Summer).

Rogers, Barbara. 1979. *The Domestication of Women: Discrimination in Developing Societies*. New York, NY: St. Martin's Press.

Rosaldo, Michelle Zimbalist. 1974. "Woman, Culture, and Society: A Theoretical Overview." In Michelle Zimbalist Rosaldo and Lousie Lamphere, eds. *Woman, Culture and Society*. Stanford, CA: Stanford University Press. 17–42.

Rosenfelt, Deborah Silverton (commentary), and Michael Wilson, (screenplay). 1978. *Salt of the Earth*. New York, NY: Feminist Press.

Rothenberg, Paula S. 1992. *Race, Class, and Gender in the United States: An Integrated Study* (second edition). New York, NY: St. Martin's Press.

Rowbotham, Sheila. 1973. *Woman's Consciousness, Man's World*. Baltimore, MD: Penguin Books.

Rubin, Lillian. 1976. *Worlds of Pain*. New York, NY: Basic Books.

Ruddick, Sara. 1980. "Maternal Thinking." *Feminist Studies.* Vol.6. No.2. 342–367.

Ryan, William. 1971. *Blaming the Victim.* New York, NY: Pantheon.

Sacks, Karen. 1975. "Engels Revisited: Women, the Organization of Production and Private Property." In Rayna R. Reiter, ed. *Toward and Anthropology of Women.* New York, NY: Monthly Review Press. 211–234.

Safa, Helen Icken, "Women's Social Movements in Latin America." *Gender & Society.* Vol.4. No.3. 1990. 354–369.

Sargent, Lydia, ed. 1981. *Women and Revolution: A Discussion of the Unhappy Marriage of Marxism and Feminism.* Boston, MA: South End Press.

Sassen-Koob, Saskia. 1988. *The Mobility of Labor and Capital.* Cambridge, England: Cambridge University Press.

Scott, James C. 1985. *Weapons of the Weak: Everyday Forms of Peasant Resistance.* New Haven, CT: Yale University Press.

Scott, Kesho Yvonne. 1991.*The Habit of Surviving: Black Women's Strategies for Life.* New Brunswick, NJ: Rutgers University Press.

Schutz, Alfred. 1967. *The Phenomenology of the Social World.* Evanston, IL: Northwestern University Press.

Sebsted, J. 1982. "Struggle and Development Among Self-Employed Women: A Report for SEWA." Washington, DC: USAID.

Sen, Gita, and Caren Grown. 1987. *Development, Crises, and Alternative Visions: Third World Women's Perspectives.* New York, NY: Monthly Review Press.

Shifflett, Crandall. 1991. *Coal Towns: Life, Work, and Culture in Company Towns of Southern Appalachia, 1880–1960.* Knoxville, TN: University of Tennessee Press.

Sinclair, M. Thea. 1991. In Nanneke Redclift and M. Thea Sinclair, eds. *Working Women: International Perspectives on Labour and Gender Ideology*. London, England: Routledge. 1–24.

Smith, Dorothy E. 1974. "The Ideological Practice of Sociology." *Catalyst*. 8. 39–54.

Smith, Dorothy. E. 1987. *The Everyday World as Problematic: A Feminist Sociology*. Boston, MA: Northeastern University Press.

Spelman, Elizabeth. 1988. *The Inessential Woman: Problems of Exclusion in Feminist Thought*. Boston, MA: Beacon Press.

Stanley, Liz. 1990. "Feminist Praxis and the Academic Mode of Production." In Liz Stanley, ed. *Femininst Praxis: Research, Theory and Epistemology in Feminist Sociology*. London, ENgland: Routledge. 3–19.

Stanley, Liz, and Sue Wise. 1983. "Feminist Research, Feminist Consciousness and Experiences of Sexism." *Women's Studies International Quarterly*. 2. 359–74.

Thorne, Barrie, with Martha Yalom. 1982. *Rethinking the Family: Some Feminist Questions*. New York, NY: Longman.

Tickamyer, Ann. R., and Cecil Tickamyer. 1991. "Gender, Family Structure, and Poverty in Central Appalachia." In Bruce Ergood and Bruce E. Kuhre, eds. *Appalachia: Social Context Past and Present* (third edition). Dubuque IA: Kendall Hunt. 307–315.

Tinker, Irene. 1990. "The Making of a Field: Advocates, Practitioners, and Scholars. In Irene Tinker, ed. *Persistent Inequalities: Women and World Development*. New York, NY: Oxford University Press. 27–53.

United Nations. 1991. *The World's Women: Trends and Statistics, 1970–1990*. Social Statistics and Indicators, Series K. No.8. New York, NY: United Nations.

United States Department of Commerce, Bureau of the Census. 1986. "County and City Datebook." Washington, DC: US Government Printing Office.

USAID (United States Agency for International Development). 1983. "Policy Paper on Women in Development." Washington, DC.

Vocational Gender Equity. 1989 (pamphlet). Big Stone Gap, VA: Mountain Empire Community College.

UMWA. 1990. *United Mineworkers Journal*. January. No.23.

Walby, Sylvia. 1986. *Patriarchy at Work: Patriarchal and Capitalist Relations in Employment*. Minneapolis, MN: University of Minnesota Press.

Waller, Maxine, Helen M. Lewis, Claire McBrien, and Carroll L. Wessinger. 1990. "It Has to Come from the People." In John Gaventa, Barbara Ellen Smith, and Alex Willingham, eds. *Communities in Economic Crisis*. Philadelphia, PA: Temple University Press. 19–28.

Walls, David S. 1976. "Central Appalachia: A Peripheral Region Within an Advanced Capitalist State." *Journal of Sociology and Social Welfare*. 4 (November 1976). 232–247.

Walls, David S., and Dwight B. Billings. 1991. "The Sociology of Southern Appalachia." In Bruce Ergood and Bruce E. Kuhre, *Appalachia: Social Context Past and Present* (third edition). Dubuque, IA: Kendall Hunt. 49–59.

Warren, Kay B. 1991. "Transforming Memories and Histories: Indian Identity Reexamined." (unpublished essay).

Weber, Max. 1958. *The Protestant Ethic and the Spirit of Capitalism*. New York, NY: Charles Scribner and Sons.

Weiss, Chris. 1990. "Organizing Women for Local Economic Development." In John Gaventa, Barbara Ellen Smith, and Alex Willingham, eds., *Communities in Economic Crisis: Appalachia and the South*. Philadelphia, PA: Temple University Press. 61–70.

Weller, Jack E. 1965. *Yesterday's People: Life in Contemporary Appalachia*. Lexington, KY: University of Kentucky Press.

Westcott, Marcia. 1990. "Feminist Criticism of the Social Sciences." In Joyce McCarl Nielsen, ed. *Feminist Research Methods: Exemplary Readings in the Social Sciences*. Boulder, CO: Westview Press. 58–68.

Wharton, Amy S. 1991. "Structure and Agency in Socialist-Feminist Theory." *Gender & Society*. Vol.5. No.3. Sept. 373–389.

Wolpe, Harold, ed. 1980. *The Articulation of Modes of Producion*. London, England: Routledge and Kegan Paul.

World Bank. 1979. *Recognizing the Invisible Woman in Development: The World Bank's Experience*. Washington, D.C.

Yancey, Dwayne. 1990. "Thunder in the Coalfields." Roanoke, VA: Roanoke Times and World News. Sunday, April 29. Special Report.

Yarrow, Mike. 1991. "Voices from the Coalfields: How Miners' Families Understand the Crisis of Coal." In John Gaventa, Barbara Ellen Smith, and Alex Willingham, eds. *Communities in Economic Crisis*. Philadelphia, PA: Temple University Press. 38–52.

Yllo, K., and M. Bograd, eds. 1988. *Feminist Perspectives on Wife Abuse*. Beverly Hills, CA: Sage.

Young, Iris. 1980. "Socialist Feminism and the Limits of Dual Systems Theory." *Socialist Review*. 10. Nos. 2 and 3 (March–June). 169–188.

Young, Kate, Carol Wolkowitz, and Roslyn McCullagh, eds. 1981. *Of Marriage and the Market: Women's Subordination in International Perspective*. London, England: CSE Books.

Young, Kate, ed. 1988. *Women and Economic Development: Local, Regional and National Planning Strategies*. New York, NY: Berg Publishers Limited.

Yudelman, Sally W. 1987. *Hopeful Openings: A Study of Five Women's Development Organizations in Latin America and the Caribbean*. West Hartford, CT: Kumarian Press.

Zaretsky, Eli. 1986. *Capitalism, the Family, and Personal Life*. New York, NY: Perennial Library.

INDEX